THE COUNTRY LIFE COLLECTOR'S
POCKET BOOK
OF CHINA

THE COUNTRY LIFE COLLECTOR'S
POCKET BOOK
OF CHINA

G. BERNARD HUGHES

Illustrations by Therle Hughes

COUNTRY LIFE
LONDON · NEW YORK · SYDNEY · TORONTO

Published by Country Life Books
and distributed for them by
The Hamlyn Publishing Group Limited
London · New York · Sydney · Toronto
Astronaut House, Feltham, Middlesex, England

First published 1965
New and revised edition 1977
Reprinted 1977, 1978, 1979

ISBN 0 600 31954 7

Printed in England by
Hazell Watson & Viney Limited
Aylesbury

Contents

PART I

Introduction: Chronological Summary

Collectors of pottery and porcelain have an unrivalled opportunity to observe the full range of materials and techniques developed down the centuries. Primitive processes directly traceable to the Middle Ages were still being applied on a commercial scale in the 19th century. Many techniques of the 18th century remain the basis of manufacture and ornament to this day. The beginner who wants to 'place' any ceramic specimen has to decide what processes were involved and the extent to which their successful accomplishment suggests long mastery of the required techniques.

At the same time he must bear in mind the general course of ceramic design and ornament through the centuries and especially the revivals and adaptations and wholly new ideas of the prolific 19th century. Outline illustrations in the following pages indicate the general trends through the simple outlines of the 1740s–50s, the mid-18th century development of a delight in rococo and chinoiserie fantasy, the pseudo-classical interest in the 1760s, revived heavy-handedly at the end of the century, the substantial shapes of the Regency, the late Georgian revival of chinoiserie and rococo again. He must note the 'Elizabethan' and 'Gothic' romanticism of early Victorians, the naturalistic excesses of the mid-19th century and the phase of statuesque ceramics—white figures, white relief-moulded jugs. From the early 1870s onwards there was an enthusiasm for all things Japanese and at the century's end a curious mixing of Victorian Japanese and Victorian 'Renaissance', heralded as *l'art nouveau*.

Only when the tyro-collector has some idea of the general

1. Slipware. TOP: posset pot, with decorated pads of light clay pressed upon the surface; jug with free-hand slip trailing in ladder pattern. CENTRE: tyg, Wrotham type with sprigged pads of ornament; fuddling cups with interconnected bodies, 'three merry boys'. BOTTOM: simple puzzle jug with incised or sgraffito ornament; mug with combing of different slips (*see* Figs. 40, 88).

picture and can relate his specimen to it can he derive much help from any mark of name or symbol upon its base. In the following pages each distinctive characteristic is considered in separate detail, presented alphabetically for ease of reference under general group headings and illustrated wherever this is of practical use. Throughout, the aim is to facilitate identification and give the beginner-collector the satisfaction of really knowing about his specimens—their fundamental substance and how they were produced, their all-important surface treatment and their purpose in the general chronological development of style and shape and ornament.

From primitive days the potter has shaped local clay mixtures into useful wares, incising their surfaces with simple patterns, baking them hard by fire and at the same time rendering them watertight with a hard glassy glaze. Always his aim has been to make them more pleasant to handle and better vehicles for ornament, aided mainly by access to a widening range of materials and improvements in firing methods which achieved greater heat more exactly controlled. In SLIPWARE the collector finds one of the first English attempts to introduce clays that burnt to a whitish tone as ornament upon useful wares made of the usual pliant clays that tended to burn to a red, buff or brownish tone. Crude but highly ornamental results were achieved by the mid-17th century, but the simple powdered lead glaze, essential on such porous clayware, invariably resulted in a yellowish tone. Country craftsmen made slipware by traditional methods through most of the last century, and a large amount of the striped variant known as WELSH WARE.

A wider colour range and especially the blue of cobalt was developed in England in the 17th century on what came to be known as DELFT WARE. In this, the basic buff-toned earthenware was wholly hidden by a substantial white opaque covering, the lead and silica mixture required to give it a surface

9

2. Earthenware money-boxes. TOP: vertical-slitted, 17th century; incised Nottingham stoneware; simple red earthenware with galena glaze. CENTRE AND BOTTOM: four hen-and-chicken boxes of 18th or early 19th century (the centre specimen with a whistle tail) and multiple box, usually two or three tiers. Such designs were deliberately simple and were smashed to obtain the contents. The hen motif expressed the nest-egg idea.

glaze being opacified with tin to form what is termed an enamel; hence the alternative names of TIN ENAMELLED and TIN GLAZED WARE. Here for the first time pictorial or flower ornament was brush painted upon the receptive biscuit surface, the colour range being limited to such metallic oxides as could endure the subsequent kiln heat required to fire the glaze.

From these beginnings developed the range of 18th-century earthenwares, spurred by the ever-increasing demand to meet the special needs of tea and coffee and chocolate drinkers and those who sought to give variety to their dinner tables with innumerable side dishes, sauces and pickles. At the same time the collector must note that when kiln heat could be increased it was possible to transform suitable clay mixtures into much stronger, non-porous substances known as RED and BROWN STONEWARE. Moreover, the same intense heat made it possible to use common salt as a glaze, giving a clean, reasonably smooth surface.

Brown stonewares for everyday use have never gone out of production, but when calcined flints whitened and strengthened the body and a wash of whiter refined clay covered the surface, a thinner, more gracious form of WHITE SALT-GLAZED STONEWARE was evolved. Stonewares are associated especially with clear-cut cast ornament in relief, but by the early 18th century all western Europe was involved in the quest for ceramics as fine as Oriental porcelain and by half-way through the century this somewhat brittle, rough-surfaced, white stoneware was being painted with flowers and chinoiseries in enamel colours over the glaze, the metallic oxides of these colours mixed in fluxes that fused to the surface under the low heat of the muffle kiln.

At the same time it was found that this whiter mixture of refined clay and flint, when subjected to a less intense heat-produced a cream-toned earthenware which began to become

11

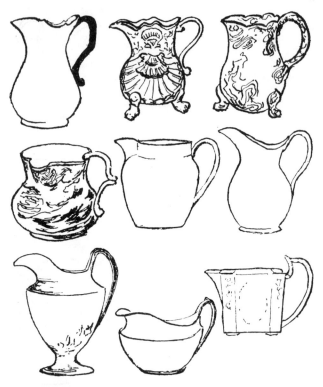

3. Cream-jugs, a chronological survey of design in useful wares. TOP: early and middle 18th century in plain earthenware, white salt glazed stoneware and agate ware. CENTRE: Wedgwood surface marbling, 1756, and two small-scale versions of serving jugs in creamware of 1770s and 1780s. BOTTOM: late 18th-century neo-classic and low pitcher shapes in basaltes, creamware.

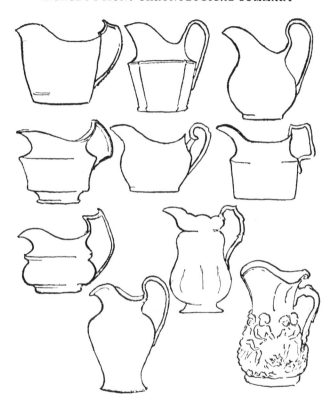

4. Cream-jugs, chronological survey cont. TOP: c. 1800–15, in jasper, New Hall porcelain and Wedgwood creamware. CENTRE: Derby, 1800s, Spode blue-and-white, c. 1810; Liverpool, c. 1820s. BOTTOM: four jugs showing gradual return to more vertical emphasis in blue-and-white, lustre, Binns' Worcester china and hard parian.

13

vastly important when a clear glaze was evolved that could be applied as a liquid dip. From the 1740s CREAM-COLOURED EARTHENWARE developed to the gradual extinction of white salt-glazed stoneware. Ornament at first followed the tradition of surface relief work and when colour was introduced it was as part of the glazing process. The collector finds low-relief patterns on the YELLOW-GLAZE and GREEN-GLAZE WARES developed by the young Josiah Wedgwood (b. 1730) and the combined yellow and green CAULIFLOWER WARE. Green leaf pickle plates have never gone out of demand. Cloudy effects of mingled metallic oxides in the glaze produced TORTOISESHELL WARE and there were various effects of surface combing and marbling in the slipware tradition. SOLID AGATE WARE is a minor exception to the general trend, colour striations being formed by mixing differently tinted clays.

On now highly valuable EARTHENWARE FIGURES of the second half of the 18th century the collector can trace the technical advance from cloudy streaks to a range of subdued glaze colours applied without mingling and thence to the brighter enamel colours painted over the glaze of the whiter earthenware then becoming available. On late-18th-century Elijah figures typical of the great religious revival, for example, or on genuine Toby jugs, the collector can note, too, the range of colours evolved by the younger Ralph Wood that could endure the heat required to fire the glaze. This distinctive and limited number of 'high temperature' colours, often though inaccurately called PRATT WARE colours, was introduced in about 1790, but continued longer into the 19th century than some collectors imagine.

Ingredients associated with porcelain had further improved cream-coloured earthenware before 1775, and in 1779 Wedgwood also evolved a whiter PEARL WARE, associated with much of the splendid blue painted and printed ornament popular in the later 18th century.

14

With the same interest in improving and enlarging the potter's craft, Wedgwood and his contemporaries at this time developed a number of FINE STONEWARES possessing the common stoneware's advantage of non-porosity, so that for ornamental purposes they required no glaze. His BLACK BASALTES, including figure ornaments, was an improvement on the more widely made EGYPTIAN BLACK STONEWARE. REDWARE sought to copy Oriental imports, but his JASPER in a number of subdued colours was his own invention. CANE-COLOURED STONEWARE or CANE-WARE, much used for PIE-CRUST WARE, is self-explanatory, as is the variant moulded in naturalistic bamboo forms and known as BAMBOO WARE.

PORCELAIN with the cherished qualities of translucency, whiteness and delicate texture was made in England from the 1740s, but only as an imitation of the Oriental; a white clay mixture was rendered translucent by the inclusion of a glass or frit substance, fused with the aid of lime or chalk. This mixture was fired at a low temperature and is known as FRIT or SOFT PASTE PORCELAIN. Some, of suitably flawless quality, was kiln-fired once and sold as a delicate white BISCUIT PORCELAIN. But most was given a low-temperature clear lead glaze either after painting with 'underglaze' colours —mainly blue—or before the application of the full range of rich enamel colours and gold, each requiring a third firing at a still lower temperature to fuse to the surface. BONE PORCELAIN (entirely distinct from bone china), incorporating the ash of calcined bones, was a stronger variant of soft porcelain used at Bow and later at Chelsea, Derby, Liverpool and Lowestoft. The inclusion of soapstone (steatite) rendered the porcelain paste more resistant to changes of heat: SOAP-STONE PORCELAIN is characteristic of the useful wares made by Worcester, Bristol (soft paste) and some from Caughley and Liverpool. Costly specimens of useful wares and England's

15

5. Development of tea jars. TOP: silver shape in white salt glazed stoneware with reliefs of tea-plant, c. 1750; pineapple in cauliflower ware, c. 1760s; Lowestoft silver-shape, raised white ornament touched with blue, c. 1760s. CENTRE, associated with teapot shapes: Derby, c. 1770s; Lowestoft, c. 1770s; Worcester, later 1770s; Caughley, c. 1780s. BOTTOM: Worcester with scale pattern, c. 1780s; Lowestoft blue painted; Leeds, painted, c. 1790s.

first delicate figures are found in the soft porcelains of Chelsea, Bow, Lowestoft, Longton Hall, Derby, Worcester, Caughley and Liverpool. A number of these firms made bone china in

6. Soft porcelain. Typical Longton Hall melon tureen (William Littler & Co., c. 1750s).

the 19th century when soft porcelain was made briefly at Pinxton, Swansea, Nantgarw and Madeley.

Only Plymouth and Bristol and New Hall made HARD PASTE PORCELAIN, the true porcelain in the Oriental manner, when the necessary ingredients were obtainable from Cornwall—china clay and china stone (the natural silicate of alumina which dispensed with the need for a glassy frit). This paste mixture was covered with a glaze of china stone rendered fusible with lime and potash and fired at a very high temperature. Results were seldom fully satisfactory and for the purpose of this brief outline the most notable feature of this development was the combination of the hard paste porcelain ingredients with the calcined bone ash first associated with Bow soft paste porcelain to produce, from the 1790s, the vastly important BONE CHINA that made translucent, white, thin yet reasonably sturdy and heat-resistant china available to countless thousands of homes in the 19th century and is still the staple 'china' of today. Great numbers of potters followed the Spode firm (subsequently Copeland & Garrett) in making bone china; among the leaders may be mentioned Coalport, Minton and Davenport.

Another development from hard porcelain, used for costly table wares, was the hard, extremely translucent FELSPAR

PORCELAIN, evolved by Spode who introduced pure felspar into a Cornish china clay and china stone mixture. Chamberlain of Worcester, Bloor of Derby and Rose of Coalport also made this ware.

Collectors find many delightful 19th-century bone china imitations of 18th-century ornaments in soft porcelain which

7. Fine bone china. Typical richly gilded work by the Davenport firm in a miniature 'watering can' with multi-nozzle spout for perfuming artificial flowers (*see* Fig. 172).

in themselves often originated as copies of hard porcelain imports from earlier 18th-century Meissen (Dresden), sometimes inspired by Chinese originals. A vast amount of 19th-century bone china ornament was produced, too, in imitation of French Sèvres hard porcelain, with splendid ground colours and lavish gilding, and this also often causes confusion to the beginner since many potters had no compunction about using other potteries' marks; and there was a fashion in the 19th century for including in the mark the date of a firm's establishment (*see* p. 351).

In the late 18th century and still more in the 19th century figure ornaments were also popular in earthenware, making little attempt to imitate the delicate detail of porcelain. Most specimens are unmarked, but sophisticated 18th-century work is associated with the father and son Ralph Wood, with Aaron Wood and his son Enoch, who continued until 1840, with the Leeds Pottery, and the partners Neale & Wilson and Lakin & Poole. Much crude early 19th-century work is associated with Walton, Salt and Sherratt and with potteries in Sunderland and Scotland. The flat-back figure group for the mantelpiece was a Victorian development.

Bone china and tougher varieties of earthenware dominated 19th-century ceramics and innumerable specimens may be found either unmarked or bearing the name or initials of one

8. Victorian figure ornament. One of several figures of Jenny Lind, c. 1847, as Maria in *The Daughter of the Regiment*, complete with red boots; typical Crimean war soldier, a flat-back design 'Scotland's Pride'; Cranmer, one of several associated with the 'No Popery' agitation around 1851, modelled in the round and inscribed 'Burnt at Oxford March 21 1556'.

of the very many potters turning out enormous quantities of useful wares. Such names as Adams, Ridgwày, Meigh and Mayer are found through much of the century. By the early 19th century the most widespread ornament was printed in a single colour from transfer paper, a cheap mass-production method introduced about 1760 which eventually became the accepted basis for hand colouring. Many collectors now specialise in the immensely popular views, chinoiseries and other series of blue-printed useful wares. Vividly coloured japan-patterned wares were introduced in the second half of the 18th century and continued popular through Victoria's reign. Lustre wares—gold, 'silver', copper, silver-resist, Sunderland—fit into the pattern of the early 19th century, but many are still made today and the term Sunderland differentiates a type made also in Staffordshire, Liverpool and Bristol.

Other collectors choose bone china flower-encrusted wares, such as the familiar baskets and the most popular—and most faked—cottage-shaped pastille burners made in profusion in the second quarter of the 19th century when naturalistic flower design dominated ornament. Others collect serving jugs, including the mid-19th-century's favourite, elaborately shaped in relief, often in a story-telling theme. Jugs can be found in the full range of bone china, IRONSTONE CHINA, STONE CHINA, semi-porcelain, opaque-porcelain and all the other improved earthenwares of the century and in the massive brown stoneware developed in Derbyshire early in the century —which included an oven-proof pie-crust ware—and later was given a new importance among the art potters.

Some collectors choose the red tones of TERRACOTTA and others the cold marble effect of PARIAN WARE, a briefly important ceramic evolved in 1842 by W. T. Copeland for making figures suggestive of carved parian marble statues at a period when Greek and Etruscan ornament of many kinds was enjoying a revival. The earliest parian was a costly, difficult soft-paste porcelain and was followed in about 1850 by a cheaper hard paste parian fired at great heat. Parian was used by a number of potters for partly-glazed useful wares. At Belleek in Northern Ireland in the 1850s fine parian was given an iridescent glaze; this MOTHER-OF-PEARL WARE was subsequently made in England too.

The full glory of rich colour and glaze was soon more popu-

9. Chronological survey of tureens, an interesting possibility for collecting. TOP: shapely Chelsea, gold anchor period; Bow, 1760s. CENTRE: view-painted melon, a shape also sometimes blue-painted, by Longton Hall, 1750s; Liverpool porcelain, c. 1770. BOTTOM: early 19th century, Nantgarw; Derby, with lion detail and small view below rich ornament in blue and gold.

21

10. Tureens, cont. TOP: classic Flaxman design in Wedgwood creamware; Spode Regency bone china. CENTRE: Spode, early 19th century (becoming more ornate); revived rococo in Ridgway's 'English porcelain', part of an 1851 exhibit. BOTTOM: compromise between classic and naturalistic in mid-19th century by J. & M. P. Bell & Co., Glasgow; corn motifs in naturalistic design by F. & R. Pratt, 1851.

lar again, however, with such wares as Minton's ENGLISH MAJOLICA, while in the 1870s designers had to widen their ideas to accept what even at the time was designated Japanesque rather than Japanese. Now even the later 19th-century art potters' wares are sought by collectors, not yet as antiques, but for the best possible reason, for design and colour and workmanship that show enjoyment and understanding of the potter's fascinating craft.

PART II

Brief Definitions of Common Technical Terms

Biscuit: earthenware or porcelain materials after being shaped, dried by artificial heat and then fired in a kiln or oven. The term is widely used to include all once-fired unglazed ware.

BISCUIT PAINTING or PRINTING: designs applied directly to the unglazed biscuit by means of enamels or transfer-printing.

BISCUIT PORCELAIN: ware heated to a temperature great enough to decompose its clay content and to produce a porous biscuit. Also the term applied to an unglazed matt surfaced porcelain known to potters as 'sculpture body' and used for white statuettes and groups. The methods of modelling and so on were the same as for the ordinary porcelain. Firing was a highly skilled operation; it was essential to prevent vitrification, which gave the statuette an unpleasant greasy-looking surface.

Body and **Paste:** the term given to the composite materials from which potter's clay is made. The term body is generally used when referring to an earthenware or stoneware. The term paste is used almost exclusively when referring to porcelain or bone china.

Bone china: a paste intermediate between hard porcelain and artificial or frit soft porcelain. Technically it may be considered as a combination of china clay and china stone made white and strong by the addition of calcined bones. Bone china, a non-frit paste, made from a basic formula standard to this day, was first marketed by Josiah Spode; the firm's old pattern

11. Mustard pots showing superficial resemblance in entirely different ceramics: Caughley soapstone porcelain, Lowestoft soft paste porcelain, Belleek mother-of-pearl ware, cheap mocha earthenware.

books prove conclusively that the first sales took place in 1794. The transparent glaze was of a texture that enabled enamel colours to sink well into it during firing so that there was no danger of flaking, as with soft-paste porcelain.

So widely did bone china differ from all preceding ceramics that it acquired an independent status in the potter's technology. Of fine texture and colour and giving enduring service at a cost far lower than the fragile soft-paste porcelains, it achieved immediate popularity, demand outstripping supply for many years. By 1800 several other potters were competing in this ware; Thomas Minton at Stoke, John Rose at Coalport, the Herculaneum Pottery at Liverpool. They were joined in about 1805 by Duesbury of Derby; by Hollins, Warburton, Daniel & Co., New Hall, in about 1810, and the Wedgwood firm in 1812. In addition eighteen lesser known Staffordshire potters are recorded as being in the bone china trade by 1818; very little of their ware was marked.

12. Coffee pots, chronological survey. TOP: rare specimen of Elers type stoneware; modified shape in sprigged salt-glazed white stoneware, 1760s. CENTRE: white stoneware in elaborate cast shape, 1760s; white with Littler's blue, c. 1755. BOTTOM: white salt glazed stoneware with enamelled ornament, c. 1760s; mottled glaze earthenware showing parallel development, c. 1760. All these are rare types found mainly in British Museum, Victoria and Albert Museum, Stoke-on-Trent Museums, etc.

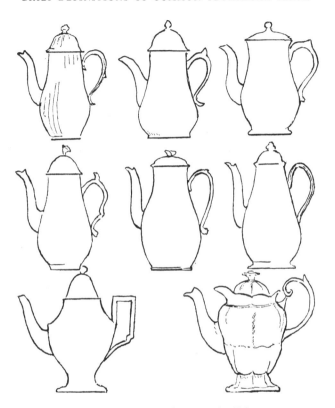

13. Coffee pots cont. Characteristic shapes in 18th century porcelains. TOP: Derby, 1760s; Liverpool, 1760s; Lowestoft. CENTRE: Worcester, 1760s; Worcester, 1760s–70s; Bristol, 1770s. BOTTOM: Pinxton, around 1800; Spode bone china, very early 19th century.

14. Coffee pots concluded. Comparable work in useful wares.
TOP: Wedgwood shell-edge shape in creamware, late 18th century;
Leeds, black, 1800s. CENTRE: earthenwares, early 19th century.
BOTTOM: around 1850; around 1880 with Japanese detail.

Carving: *see* Nottingham ware (Part III).

Casting and moulding: casting was a process of shaping hollow-ware which was introduced from the Continent in 1730, and first used in connection with white salt-glazed stoneware. This supplemented the older moulding process, which consisted of pressing the soft clay into the mould, and

15. Casting and moulding could be used to give table-ware accessories the relief ornament long associated with silverware. Typical silver outlines in two double-handled sauceboats in white salt glazed stoneware.

was used, for example, in shaping solid agate ware. In both methods the purpose was to give shape and relief ornament to wares that lacked the plasticity for easy shaping on the wheel.

For casting a master mould was carved from a block of alabaster and from this a further mould was made in porous clay or terracotta, dried and fired. An improved method was introduced in the mid-1740s, using wax models and plaster-of-paris moulds. Slip was poured into the dry mould until it was filled. The plaster immediately began to absorb moisture from the slip and when this had caused a sufficient thickness of clay to adhere to the inside of the mould the surplus slip was poured out and the mould set to dry. In drying the clay contracted, permitting the shaped piece to be removed easily. It was then carefully cleaned and the seam marks smoothed and relief work tooled where required.

China: a term applied to a wide variety of ceramics. Technically china means a hard, vitreous porcelain, translucent and cold to the touch. Originally the word was used in England to distinguish imported Chinese porcelains from native earthenware. When soft porcelain was made this also became known as china. Later in the 18th century the term was applied also to white pottery, particularly blue and white painted wares.

16. Loving cups, progressive refinement in earthenwares shown in an interesting collector's byeway. TOP: 17th century in tyg shape and in slipware. BOTTOM: mid-18th century and early 19th century with incised ornament and inscription.

apable of withstanding the full heat of the kil
rsally used cobalt blue, manganese purple, th
reen, iron red and orange and yellow fro

jugs: Ralph Wood figure of the squire; Martha
ttle and glass; conventional shape, a Salt example
with pipe in right hand.

ng the original pattern or design required to
e master mould. From a drawn design the
was produced from clay or wax with great
ll, allowance being made for shrinkage from
ware and again during the firing process.
asting.
spots: small discs of higher translucency than
f some soft-paste porcelains, such as som
a, seen when held to the light. They we
ect blending of the ingredients.
mall square box kiln in which enamel
be fired by radiation without exposir
ames. Enamelling was fired for a p
to twelve hours at temperatures be
ntigrade, according to the colour use

The term has now become generic to table ware of all kinds, from delicate porcelain cups to rough earthenware mugs.

China stone: known also as Cornish stone, is a weathered felspathic granite containing the fluxing materials essential to give hard porcelain its hard vitreous nature. It has to be blasted and quarried like granite and then ground to a fine powder.

Crabstock handles: *see* Fig. 151.

Dry edge: in some instances the glaze on an early porcelain figure, applied by dipping head-downwards, failed to reach the edge of the base, leaving the lower portion dry, unglazed and rough. This effect is also found on hollow-ware.

Earthenware: opaque ware which is porous after the first firing and which must be glazed before it can be applied to domestic use.

17. Loving cups cont. Exteriors and interiors of substantial variants containing frogs: blue-painted, c. 1780; Sunderland type, early 19th century.

18. Loving cups concluded. Typical fine quality examples from the Chubb collection. TOP: dated 1794 and 1805. TOP CENTRE: blue transfer-printed, with lid and taperstick. LEFT CENTRE: blue painted on fluted shaping. RIGHT CENTRE: dated 1807. LOWER CENTRE: dated 1839. BOTTOM: full-colour painting, 1822; cup with twisted Leeds-style handles.

Enamels: colours us
design called for sever
of materials which me
each being fixed to th
ting kiln. The pigmen
such as gold, manga
bined with lead oxi
coloured glass. These
or oil of spike laven
charring. Thick oil
to the enamel. In 1
invented, an innova
a less hazardous pr
had become widesp
Engobe: a coating
earth mixed to a
over an earthenwa
coarse texture of
easily-cleaned surf
Felspar porcelain:
Glazes: *see* Part
Green ware: unfi
This term has n
parable with the
wood.
Grog: porcelain
saggars (q.v.),
mixed with the
cally combined
body during firi
heavy earthenw
larly on soapst
High temperatu
ry glaze on d

only colours c
were the unive
rare copper g
antimony.

**19. Typical Toby
Gunn with gin b

Modelling: mak
give shape to th
original model
accuracy and sk
wet clay to gree
Moulding: *see* C
Moons or **grease**
the main body o
Bow and Chelse
caused by imperf
Muffle kiln: a s
decoration could
directly to the f
ranging from fiv
750° and 950° Ce

ware was then allowed to cool gradually during a period of about twelve hours.

Nankin: the ancient capital of China from where immense quantities of hard porcelain and stoneware painted in blue were exported to England, where it was termed 'Nankin blue' or 'Nankin china'. These became the recognised terms for blue and white porcelain, often anglicised to Nankeen in 19th-century trademarks.

Ornamenting: relief decoration shaped in a separate mould and applied or sprigged to the surface of the ceramic before firing. Clay was pressed by hand into ornamenting moulds forming figures, leaves, scrolls, and so on. The relief was lifted out, moistened and applied to the ware by the pressure of the craftsman's fingers.

Porcelain, hard paste: made from white china clay or kaolin (the plastic infusible ingredient), and fusible felspathic china stone (Cornish stone), which gave translucence. When blended together and fired at a great heat these produce a vitreous white substance, entirely hard, ringing with a sonorous metallic note when lightly struck, and breaking with a clean smooth fracture, disclosing a fine sparkling grain of compact texture. Strength and whiteness are increased by ageing the paste. The Chinese stored theirs for decades before use; in England, at Plymouth, Bristol and New Hall, seven to eight months were considered sufficient. The unfired clay was difficult to mould, and, since it softened at one period during firing, tended to collapse beneath its own weight, hence a large percentage of wasters. In an effort to prevent this the ware was made of varying thickness by a process known as wreathing (q.v.). China stone was used also for the glaze, and the paste and glaze of hard porcelain were fired in one operation, making it difficult to tell in a fractured section where the glaze ends and the paste begins.

Pottery: a soft, lightly fired opaque earthenware.

Saggar: a covered box of baked fireclay in which potters pack fine ceramics in a kiln to protect them from the direct action of the flames.

Soapstone porcelain: a soft-paste porcelain containing between 35 and 45 per cent of finely pulverised steatite (hydrated silicate of magnesium) from Cornwall, in place of china clay. Very soft and slightly plastic, it vitrified at a comparatively low temperature, producing a porcelain denser and harder in texture than other soft porcelains; it was considerably heavier and with a less undulating surface. It could withstand contact with boiling water without cracking and seldom crazed, as expansion and contraction of the glaze and paste were fairly

20. Caughley, blue ornament in this firm's most familiar Fisherman pattern.

well matched. Soapstone porcelains were made at Bristol from 1748–52; at Worcester, 1751–1820s; at Liverpool, by Chaffers and Christian, until the early 1770s; and at Caughley, 1775–99.

Soft paste porcelain: a relative term when applied to porcelain, the standard of hardness being that of Chinese porcelain. Nearly all English porcelains of the 18th century were imitations of the Chinese so far as their composition was concerned. They were translucent because they contained a vitreous frit—normally a mixture of white sand, gypsum, soda, alum, salt and nitre, melted together in a glassy mass. This was broken and pulverised and then ground and mixed with the clay. This frit porcelain was a thoroughly vitrified substance, displaying at its best a creamy or ivory tint, to which glazing gave a waxy surface.

Soft paste porcelain was first fired at a higher temperature than that required for glazing, but not by any means as high as that used for hard paste porcelain; this would have lessened porosity, making the ware incapable of retaining the glaze. Colour—blue, or rarely purple—applied underglaze sank slightly into the soft biscuit, which was then glazed and re-fired. In overglaze decoration the colours were fixed by refiring again at a still lower heat than the glazing temperature. Since these soft paste porcelains were not subject to the great heat that produced hard porcelain they emerged from the kiln appreciably softer in texture and were sensitive to sudden changes of temperature (*see* Soapstone porcelain).

21. Soft paste porcelain was made at Lowestoft from 1757 to about 1802, often dated and inscribed and bearing some resemblance to Bow, much of the ornament in blue, often copied from Worcester. At one time Lowestoft was mistakenly credited with hard paste porcelain and with the decoration of Oriental porcelain.

Sprigging: *see* Ornamenting.

Spur marks: when ware was dipped in light slip or glaze and fired in saggars (q.v.), three bit-stones separated each piece to prevent them from sticking together. These were later replaced by three spurs or stilts—triangular pieces of earthenware or stoneware. The points of the bit-stones or spurs left the three rough spots on the underside of the ware. A pottery was established in 1840 by Charles Ford, at Hanley, to specialise in the manufacture of spurs.

Throwing: the process of shaping clay on the potter's wheel. The name comes from the action of the potter in throwing a ball of soft clay down upon the revolving wheel; the ball is then centred on the wheel and worked up with the hands. Until about 1750 the wheel rested on a vertical shaft which had to be kept in motion by the thrower, who operated it with his foot. The effort required to manipulate such a machine was so great that large articles could not be made on it. In about 1750 a potter named Alsager improved the throwing wheel by fitting a rope from a pulley fixed to the vertical shaft, and linking it to a large driving wheel a short distance away. This was turned by a boy who could thus rotate the potter's wheel at whatever speed might be dictated by the size and shape of the object being thrown; this method is illustrated in the mark used by the firm of Pearson, Chesterfield (Fig. 198). Production was vastly increased by this improvement.

Turning: ware in its green or unfired state is shaved in a lathe by a cutting tool to make it lighter and more perfectly symmetrical. Tool marks are often visible.

Weathering: the clay for good quality porcelain and earthenware was weathered in rain, frost and sun for about a year. The clay was piled to a height of about three feet in such a way that undesirable soluble salts and other impurities drained away with the rain water. The frost helped to break down and disintegrate the mass and the sun dried it for handling. Weathered clay was always superior to the same clay unweathered.

Wedging: a process associated with 18th-century porcelain manufacture. Two pieces of plastic clay were continually

22. Sugar bowls or boxes, chronologically arranged for shape and style. TOP: early 18th-century earthenware; Bow porcelain, 1750s (silver shape); earthenware, 1760s–70s (silver shape); Chelsea-Derby porcelain, 1770s. SECOND ROW: earthenware, 1770s; Derby porcelain, c. 1780; Worcester porcelain, early 1780s; creamware, 1770s. THIRD ROW: Leeds creamware, 1780s; Wedgwood creamware, late 18th–early 19th centuries; Pinxton porcelain, c. 1800; Wedgwood bone china, 1815. BOTTOM: Minton bone china, c. 1820; silver lustre (silver shape), c. 1830s; revived rococo, bone china, 1840s.

slapped together until all air bubbles were removed. Any air allowed to remain expanded in the kiln and escaped during the process of vitrification, disfiguring the surface of the ware with minute depressions known as 'pigskin pitting'.

Wreathings: spiral ridges found on the interior of some hollow-ware such as hard-paste porcelain from Plymouth and Bristol and tin-enamelled earthenware. Wreathing was essential because the ware softened at one period during firing and tended to collapse beneath its own weight. The slight variation in sectional thickness provided by wreathing was sufficient to prevent this.

The term has now become generic to table ware of all kinds, from delicate porcelain cups to rough earthenware mugs.

China stone: known also as Cornish stone, is a weathered felspathic granite containing the fluxing materials essential to give hard porcelain its hard vitreous nature. It has to be blasted and quarried like granite and then ground to a fine powder.

Crabstock handles: *see* Fig. 151.

Dry edge: in some instances the glaze on an early porcelain figure, applied by dipping head-downwards, failed to reach the edge of the base, leaving the lower portion dry, unglazed and rough. This effect is also found on hollow-ware.

Earthenware: opaque ware which is porous after the first firing and which must be glazed before it can be applied to domestic use.

17. Loving cups cont. Exteriors and interiors of substantial variants containing frogs: blue-painted, c. 1780; Sunderland type, early 19th century.

18. Loving cups concluded. Typical fine quality examples from the Chubb collection. TOP: dated 1794 and 1805. TOP CENTRE: blue transfer-printed, with lid and taperstick. LEFT CENTRE: blue painted on fluted shaping. RIGHT CENTRE: dated 1807. LOWER CENTRE: dated 1839. BOTTOM: full-colour painting, 1822; cup with twisted Leeds-style handles.

Enamels: colours used for overglaze decoration. When a design called for several colours they were arranged to consist of materials which melted at progressively lower temperatures, each being fixed to the ware by a separate firing in the decorating kiln. The pigments used were derived from metallic oxides such as gold, manganese, copper, antimony and so on, combined with lead oxide glaze to form what is no more than coloured glass. These were hand-ground in spirit of turpentine, or oil of spike lavender, which volatilised in the kiln without charring. Thick oil of turpentine might be added to give body to the enamel. In 1812 a more efficient muffle kiln (q.v.) was invented, an innovation which made enamelling on ceramics a less hazardous process with far more brilliant results. Its use had become widespread by about 1820.

Engobe: a coating of white pipe-clay or other light-coloured earth mixed to a creamy consistency with water and applied over an earthenware body. Its purpose was to conceal the ware's coarse texture of red or buff colour and produce a smooth, easily-cleaned surface suitable for glazing and decorating.

Felspar porcelain: *see* Part III.

Glazes: *see* Part IV.

Green ware: unfinished clay ware which has not been fired. This term has no reference to colour and is probably comparable with the application of the term green to unseasoned wood.

Grog: porcelain and earthenware wasters and broken clay saggars (q.v.), crushed and ground to flour fineness. This, mixed with the plastic clay, gives porosity and enables chemically combined water to escape. It also lessens shrinkage of the body during firing. One part of grog to two of clay is used for heavy earthenware. It is also used in various glazes, particularly on soapstone porcelain.

High temperature colours: painted on the unfired surface of the dry glaze on delft ware, or on porcelain under the glaze. The

33

only colours capable of withstanding the full heat of the kiln were the universally used cobalt blue, manganese purple, the rare copper green, iron red and orange and yellow from antimony.

19. Typical Toby jugs: Ralph Wood figure of the squire; Martha Gunn with gin bottle and glass; conventional shape, a Salt example with pipe in right hand.

Modelling: making the original pattern or design required to give shape to the master mould. From a drawn design the original model was produced from clay or wax with great accuracy and skill, allowance being made for shrinkage from wet clay to green ware and again during the firing process.

Moulding: *see* Casting.

Moons or **grease spots:** small discs of higher translucency than the main body of some soft-paste porcelains, such as some Bow and Chelsea, seen when held to the light. They were caused by imperfect blending of the ingredients.

Muffle kiln: a small square box kiln in which enamelled decoration could be fired by radiation without exposing it directly to the flames. Enamelling was fired for a period ranging from five to twelve hours at temperatures between 750° and 950° Centigrade, according to the colour used. The ware was then allowed to cool gradually during a period of about twelve hours.

Nankin: the ancient capital of China from where immense quantities of hard porcelain and stoneware painted in blue were exported to England, where it was termed 'Nankin blue' or 'Nankin china'. These became the recognised terms for blue and white porcelain, often anglicised to Nankeen in 19th-century trademarks.

Ornamenting: relief decoration shaped in a separate mould and applied or sprigged to the surface of the ceramic before firing. Clay was pressed by hand into ornamenting moulds forming figures, leaves, scrolls, and so on. The relief was lifted out, moistened and applied to the ware by the pressure of the craftsman's fingers.

Porcelain, hard paste: made from white china clay or kaolin (the plastic infusible ingredient), and fusible felspathic china stone (Cornish stone), which gave translucence. When blended together and fired at a great heat these produce a vitreous white substance, entirely hard, ringing with a sonorous metallic note when lightly struck, and breaking with a clean smooth fracture, disclosing a fine sparkling grain of compact texture. Strength and whiteness are increased by ageing the paste. The Chinese stored theirs for decades before use; in England, at Plymouth, Bristol and New Hall, seven to eight months were considered sufficient. The unfired clay was difficult to mould, and, since it softened at one period during firing, tended to collapse beneath its own weight, hence a large percentage of wasters. In an effort to prevent this the ware was made of varying thickness by a process known as wreathing (q.v.). China stone was used also for the glaze, and the paste and glaze of hard porcelain were fired in one operation, making it difficult to tell in a fractured section where the glaze ends and the paste begins.

Pottery: a soft, lightly fired opaque earthenware.

Saggar: a covered box of baked fireclay in which potters pack fine ceramics in a kiln to protect them from the direct action of the flames.

Soapstone porcelain: a soft-paste porcelain containing between 35 and 45 per cent of finely pulverised steatite (hydrated silicate of magnesium) from Cornwall, in place of china clay. Very soft and slightly plastic, it vitrified at a comparatively low temperature, producing a porcelain denser and harder in texture than other soft porcelains; it was considerably heavier and with a less undulating surface. It could withstand contact with boiling water without cracking and seldom crazed, as expansion and contraction of the glaze and paste were fairly

20. **Caughley,** blue ornament in this firm's most familiar Fisherman pattern.

well matched. Soapstone porcelains were made at Bristol from 1748–52; at Worcester, 1751–1820s; at Liverpool, by Chaffers and Christian, until the early 1770s; and at Caughley, 1775–99.

Soft paste porcelain: a relative term when applied to porcelain, the standard of hardness being that of Chinese porcelain. Nearly all English porcelains of the 18th century were imitations of the Chinese so far as their composition was concerned. They were translucent because they contained a vitreous frit—normally a mixture of white sand, gypsum, soda, alum, salt and nitre, melted together in a glassy mass. This was broken and pulverised and then ground and mixed with the clay. This frit porcelain was a thoroughly vitrified substance, displaying at its best a creamy or ivory tint, to which glazing gave a waxy surface.

Soft paste porcelain was first fired at a higher temperature than that required for glazing, but not by any means as high as that used for hard paste porcelain; this would have lessened porosity, making the ware incapable of retaining the glaze. Colour—blue, or rarely purple—applied underglaze sank slightly into the soft biscuit, which was then glazed and re-fired. In overglaze decoration the colours were fixed by refiring again at a still lower heat than the glazing temperature. Since these soft paste porcelains were not subject to the great heat that produced hard porcelain they emerged from the kiln appreciably softer in texture and were sensitive to sudden changes of temperature (*see* Soapstone porcelain).

21. Soft paste porcelain was made at Lowestoft from 1757 to about 1802, often dated and inscribed and bearing some resemblance to Bow, much of the ornament in blue, often copied from Worcester. At one time Lowestoft was mistakenly credited with hard paste porcelain and with the decoration of Oriental porcelain.

Sprigging: *see* Ornamenting.
Spur marks: when ware was dipped in light slip or glaze and fired in saggars (q.v.), three bit-stones separated each piece to prevent them from sticking together. These were later

replaced by three spurs or stilts—triangular pieces of earthenware or stoneware. The points of the bit-stones or spurs left the three rough spots on the underside of the ware. A pottery was established in 1840 by Charles Ford, at Hanley, to specialise in the manufacture of spurs.

Throwing: the process of shaping clay on the potter's wheel. The name comes from the action of the potter in throwing a ball of soft clay down upon the revolving wheel; the ball is then centred on the wheel and worked up with the hands. Until about 1750 the wheel rested on a vertical shaft which had to be kept in motion by the thrower, who operated it with his foot. The effort required to manipulate such a machine was so great that large articles could not be made on it. In about 1750 a potter named Alsager improved the throwing wheel by fitting a rope from a pulley fixed to the vertical shaft, and linking it to a large driving wheel a short distance away. This was turned by a boy who could thus rotate the potter's wheel at whatever speed might be dictated by the size and shape of the object being thrown; this method is illustrated in the mark used by the firm of Pearson, Chesterfield (Fig. 198). Production was vastly increased by this improvement.

Turning: ware in its green or unfired state is shaved in a lathe by a cutting tool to make it lighter and more perfectly symmetrical. Tool marks are often visible.

Weathering: the clay for good quality porcelain and earthenware was weathered in rain, frost and sun for about a year. The clay was piled to a height of about three feet in such a way that undesirable soluble salts and other impurities drained away with the rain water. The frost helped to break down and disintegrate the mass and the sun dried it for handling. Weathered clay was always superior to the same clay unweathered.

Wedging: a process associated with 18th-century porcelain manufacture. Two pieces of plastic clay were continually

22. Sugar bowls or boxes, chronologically arranged for shape and style. TOP: early 18th-century earthenware; Bow porcelain, 1750s (silver shape); earthenware, 1760s–70s (silver shape); Chelsea-Derby porcelain, 1770s. SECOND ROW: earthenware, 1770s; Derby porcelain, c. 1780; Worcester porcelain, early 1780s; creamware, 1770s. THIRD ROW: Leeds creamware, 1780s; Wedgwood creamware, late 18th–early 19th centuries; Pinxton porcelain, c. 1800; Wedgwood bone china, 1815. BOTTOM: Minton bone china, c. 1820; silver lustre (silver shape), c. 1830s; revived rococo, bone china, 1840s.

slapped together until all air bubbles were removed. Any air allowed to remain expanded in the kiln and escaped during the process of vitrification, disfiguring the surface of the ware with minute depressions known as 'pigskin pitting'.

Wreathings: spiral ridges found on the interior of some hollow-ware such as hard-paste porcelain from Plymouth and Bristol and tin-enamelled earthenware. Wreathing was essential because the ware softened at one period during firing and tended to collapse beneath its own weight. The slight variation in sectional thickness provided by wreathing was sufficient to prevent this.

PART III

Alphabetical Catalogue of Wares

Agate ware: pottery superficially resembling the gemstone agate. Until the 1740s batches of buff and red burning clays were rolled and mingled at random to produce irregular veining. Then Thomas Whieldon evolved a ceramic with thin striations in several colours. This agate ware was made from a white burning clay stained green, blue and brown with metallic oxides. Until the early 1750s galena was used as a glaze. A more pleasing finish was then obtained by dipping into liquid lead glaze.

Flat agate ware was for the most part shaped by pressing into smooth surfaced moulds. Hollow-ware was assembled from pressed units. This was fired to a biscuit, hand polished and then dipped into the glaze. By 1760 the glaze was tinged with cobalt, the effect more nearly resembling chalcedony agate.

Whieldon's early productions included knife hafts and snuff-boxes. Later he made teapots. In 1773 Keeling & Morris advertised agate ware teapots, coffee pots, milk pots, sugar dishes, bowls, mugs, salts, mustard pots, cups and saucers. Demand began to decline during the 1780s and had ceased by 1820.

Agate ware was again in production during the late 19th century, prepared from a different formula and, being more pliable, could be shaped on the wheel. When leather-hard the outer crust was removed on the lathe with a sharp tool, effectively displaying the agate striations. It was then hand polished and glazed. Agate ware tumblers closely resembling horn were made by the Britannia Pottery Co., Glasgow, during

23. **Agate** and other marbled effects. TOP: solid marbling, mug, c. 1750s; agate ware teapot, c. 1740s. CENTRE: Leeds tortoise-shell, 1770s; Wedgwood surface-marbled creamware candlestick 1770; marbled knife haft, Wedgwood, 1762.

the 1920s. Unlike surface marbling, the veining in agate extends throughout the ware.

Alabaster ware: a variety of bone china resembling alabaster in translucency.

Basaltes: *see* Fine stonewares.

Bone china: *see* Part II.

Cane ware: *see* Fine stonewares.

Cauliflower ware: cream-coloured earthenware modelled and coloured with green and cream-toned glazes in imitation of a cauliflower. Developed by Josiah Wedgwood during his partnership with Whieldon 1754–59. Such pieces, usually tea ware and punch pots, display careful naturalistic modelling of the

24. Cauliflower ware. Cauliflower teapot; pineapple hot water jug.

moulded foliage in clear green. The term is also understood to include similar wares based on melons, pineapples and maize. These were imitated by many other potters of the period, especially in Staffordshire. Reproductions were made in the mid-19th century, but modelling, colour and glaze were so inferior as to make them easily recognised.

Coiled ware: primitive earthenware shapes produced by hand-rolling plastic clay into a long rod. This was coiled around a flat disc of clay which formed the base of the article, the coil being built up to serve as the walls of hollow-ware. The interior was rubbed by hand to fill in crevices, making it water-tight when fired. Ornamental coiled ware was made by obscure potters in the 18th and early 19th centuries. It is characteristic of South Africa, Uganda, New Guinea and the Andaman Islands (*see* Fig. 147).

Cream-coloured earthenware: developed by Josiah Wedgwood from the early 1760s when he lightened the deep near-yellow tinted Staffordshire earthenware by hand-washing the un-purified clays. This success was matched by his simultaneous introduction of a brilliant yellow glaze which transformed the earthenware, concealing surface blemishes as well as rendering it impermeable to liquids. In 1764 the glaze was improved to produce a harder surface better suited to withstand wear from spoons and cutlery than any earlier lead glaze. The appearance of the ware was so improved that Wedgwood secured the patronage of Queen Charlotte, consort of George III, in the following year and named it 'Queen's Ware'. Collectors recognise the yellow glaze by its oily iridescence or rainbow effect when held at an angle to the light; there is no crazing. The yellow glaze might cover relief work sprigs such as sprigs of jessamine and other flowers overpainted in natural colours. Wedgwood made every article of Georgian tableware including innumerable teapots, some decorated with land-scapes in relief, others ornamented with sprigged work or covered with a mass of impressed dots. Others were covered with tortoiseshell glaze or green glaze. The success of cream-ware astonished even Wedgwood himself.

In 1776 he improved his creamware by incorporating Cornish china clay and china stone into the body, for until then their use had been monopolised under a patent. Four years later he reduced the amount of Cornish stone, producing a cream-coloured earthenware not superseded until 1846. This body consisted of almost equal parts of ball clay, china clay, calcined flint and Cornish stone, these being mixed together in the form of slips. This ware had so profound an effect upon public taste that delft ware and white salt-glazed stoneware became almost unsaleable. It was far stronger than any earlier earthenware and was lighter in weight.

Under the influence of Robert Brown, who became a partner in the Wedgwood firm in 1846, cream-coloured earthenware was visibly improved by the installation of modern plant and more efficient cleaning methods. The body became whiter, the glaze harder, the enamelling clearer.

Wedgwood's most important rival in creamware was the Leeds Pottery. The Staffordshire Directory for 1784 lists twenty other competitors including William Adams & Co., John Bourne, Thomas Wedgwood and Josiah Wood.

Crouch ware: the origin of this term for a type of salt-glazed stoneware has been disputed. William Evans in *Art & History of the Pottery Business*, 1846, defined it as 'a kind of ware made in Burslem by mixing the marl, where the coal bussets or crops out, with the finely pulverized millstone grit of the moorland ridge. This is the *Crouch Ware*, which when glazed with salt appears compact, clean and durable; and at this day the thin pieces, by vitrescence rendered semi-transparent, excite surprise to suggest the manufacture of porcelain'.

Simeon Shaw, writing in 1837, gives a similar description, adding that crouch ware was first made in Burslem in 1696 and that 'Common Brick Clay and fine Sand from Mole Cob were first used: but afterwards the Can Marl and Sand. Some potters used a dark grey clay from the coal pits and sand'. He noted that some potters added red lead to the salt for glazing.

The late 17th-century use of the term crouch ware recorded by Shaw was for a drab or grey salt-glazed stoneware then made in Staffordshire. The name appears to have been derived from Kreussen, in the Cologne district where tall jugs in grey salt-glazed stoneware with applied relief decorations known as *cruches* were imported into England under that name. When similar jugs were made in Staffordshire the dialect converted the German *cruche* into crouch and when other articles were made of the same material they became known under the generic term of crouch ware.

Some authorities now suggest that crouch ware was a drab, salt-glazed stoneware containing among its ingredients a white-burning clay found interstratified with limestone in the Crich district of Derbyshire. This ware was faintly tinged with green owing to the presence of copper pyrites in the Crich clay.

Egyptian black: *see* Fine stonewares.

Felspar porcelain: evolved by Josiah Spode II in about 1800 and made in considerable quantity until the 1830s. He introduced pure felspar into a mixture of Cornish clay and china stone (a lesser quantity of this than in bone china) and produced one of the most translucent ceramics ever made in England. Fired at a higher temperature than either soft-paste porcelain or bone china, the resulting ware was harder than either, less liable to fracture, free from surface flaws and less subject to distortion in the kiln. Felspar porcelain was extensively used, particularly for costly table services displaying radiant colours against a brilliantly white body. Pastille burner cottages are to be found marked SPODE FELSPAR PORCELAIN. Chamberlain of Worcester, Bloor of Derby and John Rose of Coalport issued felspar porcelain as well as a number of small potters in Staffordshire. The fine quality of John Rose's improved felspar porcelain prompted him to copy Sèvres ware complete with that factory's mark of crossed Ls.

Felspathic ware: moderately hard earthenware with a white body possessing a faintly yellowish tinge and often slightly translucent. Subsidiary names include flint ware and granite ware.

Fine stonewares: fine-grained earthenwares, vitrified by firing at a high temperature, with a dense and uniform texture and matt surface, made from local marls tinted by adding colouring metallic oxides or ochreous earths.

In their more primitive forms no glaze was applied. Such

25. Ewers and basins—typical demand for hard-wearing ceramics may be noted among bedroom ewers and basins, now collected. TOP: costly and small, white salt glazed stoneware painted with enamels, c. 1760s; Derby showing the bottle shape, c. 1770s; Caughley, blue painted, c. 1770s. BOTTOM: cream ware, late 18th century; 1790s; early 19th century (Mason's ironstone) (*see* Fig. 26).

stonewares could be produced by a single firing in the kiln, emerging hard enough to endure boiling water, so that they were developed for teapots and similar serving vessels.

The collector groups these fine stonewares to include basaltes, the similar but inferior Egyptian black stoneware; bamboo and cane ware and their subsidiary pie crust ware; jasper ware; red stoneware.

BASALTES: a refinement of the earlier Egyptian black stoneware (*see* p. 52) developed by Josiah Wedgwood during the mid-1760s. This was composed of refined ball clay, calcined ochre and glassy slag from puddled ironstone, with the addition of ten per cent of manganese dioxide. This was twice fired in the kiln, being given a permanent gloss by coating with potter's varnish and refiring to a red heat. The hard surface this produced acquired a brilliant polish at the lapidary's wheel, as noted on plinths for figures and busts.

26. Ewers and basins. TOP: first half of 19th century. BOTTOM: elongated outlines in Great Exhibition specimens, 1851—J. & M. P. Bell, T. & R. Boote, Grainger of Worcester.

Wedgwood's basaltes was in commercial production by 1770 including thrown vases and tea-table ware. Ornament included sprigged motifs in relief; mould-shaped, all-over embossing; engine turning (*see* Part IV).

For the sprigged work, especially, basaltes proved an excellent body. Intricate, sharply defined relief motifs were produced by hand-pressing bats of the clay into moulds. Bas reliefs of classic figures and groups, for example, were pressed and then sprigged—that is, applied while still damp—to the surface of thrown ware. The smooth, non-undulating surface of Wedgwood basaltes was ideal also for colourful ornament

27. Wedgwood black basaltes. TOP: highly polished vase; painted coffee pot, c. 1815. CENTRE: tea cup painted red and white in encaustic colours. BOTTOM: cream jug with classical figure reliefs; engine-turned teapot with mould-shaped lion knob.

painted directly to the body. By 1769 Wedgwood had devised and patented encaustic paints in light colours and bronze: these matured to a matt surface. The demand for painted basaltes was so great that he established decorating workshops for this purpose, but the colours proved impermanent.

In 1775 Wedgwood's catalogue listed: 'Antique vases of black porcelain or artificial basaltes, highly finished with bas reliefs; lamps and candelabra; busts and small statues; boys and girls; heads of illustrious Romans and moderns; flower pots and root pots; vases and tripods; inkstands; tea and coffee services, including chocolate pots, sugar dishes, cream ewers, cabinet cups and saucers, plain and enriched; intaglios and medallions in wide variety, copied from antique gems by James Tassie'.

Several other Staffordshire potters made basaltes: Humphrey Palmer of Hanley, 1760–78; Neale & Palmer, Hanley, 1769–76; James Neale & Co., 1776–86; John Turner, Lane End, 1762–87, who was succeeded by his sons until 1806.

Marks were always impressed and included the potter's name.

Wedgwood and his contemporaries preferred the spelling basaltes: the term black basalt distinguishes modern reproductions.

CANE WARE: a tan coloured dry stoneware derived in about 1770 by Josiah Wedgwood from an earlier light buff-brown stoneware. In the late-1770s he produced a finer body by adding a proportion of Cornish stone to refined fire clay marl. Careful preparation resulted in a body of finer texture, ranging in tint from cream to buff. Wedgwood's catalogue of 1787 refers to this dry body as '*Bamboo* or cane-coloured bisque porcelain'. The bamboo ware tended to be of a darker hue than cane ware and was used in vessels shaped to suggest lengths of bamboo lashed together. Cane ware might be decorated with touches of brilliant blue and green enamels accompanied from about 1800 by red. These could be matured at a single firing in the muffle kiln.

A fine cane ware was used for potting serving jugs with ornament in relief from about 1840 until the 1870s. Ironstone

28. Wedgwood cane-coloured stoneware. TOP: bamboo candlestick; bamboo bulb pot with painted detail in red, blue and green, 1788. BOTTOM: covered sugar bowl from morning tea set, with encaustic painting; classic shape caneware potpourri bowl (*see* Fig. 175).

cane ware, possessing the important characteristics of strength and capacity for enduring oven-heat, was evolved in the 1850s and used for fireproof baking dishes, the first ever to be made (*see* p. 183).

EGYPTIAN BLACK: the more usual form of black stoneware. This was unglazed, needing only a single firing to render it impervious to liquids. Two types may be noted.

(a) Earthenware stained black with iron oxide and fired at a temperature barely sufficient to produce a vitreous stoneware. This was made between about 1720 and the 1770s.

(b) A fully vitreous stoneware stained in the Wedgwood manner with manganese dioxide, but lacking the surface texture of his twice-fired basaltes (*see* John Twemlow, Part VI).

JASPER: a dense vitrified stoneware of nearly the same properties as porcelain, developed in 1774 by Josiah Wedgwood and in production to the present day. Its finely-grained surface was never glazed and when it was thin in section it was translucent. The extremely hard body contained carbonate or sulphate of baryta. When coloured throughout the body with a metallic oxide it was termed solid jasper; when, from 1785, white jasper was coloured by dipping into a solution of coloured jasper it was known as jasper dip.

Although so hard and vitrified, jasper could be stained throughout its substance by any of seven colours that would serve as a background for applied embossments shaped in white jasper in high relief; dark blue, lavender, a bluish pink known to collectors as lilac, sage green, olive green, black and, rarely, an attractive yellow. These varied in tone for technical reasons not then under control, such as impurities in the materials and difficulties with firing temperatures. Early productions included medallions, cameos, plaques and portraits. Vases appear not to have been made until the mid-1780s. Until the 1820s Wedgwood's jasper continued to suggest satin to the touch.

Other potters contemporaneously making jasper in close imitation of Wedgwood productions included William Adams, Greengates, who from 1789 gave a violet hue to his jasper by adding gold filings to the sulphate of baryta, and John Turner

29. Jasper. TOP: Wedgwood custard cup, white on blue, 1784; Wedgwood beads; blue jasper with yellow and white strapwork, Wedgwood, 1790. BOTTOM: teapots, Adams and Neale & Co.

and his sons at Lane End, who made excellent jaspers in slaty blue, green and black.

Between about 1820 and 1846 Wedgwood made little jasper, but at the Great Exhibition, 1851, a large collection of lavender tinted ware was on view, copies of 18th-century productions. In these, the figures and ornaments were in pure white, with delicate shades of lavender appearing through the thinner parts. Solid jasper vases and plaques were reintroduced in 1856.

RED STONEWARE: a hard fine stoneware introduced in 1684 by John Dwight of Fulham whose patent, granted in that year, included 'red porcelain'. By 1690 John Philip Elers and his brother David, of Vauxhall, were using a similar formula. By the early 18th century several imitators were at work in Staffordshire, such as John Astbury and Joshua Twyford.

A harder, more finely grained red stoneware, capable of taking a high polish under friction, was patented in 1729 by Samuel Bell of Newcastle-under-Lyme. This hardness was achieved by adding powdered calcined flint to Dwight's formula, from which it was contemporaneously differentiated by the name of red china. Relief decorations were sprigged to the surface; with Bell's stoneware sharply defined intricate pat-

30. Red stoneware. Wedgwood chocolate pot. Teapot with applied sprig ornament, c. 1760s.

terns were possible. After the expiry of the patent in 1743 other Staffordshire potters competed. Red stoneware made from the Bell patent is recognised by the smooth fracture where chipped. Bell died in the early 1750s, a wealthy man.

Josiah Wedgwood in his dry stoneware experiments of the early 1760s evolved a red stoneware of more attractive colour than Bell's. This he named *rosso antico*. Much was thrown, turned on the lathe and ornamented with engine-turning. The remainder was shaped by pressing into moulds sunk with fashionable patterns. All-over gilding with lightly fired gold leaf was given a fiery brilliance by the red foundation. Among other Staffordshire potters who reproduced stonewares in Wedgwood's fine red colour were Enoch Wood, Josiah Spode and Samuel Hollins. Robert Wilson made lustrous red teapots decorated with relief work in black basaltes.

In the early 1820s highly polished red stoneware was found to be the most suitable base for copper lustre; it reflected brilliance into the film of metallic oxide.

Fire clay ware: during the early Victorian vogue for Staffordshire basaltes and Egyptian black (*see* Fine stonewares), a cheaper type of massive ware in black was made from fire clay by J. & M. P. Bell, Glasgow. Productions included vases, ewers, wine-coolers and conservatory ornaments which might exceed a yard in height. Shapes were adapted from the Etruscan and Greek styles. Two types are to be found: cast with all-over designs in relief and black enamelled; cast solid and turned, then painted with black enamel as a background for scenes of Roman soldiers with or without accoutrements

31. Fire clay ware, a Victorian alternative to the more expensive fine black stonewares. Centre and right by the Grangemouth Coal & Fireclay Works, exhibited 1851.

in highly raised white enamel. In the Greek vases the relief decoration was entirely out of harmony with the historic period. The Jury of the Great Exhibition, 1851, selected for notice among the Bells' exhibits 'vases manufactured of their excellent fireclay, which though not very remarkable in other respects, show the quality of the material to great advantage'. No reference was made to the extremely low prices. Similar fire clay vases were made by the Grangemouth Coal & Fireclay Co. who also showed specimens at the Great Exhibition.

Flint enamel ware: a white earthenware given great solidity by incorporating an inordinate amount of powdered calcined flint into its composition. Evolved in the late 1840s.

Green glaze ware: a glaze applied to shapes and decorations in various shades of green. By 1759 Josiah Wedgwood had developed a brilliantly lustrous green liquid glaze to produce a new species of coloured ware. By 1764 his productions included leaf-shaped dishes with fruiting vine in relief; tea canisters; coffee pots; leaves for the service of pickles; dishes for sweetmeats; chocolate cups; sauce boats, tureens; basins and candlesticks. This ware continued in production for

32. Green glaze ware. Basket-and-vine-leaves dish; cabbage cream jug; Wedgwood leaf and fern dish.

several decades. Until 1775 the basic earthenware was a dark-hued cream-ware; then a lighter-hued body was evolved which gave increased brilliance to the glaze. A third class of green glaze dates from the late 1790s when chromium oxide was introduced into the glaze. This resulted in more attractive tints ranging from yellowish green to emerald green and was more opaque than the copper oxide green which still continued in use. The quality of the decoration deteriorated.

Early Victorian green glaze was thicker and more crystalline and the earthenware improved. Green glaze in imitation of majolica glazes dates from the early 1860s. The final phase came in the late 1860s when Poole, Stanway & Wood applied green glaze to parian. This gave to the glaze a clarity and restrained brilliance. The green glaze ware potted by Banks & Thorley, established in Hanley during 1873, was notable for faultless craftsmanship with natural groupings of ivy, ferns and anemones embossed in low relief, with twisted rope handles. Daniel & Son, Longton, made green glazed ware from 1863 to 1875, production including stands for stilton cheese, bread and fruit dishes, butter and sardine dishes, jugs and all the 'extras' to the lunch or tea table.

Henri deux ware: elaborate inlaid pottery made at St Porchaire, France. Reproductions were made by Minton and Worcester during the third quarter of the 19th century. These were in a fine-grained nearly white earthenware usually worked to very thin walls. The decoration was produced by impressing the soft clay with stamps and roulettes and filling the impressions with black, brown or reddish clays. This was much less highly fired than cream-coloured earthenware and finished with a transparent, ivory-toned glaze.

Ironstone china: a hard durable white earthenware with a slight transparency and emitting a clear ring if lightly struck. Patented in 1813 by Charles James Mason of Lane Delf. The use of the term 'prepared ironstone' incorporated in the

33. Mason's ironstone china, continued by their successors George Ashworth & Bros.: mantel shelf vase and tall vestibule or conservatory vase; two specimens of the famous octagonal 'Mason jug'; loving cup and tureen. A ewer and basin are shown in Fig. 25 (second row, right).

patent specification caused confusion. It was realised that it is impossible to incorporate ironstone into white china. But many writers overlook the fact that at this period the top layer of molten slag taken from blast furnaces was used by the Masons. This was a pale green, glassy substance which the puddlers drew off into moulds. Later it was ground to flour fineness and added to the clay ingredients. Changes in puddling processes by the mid-1840s caused this slag to display a deep purple tinge rendering it useless for making ironstone china, although the name still continued for what Mason termed 'improved patent ironstone china'. Trade marks printed on ironstone china always incorporated this term.

Ivory porcelain: a variety of glazed parian introduced about 1856 by Kerr & Binns, Worcester, after the discovery in Sweden of pure felspar, free of all trace of iron. Groups, figures, busts and ornaments were made in the velvety ware which suggested exactly the 'soft pearly grey tint of freshly cut ivory'. Its resemblance to ivory is especially noticeable when the porcelain is accompanied by gold and matt oxidised silver decoration. Contrasted with celadon in figures and vases it was very effective. It could be potted to paper thinness for hollow-ware. No more than one in seven pieces emerged from the kiln in faultless condition: these were, of course, costly treasures. From this porcelain stemmed several other varieties of ornamental ware such as Worcester's 'Raphaelesque' porcelain introduced at the International Exhibition, 1862. This displayed a warm, almost cream-tinted glossy glaze. Ornament consisted principally of bold relief work coloured after the manner of Capo-di-Monti, but with this difference: Capo-di-Monti was a cold white porcelain, that of Worcester a soft ivory tone that tended to mellow the colours and enrich their effect.

The introduction of the Japanesque style to English industrial art in the early 1870s was well suited to a background of ivory porcelain. In this decoration a delicately tinted ivory ground contrasted with metallic films such as gold, silver and bronzes of all colours. *The Times* wrote at this time: 'The ivory Japanese porcelain is as beautiful as it is original in English ceramic art. The ivory has much the tint of the Satsuma, but it wants the little waving lines of the Japanese on it. The subjects are all from Japanese nature, animate and inanimate. The mouldings, gildings and enamellings are steeped in the Japanese

34. The Japanese style, a Worcester example, 1870s.

spirit. Lizards and dragons twine about the handles and coil themselves round the covers, couchant elephants and camels carry plates and tazzas. The shapes are all from Japan, octagons and hexagons and cylindrical forms; with open filigree work covered with native fruits and flowers.'

Ivory tinted earthenware: introduced by W. T. Copeland & Sons in about 1870 and acclaimed as one of the greatest pottery achievements of its period. It has a delicate warm ivory hue without the harshness associated with cream ware.

Jasper: *see* Fine stonewares above.

Jet ware: brownish-red earthenware given a glossy black surface sometimes touched with gilding (*see* Glazes, Part IV).

Lambeth faience: earthenware made by the Doulton firm from 1873, reviving some of the techniques of 16th- and 17th-century Italian maiolica. Vases, cups, pilgrim bottles, plaques, tiles and other shapes were issued, all the hollow-ware being individually hand-thrown on the potter's wheel. A fine textured clay was used, the body consisting of plastic Dorset clay with kaolin, china stone and ground flint. The colour of the body after firing was warmer in tone than continental earthenwares of the same class. Ornament included underglaze painting of flowers, landscapes, portraits and other motifs. Surface modelling and gilding also might be introduced. On the once-fired biscuit the design was painted with underglaze colours, fusible at a slightly lower temperature than the glaze in which the ware was then dipped. It was essential that colours and glazes were so composed as to expand and contract equally in response to variations in temperature so as to avoid crazing. The glazed ware was fired in a muffle kiln which provided protection against the direct action of the fire. Pieces decorated with gold or enamel required a third firing. Until 1900 a lead glaze with a rich warm yellowish hue was used and thereafter a leadless glaze took its place, noticeably colder and lacking in colour. Lambeth faience was discontinued in about 1914.

Technicians and artists studied examples of old maiolica and the influence of these is reflected in many examples. A great deal of entirely original work was produced, however, especially in soft monochrome tones. The technique called for sure, unhesitating brushwork because of the slightly porous nature of the biscuit. Generally speaking the development of suitable colours was more advanced than the techniques of their application, but some of the artists overcame all technical difficulties, achieving convincing effects of colours, light and shade even for a scene of mountains or moorland. Ornament was carried out by such women artists as Esther Lairs, L. Watt, Mrs Sparkes, M. G. Thompson and others. This subject receives detailed consideration in the *Royal Doulton Magazine*, November, 1957.

Lava ware: a strong earthenware containing clear slag from iron furnaces and fired in a many-chambered reverberatory furnace. Its hard, indestructable glaze, consisting mainly of flint and felspar, required intense heat to fuse it. Lava ware was coloured with oxides of iron, manganese and cobalt. It was used for heavy utility cottage ware during the early- and mid-Victorian periods. Because of its ability to stand up to travel hazards, much was exported. An improved variety was patented in 1852 by W. H. Smith. The name LAVA might be incorporated into a trade mark but the majority was unmarked.

Lustre wares: *see* Part IV.

Majolica: a ceramic evolved by Herbert Minton in 1851. It has little resemblance to the original Italian maiolica, a soft reddish or greyish earthenware of poor quality clay with painted decoration on a tin-enamelled base which was the inspiration for delft ware and the English tin-enamelled earthenware. Minton anglicised the Italian name, calling his product majolica. This was a cane-coloured stoneware moulded or pressed into high relief with details clear and sharp. This was dipped into tin enamel and fired. The cane colour so tinctured the white glaze that it enriched the coloured glazes thickly painted upon it. Colours included red, pink, blue, green, purple, mauve, orange, yellow and brown in various tints. Under gas illumination majolica displays a richly lustrous glow. Among the costly cabinet pieces in Minton's early majolica were vases, tazzas and dishes painted with religious and mythological scenes and heraldic devices adapted from Italian maiolica. Domestic majolica made by Minton and other potters from 1861 included flower vases, sometimes as much as four feet in height, jardinieres, wall brackets for trailing ivy, bowls supported by cupids, wall plaques, ladies' work baskets, umbrella stands and, in table ware, wine coolers, dessert services, Stilton cheese stands, bread trays, candlesticks and teapots. By 1862 Minton was using statuary parian as the basic ceramic for majolica figures. The creamy richness of this porcelain increased the brilliance and clarity of the glaze and gave a softness to flesh tints; crazing was avoided. Hard parian was used for a wide range of goods such as jugs,

35. English majolica. TOP: Minton ewer with embossed design, 1854; Minton bread tray with embossed holly and mistletoe in natural colours, 1862. CENTRE RIGHT: moulded ornament richly colour-glazed on hot water jug, 1860s–80s. REMAINDER: specimens by George Jones, Trent Pottery, around 1870.

36. Mocha ware: jugs, mugs, sugar bowl, cup and saucer, eggcup, peppers, salt, mustard-pot, spill vase (*see* Fig. 204 showing Excise stamp).

tripods and flower holders, butter and sardine stands and boxes, scent jars, kettles and many other productions.

Mocha pottery: known also as seaweed, fern and moss pottery.

This decoration is found on inexpensive hollow-ware such as mugs and measures and dates from the 1790s onwards. A specimen in Ipswich Museum is named and dated M. Clark, 1792. The leather-hard pearl ware or common earthenware was encircled with bands of a thin clay slip which is usually called a dip to distinguish it from the more substantial slip that has given the name to slipware. This dip might be variously coloured: parallel bands of as many as three colours might be used, from a range that included slate green, dark green, blue, orange, cane, red, grey and black. Pink dates from no earlier than 1880. Rims were coloured in chestnut brown. Whilst the slip was wet on the unfired ware, moss agate effects were produced by a diffusing agent having an acid base. A spot of this dropped upon the wet slip at once ramified into the semblance of moss, trees, shrubs or feathers by capilliary attraction. The ware was then coated with glaze. Marked examples are rare, but many are found with excise stamps for use as measures (*see* Excise marks, Part VIII).

Moko pottery: a decoration sometimes mistaken for mocha ware for which it was a substitute. It was first made in the early 1820s, of buff or red earthenware. This was covered with white slip and then mottled by splashing with slips of various colours, by means of a flexible brush made from the long hairs of a donkey's tail—which possibly inspired its name. It was then glazed.

Mother of pearl ware: iridescent glaze based on resin, given a shell-like gleam with gold chloride. *See* p. 204.

Nautilus ware: ware shaped to imitate the nautilus shell. Josiah Wedgwood's first catalogue of 1774 illustrates a nautilus shell dessert service of queen's ware composed of a centre bowl, cream bowl and plates. From about 1820 Staffordshire potters made similar shapes in bone china.

Nottingham stoneware, 1690s–1800s: in the late 1690s James Morley of Nottingham evolved a method of finishing brown,

37. Nautilus shell vessel. Early Wedgwood.

salt-glazed stoneware with a smooth surface that made for greater cleanliness. Morley's stoneware was basically a high quality brown earthenware, but he coated this with a clay slip containing oxide of iron. This fired to rich russet or bright reddish-brown tints, displaying a slightly metallic lustre. Morley obtained his clay from East Moor, Derbyshire: this contained flat sand glittering with mica. The process of glazing resulted in the remetallisation of some of the iron oxide in the slip, giving the ware its characteristic lustrous sheen, while the mica appeared as blackish glistening specks. To Morley, however, the use of this slip was important because the normal process of salt-glazing to render vessels non-porous no longer produced a mottled surface. This stoneware quickly became a formidable competitor of pewter.

China sellers would hammer Nottingham mugs against the counter board to prove their strength. They also sold large bowls, tobacco jars, puzzle jugs, bear jugs and serving jugs, often with ribbed or horizontally corrugated necks, teapots, flower-pots and capuchines—drinking vessels which, when inverted, suggested the Franciscan or Capuchin friar's pointed hood or a woman's capuchine hooded cloak.

Incised designs on Nottingham stoneware showed little variation, the most common being double or triple bands and formal flowers and foliage, especially the pink, and bands of

38. Nottingham stoneware. Mug, loving cup, jug and two teapots showing incised ornament and, bottom left, bands of crumbled clay.

scrollwork set with rosettes. Among the less common were impressed roulette ornament, stamped designs composed of geometrical motifs, wriggle work and applied reliefs. Rough-cast bands composed of fragments of clay achieved some popularity. Some decoration was produced by a resist process in which the design was in a lighter colour than the ground.

It was Morley who introduced to brown stoneware hollow-ware the process called carving. This brought about an impressive demand for double-walled vessels such as teapots, loving cups and jugs. These were made in two parts—a simple inner vessel to contain the liquid and an outer envelope that was perforated with flower and leaf shapes. This gave an illusory effect of lightness to the heavy stoneware. In some instances the pattern was hand-carved into the outer wall and not saw cut. Late in the 18th-century Nottingham ware might be decorated in colours.

The term 'Nottingham ware' became generic although production was localised in the area between Nottingham, Chesterfield, Swinton, Denby and Crich. China-sellers sold this under the label of Nottingham ware, although it was thicker in section, clumsier and less well finished.

Parian: a highly vitrified translucent porcelain evolved by Copeland & Garrett in 1842. Its primary use was for statuary figures and groups. By 1850 another variety of parian was in production and used for domestic ware and vases.

STATUARY PARIAN opened a new phase in ceramic figure work. It was a soft-paste or frit parian with a hint of old ivory in its silky surface due to traces of iron silicate in the ingredients. This could be removed by the addition of smalt, but unbleached parian was preferred until about 1870. Sharpness of detail was accentuated by shrinkage of approximately one-quarter during the manufacturing processes.

Minton recorded success in 1844 and named their version 'Parian statuary' because of its resemblance to the ivory-

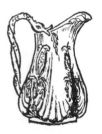

39. Domestic parian.
LEFT: marble-white, smear glazed jug, 1850s. RIGHT: registered design dated 1868 by Copeland with a glossier finish and a bright blue background to the low-relief strapwork.

tinted marbles quarried in the Greek island of Paros. At the Great Exhibition the firm displayed forty-six subjects. A year later their trade catalogue detailed titles, sizes and prices of two hundred and thirty-three subjects, naming several Royal Academicians as modellers. Nudes in parian statuary were immensely fashionable with Victorians: more than one hundred different nudes have been noted. Figures of Venus were in constant demand until the early-1860s. Copeland issued at least seven. Copeland, Minton and Robinson & Leadbeater made portrait busts by private commission and these might be tinted and gilded.

At least fifty British potters made parian statuary, with Copeland and Minton always supreme. The great potters usually impressed the sculptor's name alongside their own.

DOMESTIC PARIAN made from a standard non-frit formula was evolved during the late-1840s. This cheaper, hard-paste parian lacked the silky texture of statuary parian and was smear glazed. It proved capable of surviving boiling liquids and was ideal for potting elaborately moulded or pressed fancy ware, jugs and vases predominating.

The Mayers of Dale Hall noticed that this parian bore a superficial resemblance to jasper. Seeking a two-colour cameo effect in parian they discovered a method of applying a rich bright blue to parts of the background to set off the high relief decoration in white. The colour was restricted to flat areas in which the surface was pitted like the skin of an orange. This decoration continued popular until about 1880. Other colours were brown, sage green and very occasionally a light green relief work on a dark green ground. Sometimes the background was directly glazed, the unglazed relief work standing out as if carved in marble. Contemporary criticism was that the fine granular surface of domestic parian was easily soiled and difficult to clean. In vases and jugs in high relief with undercutting this drawback was intensified.

Cameo jugs, cups and saucers, butter dishes, teapots and candlesticks were shown at the Great Exhibition. Copeland made notably fine jugs; Minton tended to apply touches of gilding; Coalport was supreme with fine teapots, tea services, vases and wall brackets. T. & R. Boote made exceptionally tall vases in blue cameo parian decorated with flowers and fruiting vine in high relief (*see also* Ivory porcelain).

Pearl ware: a white, hard earthenware body containing a greater proportion of calcined flint and china clay than cream-coloured earthenware. It was evolved in 1779 by Josiah Wedgwood who referred to it as a change rather than an improvement of his cream-ware. Early pearl ware had a yellowish tinge: by 1790 this had been concealed by adding a trace of cobalt to the formula. Pearl ware was quickly found to be the ideal ceramic for blue transfer-printing.

'New pearl ware' was devised by Josiah Wedgwood & Sons in 1809 for a royal jubilee tea-service decorated with coloured enamels and orange transfers. When the ware was marketed many armorial services were commissioned with scroll and feather borders in gold and blue.

So-called **'pearl pottery'** was evolved in 1824. This was a dry earthenware body with a finely textured unglazed surface used only for figures and busts, which were described in *Operating Mechanic*, 1825, as 'a superb kind of elegant and tasteful ornament' and the ingredients 'blue and porcelain clay, Cornish stone and a little flint-glass cullet and red lead'. Figures in pearl pottery have been mistaken for late Derby biscuit (*see* Biscuit figures, Part V).

Pratt ware: the generic name given to a type of earthenware decorated with high temperature colours, irrespective of maker, and dating from about 1790 to the 1830s. The colour range is distinctive—thick orange ochre, pale yellow, dull blue, green, purple brown, often with a mottled or stippled effect. Wares include rustic jugs with ornament in relief, teapots, busts and primitive figures. Felix Pratt was the best considerable maker, establishing a factory at Fenton, Staffordshire, in about 1803. His impressed name is to be found on some examples and as a result collectors have classed the entire group as Pratt ware.

Queen's china: this name appears in the mark on leadless bone china made by George Warrilow & Sons, Queen's Pottery, Longton, who operated from 1875 to 1940. This should not be confused with the earthenware known as queen's ware.

Queen's ware: an earthenware of ivory or cream-colour developed by Josiah Wedgwood. The name was later adopted by other potters for a similar ceramic. In 1767 Wedgwood wrote of 'cream-coloured, alias Queen's ware' (*see* Cream-coloured earthenware).

Raphaelesque porcelain: *see* Ivory porcelain.

Red stoneware: *see* Fine stonewares.

Slipware: coarse clay ware coated or decorated with slip after shaping. Slip is potter's clay watered down to the consistency of cream. The slip was most often applied by trickling it through a quill to make lines and dots from which the operator formed figures, borders, medallions, conventional patterns and so on. A greater range of patterns was achieved by combing and marbling different coloured slips on the surface of the ware. Alternatively, the slip was applied in a slightly more solid state as pads and lines pressed into the surface of the clay vessel. A third method of slip ornament consisted of covering the entire outer surface of an article with slip and incising a pattern through this to the underlying clay of a contrasting tone. A fourth variant consisted of shaping the clay vessel, such as a plate, upon a mould and filling the surface hollows with contrasting slips.

Colour contrast between the earthenware vessel and its slip ornament largely depended upon the range of tones produced by firing different clays, but might be heightened by the use of

PETER WAKE.

40. Slipware. Four typical styles of ornament: free-hand trailing (V. & A. Museum); freehand, but with the dark outlines emphasised by white dots; sun-face from a plate with 'cloissons' shaped by moulding and filled with coloured slips; letters and stars in slip pressed into hollows shaped with printers' type (*see also* Fig. 1).

metallic oxides. All colours were considerably modified, however by the lead glaze applied before firing which gave to the body and to the slip, whatever its colour, a more or less yellow tone. Slipware potters operated chiefly in London, North Staffordshire, Kent, Derbyshire, Yorkshire, Sussex and Cheshire.

Soapstone porcelain: *see* Part II.

Sponged ware: *see* Part IV.

Stone china: a felspathic earthenware entirely distinct from ironstone china, developed by Josiah Spode II in about 1805 reputedly using a formula from J. & W. Turner. This ware is opaque, of finer texture than earthenware and extremely hard, emitting a clear ring when lightly tapped. It is double the weight of earthenware and displays a faintly blue-grey tint. In the decoration of hard porcelain the enamel colours did not sink into the glaze, presenting, as a result, a slightly uneven surface to the decorations: on stone china the enamels sank into the glaze and so did not flake in use. An improved stone china was evolved by Spode in 1810. The bluish-grey tint was lightened, but no change was made in weight or hardness. The surface was smoother, unflawed and without undulations, ideal for blue transfer printing under the glaze. Unlike earthenware of the period it did not require close ornament to conceal specks and pitting.

Best quality stone china was painted by artists in enamelling. Copies of oriental patterns were produced, but English adaptations were more popular. Then, to speed production and reduce costs, outlines were transfer-printed under the glaze and enamelled over the glaze in a limited palette consisting mainly of flat washes of pink, blue and red with touches of gilding. One outstanding success was Spode's peacock and peony pattern in which a pair of colourful peacocks confront a huge pink peony flower and a spray of prunus blossom. Equally popular was the macaw design showing the bird with an urn of flowers against a mountain and lake background.

Spode marked his stone china with a square seal containing pseudo-Chinese characters, the name SPODE across the middle and STONE CHINA below. This was usually printed in blue, but pre-1810 examples were in black. From 1810 to 1815 SPODES NEW STONE was impressed: the firm then reverted to the original mark. During the period 1833 to 1846 the mark was NEW JAPAN STONE and afterwards COPELAND STONE CHINA.

41. Stone china. Popular Spode pattern of peacocks and peony and Spode's parrot pattern in the tradition of the 18th-century dishevelled birds.

John Davenport, at Longport, was first to copy new stone china for dinner and dessert services of faultless quality. Like Spode, he adapted oriental patterns for decorations. He also painted landscapes, flowers, fruit or birds in alternating compartments of blue and white: these were usually lavishly gilded. Two marks were used by Davenport on his stone china: DAVENPORT in a ribbon supported by a pair of pillars with an anchor between and STONE CHINA beneath, all impressed; and a circular garter bearing DAVENPORT LONGPORT STAFFORDSHIRE, encircling STONE CHINA in script, all printed, with an impressed anchor.

Wedgwood made stone china for a few years, ceasing in about 1825. Examples are uncommon and marked WEDGWOOD'S STONE CHINA. These should not be confused with the wares of E. Wedgwood & Co. of Tunstall who impressed table ware STONE CHINA WEDGWOOD & CO. This firm operated from about 1860, employing about eight hundred workers.

Many other Staffordshire potters made stone china, merely impressing their products STONE CHINA without name or trade mark. Such work is usually of mediocre quality. Among the potters who named their stone china were John & William Ridgway, at Hanley, 1814–30 before the brothers separated, making stone china among finer wares, John Ridgway & Co. becoming John Ridgway Bates & Co. in 1855 while William operated several potteries in Hanley and Shelton. John Edwards & Sons established a pottery at Dale Hall, Burslem, in 1842, installing the most up-to-date machinery then available. Jewitt listed 'barley, rope, tulip, scroll and medieval' among their patterns. The printed mark consisted of an adaptation of the royal arms above STONE CHINA and the firm's name beneath. From about 1860 a dolphin entwined around an anchor was placed beneath.

Stoneware, brown, salt glazed: comes halfway between hard porcelain and earthenware. It is opaque, intensely hard, non-porous and displays a glassy texture when fractured. It was generally made from plastic clay with added silica in the form of sand or crushed calcined flint. When fired at a high temperature the clay became wholly vitrified, ensuring a closeness of texture which made it as hard as stone—hence its name—and impervious to fluids. The colour to which good quality clays usually burn at a high temperature ranges from a yellowish-buff to a dark brown. It was glazed by introducing salt into the kiln. This produced a durable, inexpensive, non-poisonous glaze which gave the surface an attractive sheen.

Stoneware, white, salt glazed: developed from a drab earthenware under the guidance of John Astbury in about 1730. He was probably the first Staffordshire potter to incorporate

42. Brown salt glazed stoneware. TOP: bellarmine; jug, of about 1800 with raised hunting motifs as on earlier work. CENTRE: spirit flask. BOTTOM: Doulton later 19th-century jug; Doulton water filter (*see* filters Fig. 92).

43. White salt glazed stoneware. TOP: teapot, cast in mould with raised ornament; puzzle jug with scratch blue ornament. CENTRE: white cream piggin and ladle; enamel-painted punch pot. BOTTOM: painted punch bowl.

crushed calcined flints into earthenware. This resulted in a stronger, dull cream body. The important difference from cream-coloured earthenware was that it was fired at a much higher temperature, producing a whiter, hard, non-porous body which, in the same process, could be glazed with salt. By 1740, though still somewhat brittle, it could be shaped into vessels sufficiently thin, translucent and white to compete with Chinese porcelain. Its salt glazed surface made it unsuitable for most table ware. By 1750 no fewer than sixty potters were producing Staffordshire salt-glazed ware, which the china sellers named flint ware to distinguish it from other stoneware. At first small objects were made by hand-pressing in moulds, such as sweatmeat and pickle leaves, plates and spoon trays. Relief ornament appeared in clear-cut detail (Fig. 83). Larger goods were made by casting and there was a considerable production of teapots in shapes resembling houses, animals, etc., with either plain, crabstock, snake or lizard handles. Coloured ornament was introduced first in the form of scratch blue (Fig. 71) in the 1740s and later in enamel painting from the 1750s (Fig. 174).

Terracotta: unglazed porous pottery in colours ranging from yellow to rich red and brown. It is softer and more porous than other earthenwares and fired at a lower temperature. Potters of this ceramic were highly skilled. It was particularly important for all ingredients to be ground to flour fineness. This ensured a smooth unflawed surface after firing. Contraction in the kiln was greater than with ordinary earthenware, ɒ defect that tended to cause firecracks and distortion resulting in a high percentage of wasters. Its slightly glossy surface was capable of holding painted decoration without glaze. The rich red colour associated with English terracotta was obtained by spraying the unfired ware with ferric chloride solution before firing. Terracotta emits a clear ringing note when struck.

The Jury of the Great Exhibition, 1851, reported that 'the

44. Terracotta. TOP: Doulton, Lambeth, 1851; Blanchard, Lambeth 1851. CENTRE: Stiff & Sons, Lambeth; Coalbrookdale flower box in a light buff tone. BOTTOM: Two specimens by J. & M. P. Bell 1851; Watcombe Terracotta Co, later 19th century with oil, paint ornament.

art of producing ornamental works was lost for centuries until Josiah Wedgwood evolved methods of duplicating the finest works . . . he left specimens of the art eagerly sought after in the present day'. None appears to have been made by any other potter until 1835 when a terracotta factory was established at Lowesby in Leicestershire. This ware was richly red in colour and decorated either with black in the Etruscan style or with enamels and burnished gilding. The pottery ceased production in 1840. The mark impressed was a fleur-de-lis with the name LOWESBY in an arc below.

Dozens of Victorian potters made terracotta. F. & R. Pratt, Fenton, made a highly vitreous terracotta, richly red and an ideal ground for enamel colours. Many of their designs were adapted from Flaxman's illustrations to the Iliad. The firm was awarded a silver medal by the Society of Arts in 1848 for the largest pair of vases so far potted in terracotta. These measured five feet in height and were bought by Prince Albert. Clock cases for drawing room mantelshelves were a feature, painted with all-over mosaic patterns in vivid colours. The printed marks included F. & R.P.; PRATT/FENTON; and, from 1847, a royal crown encircled by the inscription F & R PRATT & CO/FENTON/MANUFACTURERS TO H.R.H. PRINCE ALBERT.

M. H. Blanchard, Son & Company, King Edward Street, Westminster Road, London, established a terracotta factory in 1839. Their productions were notable for uniformity of tint: no artificial colour, such as wash, paint or stopping, was used. Much of Blanchard's terracotta, particularly urns and vases, was bought by Thomas Battam, Johnson's Court, off Fleet Street, London, for decoration in the fashionable Etruscan style with a dark liquid pigment. This was tempered with a quick-drying oil as a medium, effective adhesion being obtained at an exceptionally low temperature. In Battam's earliest work the black silhouette figures might be on either a

45. Etruscan vase, by Thomas Battam shown at the Great Exhibition, 1851.

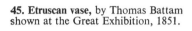

red or a buff ground. The originals from which he derived his designs consisted of historical, mythological, domestic and other scenes in red on a black ground. Every curve in the terracotta supplied to Battam was a segment of a circle. These costly vases, sometimes as much as four feet in height, were sold in pairs. Battam's painted signature has been recorded on some of these decorations. After his son joined him in partnership in the late-1860s the painted initials B S, between four spots in diamond formation, became the trade mark.

W. & T. Wills, Euston Road, London (1858–1890s) introduced two-colour terracotta, mainly combinations of deep reds and delicate tints. Goods included tall, long-necked vases with globular bodies, hand-carved all over with oriental designs. These are in a rich, almost scarlet hue intended to imitate Chinese carved red lacquer and may have gilded mounts fitted to their rims. Staffordshire terracotta in similar style failed to achieve comparable carving or colour. The name W. & T. Wills is found incised or impressed.

The Coalbrookdale Iron Company, near Coalport, established a department making terracotta in 1861. Light buff in tint, firm and hard of texture, its sharpness of detail is outstanding. Vases, tazzas, pedestals, pendants and domestic statuary were made, designed by artists employed in the celebrated cast iron section. It is impressed COALBROOKDALE.

The Watcombe Terracotta Clay Co., Torquay (1867–1901) was an important terracotta pottery. The local clay was especially suitable for this purpose and, fired at a low temperature, displayed an attractive surface bloom and, when turned in the lathe for hollow-ware, possessed an almost velvety smoothness. Watcombe terracotta was much softer than that made elsewhere and could be modelled and pressed into relief suggesting the sharpness of jasper ware. Figures were modelled in three tints of red. Vases and urns might be festooned with hand-modelled flowers. Candlesticks in florid rococo designs and parcel gilt were in great demand. Teapots and cream jug interiors were glazed and tea-cups tinted sky blue. Marks, impressed or printed in black, were WATCOMBE/POTTERY or WATCOMBE/TORQUAY. A printed mark used from 1876 was a woodpecker perched on a branch against a distant landscape and a ship on the sea, encircled WATCOMBE/SOUTH DEVON.

Other potters of collectable terracotta included George Skey, Tamworth, established 1862, who made game-pie dishes in a cream-coloured terracotta equal at first glance to those made by the Wedgwood firm in the late 18th century.

Charles Canning, Tamworth, established 1847, made flower vases, wine coolers, mignonette boxes and many other articles, some enamelled in a combination of brilliant and matt colours, impressed DELLA ROBBIA. Many fine terracotta plaques and busts were produced by Doultons.

Tin enamelled earthenware: was intended to imitate Dutch delftware. It was first made in England in 1567 by Jasper

Andries, a Dutchman who potted at Norwich until 1570 and then carried the trade to London. A century later tin enamelled ware was in production at Lambeth and within five years several competing potters were established there. Soon the trade extended to Bristol, Wincanton, Wednesbury, Liverpool and Lane Delf, Staffordshire, where from 1710 to 1750 Thomas Heath potted coarse tin enamelled ware crudely decorated. It was early in the Georgian period that the name of the Dutch town Delft was adopted in England for all tin enamelled ware. It was denser, however, more vitreous and less evenly coated with enamel. Because the body absorbed but little of the tin enamel, the latter tended to acquire a reddish or yellowish tinge rather than pure white. Lack of harmony between body and enamel caused crazing. Tin oxide was, and still is, the best opacifier for lead glaze, but is very costly.

The clay was prepared, thrown and turned, and oven-fired to the biscuit condition. This ware was dipped into the tin-opacified liquid lead glaze. The porous clay absorbed the moisture, carrying fine particles of enamel into its texture, leaving a coat of fine white powder on its surface. When this had dried, artists painted directly upon the absorbent surface. It was essential that every stroke of the brush should be placed accurately: corrections were impossible on the spongy biscuit surface into which the paint sank. The ware was then subjected to a second kiln firing. This fixed the colours and fused the glaze to the biscuit. Sometimes for extra gloss the ware was finally powdered with dust of purified lead oxide and fired yet again.

Decoration was usually in cobalt blue; manganese purple and yellow were sometimes used; less frequent were green, puce, brownish red and black. Some ware, classified by dealers as English delft, consists of a buff-brown body covered with a white engobe and a translucent glaze. This ware

46. Tin enamelled earthenware or delft ware. TOP: blue dash charger, second half of 17th century; wine bottle. CENTRE: 18th-century char-pot; handled bowl (white spots on blue). BOTTOM: 17th-century candlestick; George I plate.

resembles tin enamelled earthenware in general appearance.

All kinds of domestic ware was made as well as drug jars and pill slabs, rack plates, inscribed wine bottles, punch bowls and tiles.

Tortoiseshell ware: earthenware associated with the vogue for imitations of this shell. Because the improvements that led to the popularity of this ware were introduced by Thomas Whieldon it has become known to collectors under the generic term of Whieldon ware although it became a standard product of other Staffordshire potters and was made also at Liverpool and Leeds. The effect was obtained at first by sprinkling the green ware with powdered lead oxide and calcined flint mixed with a trace of manganese oxide. Firing produced a glaze with a highly lustrous mottled effect. In about 1750 Whieldon developed mingled colour glazes by tinting the biscuit surface with metallic oxides and then coating it with a liquid transparent glaze. During firing these blended into a range of variegated colourings. The limited palette consisted of green, yellow, slate-blue, dark brown and mottled grey. The more frequent combinations were mottled green and brownish grey; brown, green and slate-blue; mottled grey, green, slate-blue and yellow. This was Whieldon's first important contribution to the pottery trade. Production continued in a small way to the early 1820s (*see* Fig. 23).

Welsh ware: large near-oval meat dishes of coarse earthenware covered with slip combed and feathered in zig-zag patterns of contrasting light and dark tones. Such ware is usually assumed to be of 18th-century origin. The majority of existing specimens were potted in the 19th century, production continuing into this century. They were a staple production of the Isleworth Pottery from about 1795. When the firm moved to Hounslow in 1810 Welsh ware was continued until the mid-1820s: this might be impressed HN. In 1811 Richard Waters,

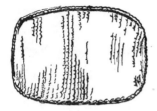

47. Welsh ware. Typical meat dish with repetitive wavy stripe ornament which eventually acquired a mechanically even finish.

Fore Street, Lambeth, was granted a patent (No. 3457) for 'making cloudy or Welsh ware by using a number of pipes for distributing the colour instead of one as formerly'.

Whieldon ware: *see* Tortoiseshell ware.

PART IV

Ornament, Including Glazes

Banding: colour bands and lines on earthenware. This was freehand work, one finger being used as a guide to regulate the distance of the band from the edge of the article. Since the early 19th century circular articles have been placed on a wheel or whirler. The loaded brush was then applied to the rotating object, and the hand steadied by an adjustable rest.

Bat printing: *see* Transfer printing.

Bocage: a widely spreading background of closely clustered hand-modelled flowers and foliage supporting a figure or group, a tree trunk being incorporated into the design to prevent collapse during firing. The plinth on which the figure stands may be moulded in rockwork with growing flowers in relief. The back of the bocage tends to be finished perfunctorily. Bocages were made in porcelain during the 1760s and later at Bow, Chelsea, Derby and Plymouth. Bow examples are recognised by their twisted leaves and petals, and are smaller than Chelsea bocages in which the leaves are flatter and the outer petals saucer-shaped. Various Staffordshire earthenware potters made crude versions during the early 19th century.

Chantilly sprig: an early pattern composed of a cornflower with two leaves and two forget-me-not sprays sometimes grouped with smaller flower sprays and an occasional insect.

Clobbering: coloured enamels and gilding applied over underglaze blue transfer-printed decoration on earthenware. Clobbered work may sometimes be detected for the blue is seldom entirely concealed. This faking produces results closely resembling early enamelled ware and the price is accordingly

48. Banded ware, at its most ornate, the horizontal banding augmented by the crude form of ornament variously known as snailing, worming or finger-trailing. A specimen at Stoke-on-Trent Museums by Copeland & Garrett has been dated to about 1835.

49. Bocage. A Chelsea gold anchor example with a musician in an arbour smothered in hawthorn flowers as support for candlesticks.
RIGHT: **Chantilly sprig.**

enhanced. It must be distinguished from the normal practice of introducing hand-colouring in the course of manufacture over transfer-printed outlines prepared for the purpose, usually in a brownish neutral tone.

Clouding: clouded, mottled or broken colour effects created with a 'clouder' tool. This consisted of a number of pieces of sponge attached by copper tacks to a wooden base about $\frac{1}{4}$ to $\frac{3}{8}$ inch wide. The tool was dipped in clean water, then into a dark coloured glaze, which was thus dabbed on the surface of the unfired earthenware. The piece was afterwards dipped in clear glaze. A stronger effect was obtained by clouding over the glaze. Clouding was quickly carried out, but the results were crude.

Cobalt blue: prepared from cobalt oxide discovered in Saxony by Schurer in 1545. This he named zaffre and a finer preparation smalt. It was used by the potters of English tin-enamelled earthenware as their chief source of decoration. In the 18th century the colour was used on white salt-glazed stoneware, soft porcelain, earthenware and, from 1796, bone china.

50. Blue transfer-print—typical of vast quantities of blue transfer-printed work—detail from the 'Fairy Villas' pattern of John Maddock, 1840s–1850s.

51. Transfer-print—elaborate transfer-printed border to the pattern above.

When applied to the unfired ware it was a dirty brown in colour; firing at a suitable equable temperature converted it into the celebrated cobalt blue. English importations from Saxony were always substantial, but from 1730 the demand for zaffre and the more refined and costly smalt progressively increased so that 180,000 lb. came into the country during 1748 and 286,000 lb. by 1754. Supplies ceased from 1756 until 1763, when Saxony was involved in war with Prussia. English deposits of cobalt were thereupon worked. Contemporaneous opinion was that English cobalt—a greyish hued metal faintly tinged with red, brittle and slightly magnetic—was finer than the Saxon, but lack of experience in producing the oxide resulted in a deep hue strongly tinged with indigo, violet or purple. Potters disliked the violet tinge of English cobalt which was inclined to appear unexpectedly in varying strength, thus making standardisation of colour on a large service hazardous. English zaffre and smalt ceased to be made from the early 1770s until the late 1790s.

The finest smalt of Saxony had been monopolised by the government on behalf of the Royal Saxon Porcelain Manufactory, Meissen, near Dresden, and export was forbidden. Medium quality Saxon smalt cost £11 an ounce in 1733. At the close of the war quantities of superfine smalt were confiscated by the Prussians, and some of this was made available to English potters at fifteen shillings an ounce.

Every porcelain factory bought largely of this 'Bristol blue', so termed because a wholesale druggist in Bristol was the sole source of supply. Dr Wall prepared this blue to such excellent advantage at Worcester that his decoration more nearly approached K'ang Hsi blue and white than did the work of Meissen. Not until the late 1820s was this colour equalled. when Josiah Spode II reproduced Wall's blue and white porcelain in bone china.

MAZARINE BLUE: Chelsea, Derby and Worcester imitations of soft porcelain of the *gros bleu* of Vincennes (forerunner of Sèvres), but less brilliant and of a deeper hue; it is also found on good quality bone china from about 1825. The smalt or zaffre was applied direct to the soft porcelain biscuit in wet washes; the brush-work resulted in the subtle gradations of tone which saved much ware from monotony, particularly when the colour was laid on thickly.

POWDER BLUE: dry, finely powdered smalt blown through a tube covered at one end with a piece of lawn, on to an oiled surface before glazing, thus producing a powdered, sprinkled effect. This method was used at Wall's Worcester pottery and may be recognised by the resultant granular effect, the bright blue being mingled with pin points of a steely blue shade.

SMALT: a preparation of cobalt oxide consisting of from two to ten per cent of high quality zaffre added to glass. While still molten this was poured into cold water and pulverised. Melting, cooling and grinding were repeated a dozen or more times, making the glass exceedingly hard. The resulting fragments were finely ground in a series of mullers until of flour fineness. This powder, smalt, was stored in small bags of white leather.

ULTRAMARINE: a colour prepared from the azure stone lapis lazuli, used for decorating porcelain. This produced a paler and more delicate sky blue than the Saxon smalt. It was used rarely on English porcelain and then sparingly and at great cost. Obtainable in the early 19th century only from Siberia and sold to potters at £20 an ounce in 1848. Artificial ultramarine was discovered in about 1802, its colour resembling the bright blue of genuine ultramarine. Because of its low price it could be applied plentifully and formed the basis of the lovely blue found on Staffordshire earthenware figures from the 1830s to the 1870s. By the late 1830s artificial ultramarine had superseded smalt and zaffre for decorating ceramics, costing one shilling and three pence a pound when poor quality zaffre was being sold by the refiners at six shillings a pound.

ZAFFRE: cobalt oxide produced by roasting cobalt at great heat. At first it contained many impurities. In the late 17th century the blue colour was improved, the oxide being cleansed of insoluble matter by dissolving it in hydrochloric acid and recovering the clean zaffre. This process was repeated several times to produce fine quality for making smalt. Further purifying treatments were progressively evolved, all tending to produce smoother and bluer blues. By the 19th century all traces of copper, lead, iron, bismuth and nickel were removed.

The resulting zaffre gave a less attractive tint, however, and this is noticeable in reproduction decorations of today.

Émail ombrant: porcelain decoration developed in 1842 from the lithophane by the Baron A. du Tremblay, who had acquired the French patent rights of the lithophane for the Rubelles porcelain factory in 1828. The design was impressed in sharp relief as in the lithophane (Part V), but in reverse with the projections introduced where the picture required highlights and cavities for shadows. This irregular surface was flooded with coloured transparent glaze, usually green, to level the surface once more. This caused the cavities of the design to appear as deep green shadows of varying intensities, while the parts in highest relief, coming near the surface, appeared palest in the design. Rubelles' dessert and table services in *émail ombrant* at the Great Exhibition, 1851, were awarded a gold medal, the Jury commenting upon the unusual beauty of the ware and its low price. The process was acquired by the Wedgwood firm in 1873.

Enamel colours, Enamelling: *see* Part II.

Engine Turning: complicated decorations incised on the surface of ceramics by means of a lathe fitted to operate with an eccentric motion. This was developed by Josiah Wedgwood in 1763 on dry stonewares such as red ware, basaltes, caneware and jasper. A lathe was equipped with a contrivance which converted the rotary movement into an eccentric oscillating motion. The article moved in various directions, rotating against a stationary tool of steel. This cut shallow incisions without tearing the surface of the stoneware and could be adjusted to design many hundreds of close, repetitive patterns such as chevrons, checkers, diamonds, dicing, fluting, strawwork and bands of wavy horizontal lines.

Engine turning had a passing vogue during the third quarter of the 19th century when several Staffordshire potters made dry bodies, chiefly for export.

52. Engine turning. TOP: Wedgwood terracotta vase with basket-weave effect, about 1810; cube effect on Wedgwood red coffee pot. BOTTOM: red stoneware (Victoria and Albert Museum); Wedgwood dice pattern, blue dip removed by lathe to show white jasper, with added flowers of contrasting jasper.

Famille rose colours: a series of rose colours obtained from purple of cassius, a European discovery produced from gold chloride and tin chloride and developed by Chinese potters early in the 18th century, and hence a style of ornament in delicate opaque enamels. Such ornament may include a number of other colours and often the rose-pink tones make only a minor contribution to the theme. The discovery was particularly valued because of the range of rose-colour tints obtainable, also purple and violet. As the temperature in the muffle kiln increased, the hue of the enamel changed, starting with red-brown, at 650° C; bright rose, 800° C; through rose-purple, rose-violet, pale violet, very pale violet, until all colour vanished at 1000° C. The bright rose colour was used on early Bow, Chelsea and Worcester porcelains, and on bone china from about 1820.

Famille verte colours: Chinese porcelain of the K'ang Hsi period painted over the glaze with vivid green, strong rust red, yellow, manganese purple and violet blue enamels, the green predominating, sometimes with gilding added. These colours were copied on fine quality bone china from about 1815.

Flown blue: a light blue evolved by the Wedgwood firm in about 1820 by using a special glaze which gave a rich, almost flowing appearance. Before firing, a mixture of saltpetre, borax and white lead was introduced into the saggars. This caused the blue to flow into the surrounding glaze with an effect suggesting a halo. Almost invariably this was in blue, but rare examples are known in brown, green and yellow, dating to the 1830s. Some exceptionally fine flown blue bears the Minton marks of the 1860s.

Gilding: progressive changes in the processes of decorating ceramics with gold make it possible for collectors to group specimens into well-defined classes. For example, soft porcelain decorated with mercury gilding dates later than 1790; bone china was never honey gilded; liquid gold is found only on wares from 1855 onwards.

OIL GILDING: this was the earliest English gilding and was used on unglazed red stoneware, Staffordshire white stoneware and early English porcelain. The gold leaf used was hammered from 23½ carat ingots. The pattern to be displayed in gold was painted over the glaze with a preparation of linseed oil, gum arabic and mastic, and allowed to dry for two or three days. Its surface could then be made slightly tacky by breathing upon it. Gold leaf cut to shape was blown upon this and pressed with a pad of cotton wool. The ceramic was then fired for two or three hours at a low temperature. Oil gilding could not be burnished and was very impermanent, yet it was used in Staffordshire until the 1790s.

53. Gilding, at its most lavish on 19th-century vases. TOP: Derby, late Duesbury, painted with birds; Derby, Bloor, with large 'view' in elaborate arabesque setting; Worcester, Flight & Barr, with gilded eagle handles. BOTTOM: Coalport, with coiled snake handles, 1860s; Worcester, Chamberlain, with tiny country house in elaborate setting; Minton on classic lines with cupid ornament; ornate Copeland exhibit for 1862 International Exhibition.

JAPANNED GILDING: devised during the 1740s, was more permanent than oil gilding and could be burnished. The gold leaf was fixed with japanners' size and could be fired without hazard in a small reverberating furnace. Direct application of the burnisher, which might be a bloodstone, an agate or a dog's or wolf's tooth set in a handle, tended to tear the gold from the japan, so it was rubbed over a piece of thin, calendered paper laid over the gold.

HONEY GILDING: harder and longer wearing than leaf gilding, has decorated English ceramics from about 1755. Gold leaf was ground with one-third its weight in honey, tempered with oil of lavender, and painted over the glaze. It was then fixed at a temperature considerably less than 1045° C., the temperature at which gold fuses. The honey reduced the rich brilliance of the gold, resulting in a slightly dull appearance, even after burnishing. Such gilding, when thickly applied, could be chased with a metal point.

MERCURY GILDING: this was the first gilding capable of withstanding hard firing. It was introduced from the Continent in the late 1780s, although the basic processes had long been known, and produced a harder film of gold than did the former methods. The gilder prepared an amalgam of grain gold, a brown granular metal less pure than gold leaf. This was rubbed into alcohol and a little bismuth subnitrate for twenty-four hours, and then dried at a temperature of 100° C. It was then rubbed with fat to a soft paste and brush applied to the ceramic. The mercury was removed in the form of vapour by firing. This left a film of pure gold which was laboriously burnished, resulting in gilding harder, more brilliantly lustrous and more permanent than other methods. Collectors recognise mercury gilding by its excessively brassy appearance. A pounce or stencil was used to secure uniformity in intricate patterns on every piece of a complete service. The outline was dusted through with charcoal powder.

UNDERGLAZE GILDING: occasionally used on early 19th-century earthenwares. The gold, cut to shape from the leaf, was attached to the ware by an adhesive such as resin and then fired. It was then brightened by covering with a film of glaze, dusted with pure sand and refired. The design was regilded and the surface granulated by stippling with a short-haired brush. Protective transparent glaze was then applied in the usual way.

SOLID GILDING: this process was introduced to Staffordshire in 1810 by Henry Daniel, a gilder employed by Josiah Spode. On fine quality bone china the burnished gold glittered with spectacular effect; on less important work it was bright and hard. Handles, knobs and other raised surfaces might be left with a dull surface.

RAISED AND TOOLED GILDING: also introduced by Henry Daniel in 1810. Scrollwork and other intricate patterns were obtained by modelling or painting white composition in relief on the biscuit. This was fired, gilded, refired and burnished. The final effect suggested solid gold.

TRANSFER GILDING: a process patented in 1810 by Peter Warburton, Black Hill Pottery, Cobridge. Examples are rare and recognised by a printed mark in mauve; WARBURTON'S PATENT, beneath a crown. Some excellent transfer gilding on blue enamelled grounds was made by Josiah Spode II after the death of Warburton in 1813.

An improved method of transfer gilding was invented in 1835 by Godwin Embrey, who sold ready-made transfers to the leading potters of the period. Examples are uncommon, but the gilding is as brilliant as when made, having withstood burnishing after firing.

A third method of transfer gilding was patented by Charles Breeze in 1853. Complicated filigree patterns in gold were produced and even pictorial engravings with gold lines. Gold leaf was laid upon isinglass painted over the glaze and dried.

The required pattern was printed on transfer paper in an ink composed of asphalt, oil and gold size and thus conveyed to the gold upon the ceramic. When dry, superfluous gold leaf was washed away with water, leaving only that covered by the transferred lines. When this protective covering was removed with turpentine it left the pattern in bright gold. This was fired in the usual way.

LIQUID GOLD: was little used in England until the early 1850s, when potters began using it on felspathic earthenwares. Although extremely brilliant it was not wear-resistant. Processes were secret, but were based on the ability of various sulphur-impregnated oils to dissolve gold or retain it in suspension. The resulting gloss was so brilliant that no burnishing was required.

BROWN GOLD: a gilding paste patented by William Cornelius in 1853, but little used until the late 1860s. This produced gilding of richer brilliance than any other method. A thin paste composed of gold chloride, bismuth oxide, borax and gum water was painted on the ceramic, chiefly stone china. The surface was dull after firing, but cleaning with vinegar followed by burnishing produced a handsome brilliance.

ACID GILDING: a process patented in 1863 by James Leigh Hughes for producing gold patterns in bas relief on white glaze. The sole rights of manufacture were acquired by the Minton firm. The pattern was engraved on copper with lines more deeply incised than for ordinary transfer work. Instead of coloured ink an acid resistant compound was used, printing black upon white glaze. The porcelain was then immersed in hydrofluoric acid, which ate into the exposed glazed surface, that is, the parts unprotected by resist were affected by the acid, the ornament showing against a recessed background. It was essential that the acid penetrated evenly and not beyond the exact depth required. The acid and resist were then cleaned off, leaving the design as a lacy pattern in white glaze raised above its background. The whole area of the pattern was mercury gilded, then fired, scoured and burnished. A second and thicker coating of gold was then applied and the processes repeated. The burnishing tool contacted only the raised part of the pattern where the glaze had been protected by the resist. The sunken background, from which the glaze had been removed by the acid, remained a contrasting matt gold.

Glazes

BRISTOL GLAZE: evolved in 1835 by William Powell, Temple Gate Pottery, Bristol, for use on brown stoneware. It is a leadless glaze differing from salt glaze in being even of texture, uniform in colour, richly smooth and easy to clean. The green stoneware was double slip-glazed, that is, the upper part of the unfired vessel was dipped into a liquid glaze which would mature to a rich brown colour when fired. Then, when dry enough for handling, the lower part was dipped into another glaze which would fire to a creamy yellow. Variations of tint could be obtained. The dippers were skilled in making the two glazes overlap exactly the correct amount, but collectors will occasionally notice an unglazed space between them. Firing matured the colour and in the course of the process the ochre or brown on the upper part of the vessel flowed over the yellow. Stoneware glazed in this way became known to the trade as 'Bristol ware'.

COLOURED GLAZE: a colour or stain mixed into transparent glaze and applied to the biscuit earthenware, either to the whole surface of an article or to parts, the remainder being decorated by a different method.

Coloured lead glazes, side by side, or applied upon one another so that they flowed over each other, created attractive mingled effects when fused by the firing process. Brilliance of glaze was enhanced by ensuring that the colours did not reduce transparency. There was little irregularity of surface if the colour was added before fritting. Such a glaze applied to a smooth horizontal surface matured to a uniform colour, but on a curved or moulded surface tended to flow downward and accumulate as dark tones in hollows. The addition of a metallic oxide colour made the glaze more fusible.

Leadless glaze stained with a metallic oxide matured to a different colour from that of a lead glaze similarly stained. For instance, copper oxide mixed with a 19th-century leadless glaze matured to turquoise blue, but to moss green in a lead glaze.

CRAZING: a network of thin, irregular lines crossing each other in the glaze and resembling fine cracks. This might be confined to the surface of the glaze, or might go so deep that food penetrated to the ceramic beneath, causing discolouration impossible to remove. This crazing took place through the years and was due to endless changes in atmospheric conditions, the paste or body and the covering glaze contracting or expanding in response to these changes at differing rates. It was not until 1885 that potters fully overcame this defect. In fake crazing the lines tend to be widely spaced.

GALENA GLAZE: natural sulphide of lead crushed to a powder and sprinkled over the shaped, unfired clay. When fired in the kiln the galena took on a rich yellow hue. Used until the introduction of liquid lead glaze in about 1750, but continued to a minor extent ever since.

GREEN GLAZE: a lustrous green liquid glaze introduced by Josiah Wedgwood by 1759 to produce a new species of coloured ware. *See* Green glaze ware (Part III).

JET: rich cobalt glaze applied to brownish-red biscuit earthenware, by dipping, and fired in a smother kiln until jet black. The carbonaceous smoke from the fuel came into direct contact with the earthenware, thus deepening surface blackness. The lustrous black glaze might be touched with gilding. It was first used at Jackfield in Shropshire from 1751 to 1772. It was revived by the Staffordshire potters during the third

54. Jet glaze or black ware. TOP: with painted ornament, 18th century; with relief ornament, probably Staffordshire. BOTTOM: early 19th century.

quarter of the 19th century in a much harder red earthenware, large quantities being made.

OPAQUE GLAZE: opacity in ceramic glazes was produced by the addition of costly tin oxide to clear lead glaze. This tended to increase the viscosity of molten glaze and so increased its tendency to crawl. Applied to calcareous bodies and fired this glaze scattered and reflected light. Unless the earthenware contained marl or chalk, calcium carbonate was added to the clay or to the glaze.

ROCKINGHAM GLAZE: a lead glaze heavily stained with oxide of manganese producing a purple brown; this is lighter on the neck of a piece and deepens towards the base through running during firing. Fine examples display an attractive bloom. A wide range of tints may be found in tea and coffee pots, dessert services and cadogan teapots. This glaze, used on brown earthenware, was evolved in about 1790 at the Rockingham Pottery, so named because the land was owned by the Marquis of Rockingham. It must be realised that the term specifies merely the type of glaze and does not imply that a piece of this ware has any direct association with that pottery. From about 1825 this glaze is usually found on red earthenware.

SALT GLAZE: a hard, translucent, non-porous glaze imposed on the surface of stoneware by the action of common salt upon the red-hot surface of the clay. The shaped ware was enclosed in saggars perforated with large holes, piled one above the other in a specially designed furnace. Salt was shovelled into the kiln at the moment of peak temperature. The perforations permitted the fumes from the volatilised salt to reach the stoneware, when chemical changes caused a fine coating of silicate of soda. When cold this appeared as a thin, intensely hard film of transparent soda glass. Brilliant and durable, salt glaze is characterised by tiny pin-holes or granulations giving a roughness better suited to jugs than to drinking vessels or flatware. *See* Stonewares, brown, white (Part III).

SMEAR GLAZE: an almost invisible glaze displaying a suggestion of dull polish, as on domestic parian ware. This glaze was not applied directly to the biscuit by dipping, but introduced into the saggar containing it in the glazing kiln. Whether placed in a small cup or thickly painted over the walls of the tightly-sealed saggar, the glaze melted as the temperature increased, its vapour settling as a fine mist on the ware. Hollow-ware intended to contain liquids might have the interior lead glazed and the exterior smear glazed. Smear glaze collected dust, hence its limited use.

THUNDERCLOUD: the dark bluish-grey shading seen where cobalt-tinted glaze has collected in crevices.

Green, chromium: a colour prepared from chromium oxide, discovered in 1749, but not brought into use for decorating English ceramics until the early years of the 19th century. Formerly copper oxide was used in preparing green enamels which could only be used overglaze. The chromium greens are less transparent than the copper greens and are slightly yellowish in tone. Chromium greens were never used on soft porcelains of the 18th century.

Ground laying: covering a border or a large surface area with a single colour. Until about 1830 this was carried out with a flat brush. Difficulty was experienced in avoiding brush marks in the application of most colours to a smooth surface. Yellow was less difficult than the majority, accounting for its frequent appearance in early grounded work. Peach-bloom, fawn and pale red could also be laid easily, as they were so thin as to be little more than stained oil.

In 1826 Henry Daniel of Shelton introduced a method of applying an even coating of colour by dusting dry powdered colours over an oiled surface made even by dabbing with a white silk boss. The colours most commonly used on bone china were dark blue, apple green, deep yellow, canary yellow, grey, turquoise, crimson, salmon, rich yellowish green, lavender, cane colour, marbled brown, marbled blue, striped red and gold. Ground laying was carried out with colours less fusible than enamels and fired at a higher temperature to give a level glassy surface. They were thus unaffected by the subsequent firings required for the decoration.

Henri deux ware: *see* Part III.

Japanesque: a style of decoration introduced in the early 1870s. This decoration was on a delicately tinted ivory porcelain contrasted with metallic films such as gold, silver, bronzes of all kinds, and so on.

Japan patterns: first appeared on 18th-century porcelains of Chelsea, Bow, Worcester, etc., first in the delicate Kakiemon

55. Japan patterns (*see* Figs 56, 57). TOP: typical Bow and Worcester Kakiemon style; Kakiemon-inspired Bow flower and below it a typical brocade background detail; Chelsea sunflower pattern, Imari style. CENTRE: Spode tray, c. 1795; Spode potpourri jar in famous 967 pattern. BOTTOM: Chamberlain vase; typical Chamberlain flower detail with plumage effect; Derby pattern on Davenport jar, the flowers in red, blue and gold among meaningless whirls of curling lines and dots.

56. Japan patterns on cups. TOP: Bow, Kakiemon style of rock, flowers and branches; Derby, Kakiemon style including typical rice-stalks motif. CENTRE: Worcester, alternating panels of diapers and prunus sprays; Worcester 'fan' pattern with brocade diapers. BOTTOM: Minton, c. 1820–25; Spode, pattern 1645, later 18th century.

57. Japan patterns on cups cont. Derby brocaded; Derby at its most ornate; Derby, a late conventional pattern as used by Davenport in Fig. 55.

manner and then in the richer styles, now vaguely classified as Imari, taken from Japanese export wares. In bone china they date from about 1800, when many more people than ever before could afford handsome table wares, cheaper, more enduring and whiter than soft porcelain. For many years bone china tended to come from the kiln with surface defects which were concealed beneath all-over decoration. Japan patterns were found ideal for this purpose. Colours were gay and gilding profuse. These japan patterns may bear a superficial resemblance to Japanese export Imari ware with flowers and shrubbery in abundantly used deep velvet blues, vivid patches of scarlet and gilded tracery. In addition cold blues, yellow, pink, purple and greenish turquoise might be used. On early ornamental pieces delicate tree and dragon motifs might be surrounded by a wonderful range of inventive diapers. On useful wares the design typically consists of radiating panels centring on a circular flower-painted reserve and much work was issued patterned profusely, but incoherently, with scrolls and flower-heads.

Pattern books prove the use of japan patterns on bone china by Josiah Spode II from 1803; Minton from 1805; Chamberlain of Worcester from 1811; Bloor of Derby from 1816. At Derby, women were employed to paint the blue portions of these patterns underglaze. The remaining colours and the gilding were applied by men. The Davenport firm from 1815 applied sumptuous japan decorations in colour and gold. By 1825 japan patterns were beginning to deteriorate in the face of increased competition and lower prices. A revival of better quality came late in the 19th century.

Jewelled porcelain: a Victorian decoration introduced to English ceramics by W. T. Copeland in 1850 in the style of the earlier jewelled porcelain of Sèvres. The Jury of the Great Exhibition commented on Copeland's 'porcelain in which the effect of inlaid pearls and other jewels is rendered with conspicuous success. This novel style undoubtedly exhibits much skill in the process of manufacture'. Jewelled work at Sèvres

58. Jewelled porcelain. Cream jug from a Worcester service—an 1876 replica of a piece made in 1865.

was carried out by stamping pure gold foil into circles, ovals and other shapes for the reception of coloured enamels which were pencilled on and then fired. These 'jewels' were then attached to the surface of the porcelain with a glaze and the piece re-fired. This vitrified them into imitations of rubies, emeralds, turquoises and so on. Adhesion was unsatisfactory and the jewels tended to flake away.

W. H. Goss in 1872 patented a method of jewelling porcelain with permanency. Designs for cut gem stones were indented in the damp clay and the jewels were inserted into these. Contraction of the paste in the kiln during firing secured them permanently. Goss's process resulted in brilliant effects formerly impossible. Jewelled porcelain was also made by Minton, Worcester, E. Wedgwood & Co., and W. T. Copeland, whose mark was 'Copeland's Jewelled Porcelain' in script, but with dots of enamel as 'jewels'.

Lacework: finely perforated lacework decorated the flower-decked dresses of some parian statuary. The technique, originally used at Rouen, was to soak machine-made lace in lawn-filtered slip. The lace held the particles of slip until they became vitrified in the kiln. The heat destroyed the threads of cotton, leaving only the lacy ceramic. The Minton catalogue of 1852 records the following parian statuary 'with lace', but the process was in use by 1847: 'Cleopatra', £3 10s; 'Ophelia', £3 10s; 'Taglioni', £4 4s; 'Fanny Ellsler', £4 18s; 'The Four Seasons', £1 1s each.

Long Elizas: the delft potters of Holland copied slim ladies

59. Long Elizas, blue-painted Worcester.

from Chinese porcelain and named them *lange liszen*—slender maidens. This was anglicised to Long Eliza. Every English pottery and independent decorator painting in blue and white incorporated these ladies into genre scenes and landscapes, or as single motifs usually alternating with floral subjects.

Lustre: an English commercial adaptation of Hispano-Moresque pottery, not manufactured successfully until the early years of the 19th century. Diffracting effects were produced in a film of lustre fired in a reducing atmosphere for eight to twelve hours. The basic metallic oxides were mixed with balsam of sulphur and oil of turpentine thinned to the required consistency with oil of lavender. This liquid, with the metal held in suspension, was brush-applied to the ware, which was then fired in a muffle kiln. Heat dissipated the oxygen and destroyed organic matter in the metallic coating, leaving a hard, fast film of lustrous metal. Lustre was applied to cream-ware, common earthenware and bone china. Decoration was usually restricted to unlustred reserves with white or coloured grounds. These might display blue transfer-printed designs; paintings in sepia or purple lustre or enamels; black transfer-printed work often over-painted with colours or thin purple lustre. Sprigged ornament in relief came into use on lustre about 1820, at first meticulously modelled in continuous scenic bands with such themes as huntsmen, hounds and fox. It was enriched by colouring with purple lustre and enamels, and usually broadly banded with plain lustre.

Although the list of makers is extensive, little lustre ware seems to have been marked. One firm established in 1831 to make silver lustre has continued its manufacture ever since, using original formulae, processes and shapes. Other potters are now making gold and silver lustres.

GOLD LUSTRE varies in colour from yellow guinea gold to reddish gold, and the not very durable ruby. It was produced from gold oxides, widely different hues resulting from gold of different carats. The more copper in the gold alloy the more suggestive of bronze was the lustre. Until 1823 gold lustre was applied to glazed ware; later, often directly to a specially prepared reddish-brown clay finished with a smooth mirror-like surface that gave consistent depth and richness of tone to low-carat gold lustre—then termed copper lustre. In high quality work the biscuit was covered with a glaze stained purplish pink with purple of cassius; this made the lustre sparkle like shot silk. In other ware a first coating of purple lustre might be given to increase brilliance.

PURPLE LUSTRE was produced from purple of cassius—a mixture of gold chloride and tin chloride—suspended in an oily fluid prepared by dissolving sulphur and venetian turpentine in ordinary turpentine. This was thinly brush-painted over the glaze, oil of lavender being added to make it the required consistency, and fired in a muffle kiln. The tint varied with the gold-tin ratio, one to four producing light purple, one to five a rose shade. It was used chiefly for ornamental banding, conventional motifs and painted scenes. The lustre was greatly used by the Sunderland potters.

MARBLED OR MOONLIGHT LUSTRE effects were introduced by Wedgwood in 1810 under the name of moonlight lustre. Evolved by mingling various tints of purple lustre, it was immediately copied by other Staffordshire potters.

SPLASHED OR MOTTLED LUSTRE effects were produced by applying purple lustre over the glaze and spraying it with oil blown through a tube, of which the end near the lustre was covered with fine muslin. The oil expanded in the muffle kiln, forming tiny bubbles which burst and produced irregular spots, waves and splashes. In most instances panels were reserved for printed or painted decoration over the glaze. This ware is associated chiefly with Sunderland, but Staffordshire, Liverpool and Bristol used the same process.

SILVER LUSTRE was obtained from platinum oxide. The

60. Silver lustre: teapots in outlines and surface ornament to suggest solid silver, from the early 19th century to the revived rococo of the 1840s.

Wedgwood firm began manufacture in 1805, introducing narrow bandings encircling the ware, often in association with coloured enamels. Manganese oxide added to the platinum produced polished steel lustre. All-over silver lustre on vessels

61. Silver lustre. Candlestick, serving jug, sugar bowl and cream jug entirely silvered, the serving jug with raised vine ornament, the sugar and cream with elaborate silver-style detail in relief; goblet and bottom candlestick with some resist ornament.

shaped and relief-ornamented to resemble sterling silver plate was seldom made before 1823. Earlier silver lustre now tends to display a greyish black hue. White, yellow and light grey clay mixtures were then introduced, two films of platinum in different qualities being applied to the biscuit. Three-piece tea sets of teapot, sugar bowl and cream jug, rectangular on plan, were popular and a wide variety of domestic ware was issued during the following forty years. Early productions were of good quality and were without relief work apart from silver-style fluting and beaded edges. After about 1845 interiors might be lined with a white glaze and exteriors painted with gaudy flowers or banded in horizontal rings of blue, cream or pink. Electro-metallurgy produced a cheaper silver lustre, invented in 1852 by John Ridgway & Co. The film of platinum was so thin that it failed to stand up to wear and production had been abandoned by the early 1860s.

STENCILLED LUSTRE was evolved in 1806 by John Davenport of Longport. Cut-out paper patterns were pasted upon glazed ware and the entire surface waxed. When the wax-coated patterns were removed the design remained exposed on the glaze. This was coated with lustre. When dry the rest of the wax was removed with benzine and the ware fired. Silhouettists were employed as paper pattern makers, cutting so skilfully that hair-line details were of pen-and-ink fineness.

RESIST LUSTRE dates from 1810, the stencil process described above being used in reverse. The white glaze, or a ground colour, was used for the intricate, detailed pattern, brilliantly displayed by the setting of metallic lustre. The pattern was painted over the glaze with a resist material, such as china clay mixed with honey or glycerine. This resisted the metallic oxide solution, with which the ware was then painted, so that the solution did not adhere to the protected area. The resist was later washed away, leaving the metal on the glaze ready for firing in a muffle kiln. Designs appeared almost invariably in white or cream glaze until about 1831, exceptions being hand-painted grounds, which included buff, pink, apricot, blue, rose and canary yellow. Patterns included all-over fruiting vine designs, formal scrolls and the purely English inspirations

62. Lustre—two typical jugs, bulb pot, goblet and mug in silver resist; vase in painted silver lustre.

featuring song-birds, roses, strawberries, thistles, ivy, fuchsias (after 1850) and also sporting scenes and many others.

TRANSFERRED LUSTRE in gold and platinum was patented

115

63. Copper lustre, with raised ornament touched with colour.

in 1810 by Peter Warburton of New Hall. An impression was taken in oil from a copper plate by means of a glue and isinglass bat. The oil impression was transferred to the ware and sprinkled with the powdered preparation of gold or platinum, and then fired.

116

64. Copper lustre, in shapes of the 1840s–50s.

COPPER LUSTRE, so-called (*see* p. 111) was introduced in the mid-1820s and was often disfigured with specks, pin holes, pimples and bubbles. The earthenware was appreciably heavier than lustred cream-ware (*see also* Fig. 173).

117

Marbling: earthenware surface-decorated in imitation of marble. The marbled effects were obtained on vases and useful wares by laying on lines and splashes of contrasting coloured slips or glazes and combing them together. These are classed into three groups; slip marbling or combed ware, glaze marbling and underglaze painted marbling.

SLIP MARBLING dates from the 16th century onwards and decorated coarse earthenware. While leather-hard the ware was decorated with alternating lines of light-burning and dark-burning slips of equal consistency. The slips while moist were mingled together in wavy and zig-zag patterns by means of a many pointed tool known as a comb, or a brush of leather or wire. The usual contrasts were red and drab, red and brown, light red and buff, buff and brown. Great skill was eventually acquired, as is demonstrated in the collection of early owl jugs in the British Museum. By the 1750s almost pure white slip had been evolved and this was mingled with three or four tinted slips. Slip marbling continued until the end of the 18th century. It was revived on closer textured earthenware during the third quarter of the 19th century in 'antique forms' intended for collectors' cabinets.

GLAZE MARBLING simulating quarried marbles and granite was evolved by Josiah Wedgwood in about 1770. Four standard variegated glazes were produced; marbled, granite or mottled, sprinkled porphyry and agate. Marble imitations were secured by applying lines and splashes of colour oxides mixed in slip glaze to the shaped cream-coloured earthenware biscuit. This was combed. When fired the mingling of the colours produced handsome surface effects. The appearance of granite was obtained by using grey and bluish mottled glaze. Vases resembling agate in appearance were made by covering the glaze with a mixture of coloured glazes in hues of brown, grey, blue, green and fawn. Handles were gilded. Such vases might stand upon square plinths of white jasper or black

65. Marbling, surface, by Wedgwood on a vase with applied motifs in classic style. 1783.

basaltes. Glaze marbling of fine quality was also produced by Henry Neale & Co., and John Turner.

PAINTED MARBLING decorated cream-coloured earthenware and pearl ware from about 1815 until about 1840. Streaks and curls in yellow, reddish brown and chocolate high temperature colours covered the earthenware in the manner of the freer type of paper marbling and were then glazed. Hollow-ware such as bowls and mugs might be encircled with narrow moulding around brim and foot, thinly coated with bright green glaze. Painted marbled ware was made in Staffordshire, at Leeds and the Don Pottery, Yorkshire, and in Scotland. Rarely is an example of surface marbling found with a mark, apart from the fine examples impressed Wedgwood and Bentley or, after 1780, Wedgwood.

Medallion cutting: four types of machines were capable of 'rapidly and faithfully copying medallions even to the inscriptions and dates'. A tracer passed over the indentations and mouldings of a pattern, giving motion to a steel tool which rose and fell in harmony with the relief work. Medallion machines were used for cutting in relief on fine stonewares, particularly basaltes.

Majolica: *see* Part III.

Mocha ware: *see* Part III.

119

Moko ware: *see* Part III.

Oeil-de-perdrix or **Partridge eye:** decoration composed of small circular spots in sea-green or bright blue, with points of black on a white ground. Gilded moulding surrounded

66. Oeil-de-perdrix pattern.

reserves to separate the more important decoration from oeil-de-perdrix background. Alternatively, tiny rosettes surrounded by gold and blue circles might be scattered over the entire surface.

Painting: overglaze decoration on early soft-paste porcelain with cold pigments of various colours. This was less costly than enamelling for no greater heat was required for fixing than a few hours in a warm oven. Such painting was impermanent for it adhered poorly to the glaze and eventually flaked away. In the 1750s advertisements distinguished between 'true enamelling' and the cold pigment variously termed painting, varnishing and japanning. White porcelain occasionally shows traces of unfired oil colours. Painting is a term also applied to high temperature colours applied under the glaze (*see* Underglaze painting (Part IV) and Pratt ware (Part III)).

Pâte-sur-pâte: (paste on paste), a type of decoration developed at Sèvres and made by M. L. Solon for Mintons from about 1870. The process, demanding great skill, consisted of painting the subject on an already coloured, but unfired article of porcelain, using white slip as the medium. A thin wash of the slip appeared as a semi-translucent film over the ground colour, which might be green, blue, black or dark grey. The design was built up in layers of slip, each perfectly dry before another was applied, details and final embellishments being accomplished with a sculptor's tools. The article was then fired for the first time, when the decoration became an integral part of the body, ranging in tone from intense white, where the slip was thickest, to subtle shadow effects, where the ground colour was only partly obscured. It was finished by glazing and gilding.

Pierced ware: decoration resembling fret-work. Made by perforating clay with holes of various shapes arranged in near-symmetrical designs, or with rectangular pales encircling flat-ware rims. This process resulted in some exceptionally light-weight porcelain and earthenware, such as cream ware made at Leeds. Common ware was usually pierced with hollow steel punches, but fine pieces were perforated with a series of sharp, fine-pointed knives. Lozenge-shaped perforations were probably the most common, although requiring great skill to cut without damage to adjoining perforations. Simple, but effective, patterns were achieved, using only the one shape of perforation. It was essential not to reduce the strength of the ware so greatly that it would warp during firing.

Perforations were almost invariably cut into green (unfired) ware, but in some instances were cut into a soft biscuit which had been fired at a low temperature, about 600° C. A hollow-ware vessel might have a pierced outer shell covering an inner, unpierced container (*see* Nottingham stoneware, Part III). A variation might be obtained by allowing the glaze to fill the perforations, to appear translucent against the light. Small lozenge perforations treated in this way are termed rice-grain decoration and are found in Chinese porcelain and in Persian Gombroon ware.

Pot-lid pictures: lids from white glazed earthenware vessels made to be sold filled with either bear's grease, pomade or macassar oil, or with fish pastes or potted shrimps. The distinguishing feature is their decoration consisting of pictures printed not in familiar monochrome, but in multicolour, the

67. Pierced or perforated wares. TOP: plain white salt glazed stoneware of 1750s, also detail of the moulded flowers at the intersections; teapot with perforated outer walls. UPPER CENTRE: Wedgwood creamware lid as found on early fruit bowls and on 19th-century *hors d'oeuvre* and chestnut bowls; diamonds, hearts, circles and petal-shaped perforations on Leeds bowl, later 18th century. LOWER CENTRE: Worcester and Derby style with painted flowers in relief at intersections; Spode blue and white. BOTTOM: details of perforations, from Worcester vase, hand cut, 1892; two patterns from vases by Senior of Leeds, 1888.

majority being made by F. & R. Pratt, Fenton, Staffordshire, between 1846 and 1880. Until early in 1849 lids were flat-topped, uneven of surface and printed in two colours. Afterwards they were slightly domed, smooth surfaced and decorated with pictures in four or five colours. At first such pots were used as containers for the hair oil sold as bear's grease, and a series of twelve were issued ornamented with bears, most often performing bears. The first firms to realise the value of these colourful lids for pots of fish paste were Tatnell & Son, and S. Banger, both of Pegwell Bay, near Ramsgate;

68. Pot-lid pictures. TOP: lidded pot as sold containing hair pomade or shrimp paste, and two lids—'Bears on a Rock', and 'Pegwell Bay' showing Banger's shrimp sauce manufactory. BOTTOM: the same printing process applied to a toilet water bottle, a cup, and an exhibition plate 'The Queen of the Hops' after Witherington, by F. & R. Pratt.

about eighteen lids are known displaying picturesque scenes in the Pegwell Bay district, including a street scene showing a shrimper with his net approaching a tall double-fronted shop liberally decorated with signs drawing attention to Banger's original shrimp sauce manufactory.

Multi-colour printing was perfected in 1848 by Jesse Austin, head engraver of F. & R. Pratt, and developed on earthenware pot-lids. The process was underglaze transfer-printing by a method in which as many as five transfers were superimposed one upon the other in different colours. Stippled transfers were used for the first three or four colours—buff, blue, pink and red were usual—with a final transfer in brown from a line-and-stipple engraving, the flesh portions only being stippled. Green was occasionally used. The colours were applied as for ordinary transfer-printing and were prevented from blurring by accurate registration, a tiny circle on each side of the transfer being used for this purpose. Slightly raised patches of colour sometimes found on completed pictures are the result of finishing by hand-painting. This feature does not appear on reproductions. About fifty of the five hundred colour prints issued from this factory are signed J. AUSTIN SC or J A SC. Four examples of Pratt lids have been found bearing the signature of T. Jackson.

Mr H. G. Clarke, an early writer on pot-lids, divided the subjects into ten main groups; bear motifs, view of the Great Exhibition, military subjects, Shakespearian, portraits of celebrities, nautical scenes, London views, topographical scenes, sports and pastimes, and landscape and general pictures.

The Pratts' successors discovered the original copper plates of some two hundred pot-lid pictures engraved under Austin's supervision. These have been extensively re-issued on a harder earthenware than that used for the originals. It is not difficult to distinguish between the old and the new. Colours on original lids have brilliancy and depth of body, particularly in reds and blues and are covered by fine crazing. A pot-lid can be tested by allowing it to hang from the finger and tapping it with another lid. If it sounds dull, as if it were cracked, the lid is likely to be genuine; a clear ringing tone suggests twentieth century origin, although artificial crazing tends to dull this.

Multi-colour printing was applied to a wide variety of work in addition to pot-lids of earthenware, such as dessert services, cups and saucers, plates, mugs, jugs, vases, boxes and bottles for the toilet table, all in bone china. Many of these were decorated with copies of pictures by celebrated painters such as Gainsborough, Landseer, Wilkie and Mulready. This new method of ceramic decoration, when displayed at the Great Exhibition, 1851, attracted the attention of the Prince Consort. Subsequently a royal crown was added to the firm's mark, followed by the inscription MANUFACTURERS TO H.R.H. PRINCE ALBERT. Few examples of multi-colour printed work are marked, but F & R PRATT & CO/FENTON with a pattern number has been noted.

Queen Charlotte's pattern: an elaborate form of strohblumen-muster design used by Meissen to decorate plates from about

69. Worcester (Flight) Queen Charlotte, or royal lily pattern.
70. Worcester Queen's, wheel, whorl or spiral pattern (*see* Fig. 134).

1740, and adopted by Worcester and Caughley from about 1780. The original Meissen design was divided into six radiating and exactly symmetrical floral panels, which became eight at Worcester and ten at Caughley. Painted in blue and gold the flowers were large with scrolls and foliage filling the background. This pattern was selected by Queen Charlotte when, with George III, she visited the Worcester factory in 1788.

Queen's pattern: a design, evolved at Worcester in about 1770, consisting of alternate radial whirling bands of ornament in red on white and white on blue with gilded enrichments. Known also as the 'spiral' or 'catherine wheel' pattern.

Roulette work: simple repetitive line ornament, noted, for example, emphasising the outlines in some slipware ornament. It was produced with a revolving toothed wheel set in a handle. This cut bands of light incisions into the soft clay before firing.

Scratched blue: types of graffito ornament in which patterns in blue lines decorated white earthenware or stoneware.

1. Body coated with blue and then covered with a white or cream engobe. Body and slips were of almost equal composition to prevent crazing by expansion and contraction. The

71. Scratched blue or graffito ornament, on white salt glazed stoneware (*see* Fig. 43).

design was then scratched with a sharp tool upon the outer stratum before firing, thus revealing the pattern in blue lines.

2. The design was scratched directly into the body—usually white stoneware—and finely powdered blue-stained glaze or

zaffre dusted into the incisions. After firing in a salt-glaze kiln the pattern was seen in dark blue against a white ground.

3. The traditional slipware potter's method of dipping coloured earthenware into white clay slip and incising a design through the coating to display the pattern in dark colour.

Slip: potter's clay watered down to the consistency of cream and used to ornament common clay wares (*see* Slip ware, Part III).

Snail horn ware: a Yorkshire novelty of the 19th century consisting of yellow and brown pottery mixed to produce striped and banded effects.

Sponged ornament: strong earthenware such as granite ware and ironstone china decorated with stipple effects by dabbing the biscuit with a sponge or roll of rags dipped in colour. Birds, flowers, trees and houses incorporated in the design were outlined black in freehand lines and coloured with a

72. Sponged ornament, with characteristic bold motifs against backgrounds of lines and spatters (*see* Fig. 156).

brush. Sponging might be in monochrome or polychrome, the colours being blue, pink, green, brown and purple. The backward-glancing Asiatic pheasant, for instance, was a popular quickly-painted motif drawn in outline with a plumed tail and usually perched on a branch of sponged work. Sponged decoration for the most part decorated table ware. Hexagonal hollow-ware was common and lids to teapots and sugar basins were highly domed with knob finials.

Few pieces were marked, but the following have been recorded: B & T—Blackhurst & Tunnicliffe, Burslem, from 1879; ELSMORE & FORSTER, TUNSTALL, 1853–71; P W & CO —Podmore, Walker & Co., Tunstall, 1834–55; HARVEY— C. & W. K. Harvey, Longton, 1835–53; B B—Barker Bros., Longton, who made 'fancy sponged' in the 1870s. (*see* also Fig. 155).

Sprigged decoration: relief ornament shaped in a separate metal or hard plaster mould, removed and immediately applied, or sprigged, on to the body of the ware before firing.

Transfer-printing: a process of applying engraved decorative designs to ceramics. Its earliest use was at the Battersea enamel works in 1753, the three partners each having made a contribution to its success; Stephen Theodore Janssen perfected the strong, hairless, pinhole-free transfer paper, John Brooks initiated the special technique required for engraving the copper plate, and Henry Delamain (*see* Dublin) was responsible for preparing enamels with printer's ink in such a way that firing fused the design to the white enamel surface.

Battersea failed in 1756 and it is thought that Robert Hancock, experienced in engraving for transfers, carried the process first to Bow and later in the same year to Worcester. This process of transfer-printing began with engraving the design in such a way as to produce sharp, clear lines on a thin copper plate, rendered hard-textured by long beating with a hammer.

This early form of transfer-printing was applied over the glaze of soft-paste porcelain, which was then fired at a low temperature hardening-on kiln. The resultant print consisted of a simple design in black, brick red, dark purple or brown,

73. Transfer-printing—typical borders found on transfer-printed use-
ful wares, early 19th century. TOP: by Joseph Stubbs, Burslem; by
J. Rogers & Son, Longport. SECOND ROW: by Joseph Heath &
Co., Tunstall; by Bourne, Baker & Bourne, Tunstall. THIRD ROW:
William Adams, Stoke; Rockingham, Swinton. BOTTOM: 'Tri-
umphal car' border by J. & M. P. Bell, Glasgow.

and might be overpainted by hand with washes of near-transparent colour.

BLUE UNDERGLAZE was originated by Robert Hancock at Worcester during the early 1760s, developed by Thomas Turner at Caughley and perfected by Josiah Spode in about 1781. The transferred design was applied to the biscuit, fired and afterwards glazed to give the decoration a protective coat with a lifetime of hard wear resistance. The clarity of outline

74. Blue and white transfer-printed borders, cont. TOP: by Thomas Mayer, Stoke; by Andrew Stevenson, Cobridge. SECOND ROW: both by E. Wood, Burslem. THIRD ROW: by E. Wood; by James & Ralph Clews, Cobridge. FOURTH ROW: both by J. & R. Clews, left also by Adams.

and brilliance of colour on an earthenware notably whiter than that of competitors brought Spode immediate popularity. Until 1805 patterns followed the established convention of adaptation from Chinese porcelain. Not until about 1800 was an improvement made in the slightly smudgy effect of cross-hatching associated with 18th-century blue underglaze-printing. In the early 1800s engraved lines were thinner, making possible a variation in tone and introducing dark shades and high-lights. From 1810 finer tone variations were secured by combining line and stipple engraving on a single copper plate.

The colour particularly associated with underglaze transfer-printing is blue against a white ground. The blue obtained from cobalt oxide was the one colour unspoiled by glaze firing and was also capable of producing numerous gradations of tint. In some early 19th-century examples dark and light blue transfers might be used on a single piece of ware. Until 1830 shades of cobalt blue continued under such trade names as Canton blue, zaffres, willow blue, flown blue, flower blue and mazarine. Deterioration in quality is observed in blue and white made after 1830, the blue being lighter and patterns less meticulously engraved.

The collector will distinguish between the soft cobalt blue of early blue-printed ware and the harsher synthetic blue used from about 1802. Lightweight earthenware usually belongs to the late 18th century. If the glaze of the blue-printed ware is examined, with the light falling obliquely upon it, the surface of an old piece appears to be finely dappled, rather resembling the appearance of smooth sea-sand after a shower of rain. Once recognised, dappling is unmistakable and is a feature that has not been reproduced. It is seldom visible on ware dating from 1800 and never after 1820.

Among the two hundred or so potters who made Staffordshire blue probably no more than twenty issued fine quality ware and it is this that the collector seeks, for most of it is

75. Blue and white transfer-printed borders, cont. TOP: both by Wedgwood. SECOND ROW: both by Spode, on Italian series and on tower pattern. THIRD ROW: both by Spode, on gothic castle pattern and on Lucarno pattern. BOTTOM: by Spode on willow pattern.

impressed or printed with trade marks. Some firms had their own range of exclusive border designs; typical specimens are illustrated on pages 90 and 129–34.

The names most frequently encountered are Josiah Spode, Enoch Wood, Joseph Stubbs, Charles Meigh, J. & J. Jackson, Andrew Stevenson, T. Mayer, Wedgwood and Minton. Frequently the title of a pattern is given in a cartouche incorporating the initials of the firm and many of these have been elucidated (*see* Part VII).

The blue transfer-printed pottery from the Spodes and their successors the Copelands is now regarded by collectors as technically almost perfect, the engraving, colour and glaze all being outstanding. Their designs have been grouped into five main classes: Indian influence; Caramanian patterns; Italian patterns including Tiber, Castle, Tower, Lucano, Blue Italian; Chinese patterns such as willow, India, mosaic, two birds, hundred antiques, net, Nankin, Gothic castle, old peacock; general subjects including Waterloo, milkmaid, woodman, geranium, Warwick vase, filigree, Greek, Persian, blue rose, Union wreath, girl at the well, country scene. There are numerous variations in each group.

Enoch Wood and his sons (1784–1846) were probably the most prolific makers of Staffordshire blue and were responsible for some outstanding examples between 1819 and 1840. Their printing was always in dark shades of blue, but late printing was in a tint too dark to give perfect clarity to the pictures. They issued a range of more than five hundred English, American and French views; in addition more than three hundred miscellaneous pictures have been recorded. Sea shells frequently appeared in the borders, with the cockle conspicuous. Flowers, however, were Wood's favourite border motif until about 1830, when a change was made to compositions of fruiting vine and oak leaves, edged with a narrow, twisted border. Common during the 1830s was a flower and scroll border containing several reserves—usually six—separated from the central view by a narrow ornamental ribbon.

John & William Ridgway, Hanley (*see* Fig. 76) from 1817 to 1824 printed in blue paler than that of their contemporaries, but with unblurred tone differentiations. Exported wares included their Beauties of America. They made the long series of Oxford and Cambridge University views set in eight-sided

76. Blue and white transfer-printed borders, cont. TOP: both by Ralph Stevenson & Williams, Cobridge (*see* Fig. 89). SECOND ROW: both by J. & J. Jackson, Burslem. THIRD ROW AND BOTTOM: by J. & W. Ridgway, Hanley.

panels, bordered with medallions of children and flowers. A series of Zoological Garden scenes was issued in the late 1820s, with elaborate borders of twisted scrolls. All blue-printed ware was impressed J & W RIDGWAY with the name of the view printed in blue.

BAT PRINTING was an overglaze process producing pictures and designs of extreme delicacy, introduced to England in the early-1760s, but little used until the 1780s. The copper plate was stippled with a fine point, short lines also being included, but being subsidiary to the stipple dots. The design was printed in oil upon a bat—a flexible sheet or pad composed of glue, treacle and whiting, about ¼ inch thick. This oil outline was transferred to the ware and dusted with the colour required, any surplus being removed with cotton wool. Bat printing was little used from about 1800 until 1825, when a special transfer paper was evolved for the purpose, the results being equally fine.

COLOUR UNDERGLAZE dates from 1828, when it was found that by mixing finely powdered green, yellow, red and black enamel with barbadoes tar it was possible to apply transferred designs in various shades of these colours without distortion. Two or more of the colours might be printed on a single piece, a separate firing being required for each transfer. This increased the cost and examples are uncommon.

MULTI-COLOUR UNDERGLAZE was invented in 1848 by F. Collins & A. Reynolds, Hanley. By this process three colours —blue, red and yellow—could be fixed from a single transfer requiring one firing. Brown and green were added from 1852. The process continued in use until the 1860s (see Pot lids).

GILDING: see page 98.

LITHOGRAPHY was first used on ceramics in 1839 in light blue carried out with artificial ultramarine under the glaze. From 1845 lithography was carried out in multi-colour, pink, green, purple, grey and black all being incorporated into single pictures. Examples made before the late-1850s are recognised by their dull, uninteresting surface caused by the small amount of colour used. The impressions were taken from lithographed

135

stones, but, instead of ink, potter's varnish was used. This was transferred to the paper and thence to the surface of the glazed ware, and dusted with colour powder.

Underglaze painting: metallic oxide colouring agents used as decoration between the body and glaze, thus ensuring permanency. The pattern was painted on the once-fired biscuit ware, which was then fired at a low temperature capable of burning out the varnish and setting the colours. This was known as hardening on. The ware was then dipped into transparent glaze and fired in a glost or glazing kiln. The palette was limited and eventually included cobalt blue, nickel brown, chromium green and red, manganese brown and violet, iron yellow and red, platinum grey, iridium black. Rich reds were obtained from oxide of gold.

Uranium: this rare metallic element was obtainable from Cornwall and Saxony by the 1840s, extracted from uranite and pitchblende. Its oxide was found to be successful in preparing a golden green enamel; late in the century it was used to produce brilliant tangerine and vermilion red glazes. Its use is now prohibited as this oxide is a health hazard. Hence reproductions are impossible.

Widow knobs: these ornamented the lids of many teapots, coffee pots and other fine stoneware hollow-ware for more than half a century from the 1760s. The original model, believed to have been designed by William Greatbach, depicted a young woman wearing a bonnet and shawl. In a later version she is seen with a flat-brimmed hat, and in a third as an older woman with folded arms and her head covered with a shawl arranged as a cowl; the fourth version is a younger woman with a coif not entirely hidden by a shawl. Other and later versions have been noted.

Willow pattern: a pseudo-Chinese design in blue underglaze evolved from the 1760s and now associated with Thomas Turner of Caughley. The original copper plates as used on

77. Willow pattern. TOP LEFT: Spode's earliest, with one figure on the bridge and no birds. TOP RIGHT: by Herculaneum, Liverpool. CENTRE RIGHT: less common, with two figures and the familiar birds. BOTTOM LEFT: Leeds (and noted almost identical on Swansea). BOTTOM RIGHT: Davenport, with two figures on the bridge and two huge birds swimming on the water.

137

earthenware engraved by Turner, with his signature in the margins, are preserved in the British Museum. In this design Turner placed the pagoda on the right surrounded by six types of conventionalised tree—interpreted as willow, beech, fir,

78. Later willow pattern. By Davenport, with three figures on the bridge and flying birds. Typical design by Spode, Minton, etc. Typical detail of later figures: this from a version by J. & E. Baddeley, Shelton.

plum, the mysterious tree with dark circles and the tallest of all bearing thirty-two apples arranged in three tiers. No figure appeared on the bridge and the zig-zag fence extended from the water to the right-hand edge of the design. On Caughley porcelain the design was different; the pagoda was on the left of the picture. But this was only one of several Caughley variations on the popular theme.

Thomas Minton, while an apprentice engraver at Caughley, cut many of the willow pattern copper plates, and when he left and set up as a freelance engraver in Stoke he designed and engraved variants for other potters, retaining the main motifs, but altering the fence patterns, the number of apples on the tree and the rim and bouge designs. Josiah Spode I made willow pattern from 1785, using a design very similar to that on Caughley porcelain, but applied to earthenware only. From about 1800 a slightly different pattern was adopted with thirty-two apples on the tree. Wedgwood issued willow pattern from 1795, the design being a close adaptation of Caughley with the pagoda on the right, the fret of the fence different and thirty-five apples in the design used on plates and more on dishes. In about 1830 the Wedgwood firm produced a small quantity of willow pattern earthenware printed in black and sometimes enriched with gilt bands.

William Adams, Stoke on Trent, made large quantities of willow pattern, the tree bearing thirty-two apples and, after about 1830, fifty apples. John Davenport's trees bore only twenty-five apples; these dated between 1793 and about1830. The Swansea willow pattern had thirty apples and might be printed in dark and light blues, also, occasionally, in black and brown. There were nearly two hundred makers of willow pattern in underglaze blue by 1830. The only way to attribute a piece accurately is by the mark, or by comparison with a marked piece.

Zaffre: *see* Cobalt.

PART V

Items for the Collector

Bellarmines: coarse salt-glazed stoneware bottles, bearing on the neck a crude bearded mask so ugly that some saw a resemblance to Cardinal Bellarmine (1542–1621), who was disliked in Protestant countries. Known in England as greybeards, such bottles were being made in London for use in the royal household by the late 1570s. In shape the vessel is full bellied, short in proportion to the narrow neck that bears the mask, and below it sometimes a coat of arms in relief. They were made until the mid-19th century in four sizes: gallonier (gallon); pottle pot (half gallon); pot (quart); little pot (pint). Reproductions are now being made (*see* Fig. 42).

Bird tureens: shaped as sitting hens, ducks and drakes, swans, fighting cocks, rabbits, fish, imposing boars' heads, partridges and so on, in at least twenty types, these have been wrongly assumed to have contained food associated with their outer form. Originally, however, they were included in the service of

79. Bird tureens. Typical 19th-century hen on basket—mould-shaped in parian. Typical porcelain partridge, Chelsea.

dessert at a period when this might be an ornamental repast for a social gathering. The vogue for bird tureens was initiated by Meissen in the 1740s. They were made in porcelain in England from the early 1750s and some may date as late as 1775. Those made after about 1763 were inferior in modelling and enamelling.

CHELSEA: appears to have been first to copy the Meissen style in England, cataloguing them singly and in pairs. Particularly desirable were 'tureens in the shape of a hen and chickens as large as life in a fine sunflower leaf dish'. The hen is in a sitting position with a chicken perched on her back, three others peeping from beneath her left wing and three snuggling against her breast. Colouring is in shades of purple, with dashes of brown and blood red. The hen is divided horizontally from the upper tail feathers to the breast, the upper portion forming a lid with a chick for a knob. The dish upon which it rests is composed of three large sunflowers in full relief, several small flowers, and a border of leaves in relief.

Fighting cocks, plucked, cropped and spurred and in the attacking posture; graceful swans appearing to float in their flat oval dishes; crouching rabbits with raised ears; crested ducks and drakes; boars' heads; carp naturalistically coloured in purple and brown with a greenish slime tint around the gills were all made at Chelsea. Partridge tureens, smaller and less imposing than the others, were made in greater numbers as sweetmeat containers and might be sold already filled; one Chelsea series consisted of two birds sitting on a single dish.

BOW: made pairs of partridge tureens with dishes from 1756, copying a Meissen original and adapting from it several other models and sizes. Bow partridges are less realistically modelled than those of Chelsea, but colouring is more naturalistic. Pigeon tureens were made also.

DERBY: made partridge tureens with the birds sitting on plain embossed nests bordered with overlapping rings. These date from 1756 onwards. Pigeon tureens were made also.

BONE CHINA: during the second quarter of the 19th century there was a revival of bird tureens shaped as hens sitting on bowls representing wicker basket nests. Those marketed during the early 1820s were rather smaller than life size and vividly enamelled. These were filled with delicacies and presented to mothers during their confinement. In the 1830s a smaller size was made to contain a Valentine gift. Small sitting hens in coarse pottery belong to the 1840s to 1860s when they were filled with sweets and offered as prizes at country fairs.

Life-size sitting hens of finely modelled bone china served a different purpose. They were warmed and carried to the breakfast table containing hot boiled eggs in their egg-cups. They were also made in parian ware by Charles Meigh & Sons, Hanley, and T. J. & J. Mayer.

Biscuit figures: unglazed figures and groups in white porcelain. These were in production at Derby from 1773 to about 1830. They were sculptured in lines cleaner and more distinct than figures made by any other English potter. Folds of garments were often knife-edged. The surface of the biscuit needed to be absolutely flawless. So few were the perfect examples coming from the kiln that prices were high: for instance, the group *Two Virgins Awakening Cupid* in 1796 cost two guineas enamelled and gilt, and three guineas in the biscuit.

Derby biscuit figures are classed in three groups: 1773–1795, unglazed frit porcelain. The paste was close-textured light ivory-white in tint and slightly translucent in places. 1795–1815, smear glazed frit porcelain. This is slightly velvety to the touch. 1815–c.1830, non-frit biscuit. This displays a dry-looking chalky surface and by 1820 had deteriorated to reveal itself as unglazed non-frit bone china. Figures were carelessly modelled, even when Duesbury's original models were used. It is doubtful if any biscuit figures were issued after 1830.

Blue dash chargers: a term given in 1919 by E. A. Downman to large plaques of tin glazed earthenware on which the deep rounded rims are decorated with broad dashes of cobalt blue applied with a sponge to suggest twisted rope. This style was copied from the Dutch by the Bristol decorators. The plaques bear crudely painted pictures such as Adam and Eve, Stuart kings and queens, equestrian figures, popular celebrities and floral designs such as tulips and carnations in blue, green, orange yellow and purplish brown. Such a plaque measures twelve to eighteen inches in diameter. A point to note is a flat foot-rim on the back shaped with a groove or with two holes intended for a hanging cord (*see* Fig. 46).

Boot warmers: hollow vessels in the shape of boots with screw stoppers. These were filled with hot water—a passing mid-Victorian notion.

Buttons: bone china was used for buttons during the early 19th century with little success. In 1840 Richard Prosser of Birmingham patented a process by which buttons could be pressed with relief patterns in a dull, felspathic porcelain. This was composed of finely powdered felspar, bone ash and colouring matter to which grease was added to give plasticity. Milk was added to make a paste and the buttons were shaped by pressing, five hundred being made by a single stroke of the press. After firing for only ten minutes they were allowed to cool and then enamelled. Cameos and mosaics were also made by this method. The process was taken up by Minton & Boyle and productions continued from 1841 until 1848.

Cabaret sets: the name given by collectors to porcelain or earthenware tea sets for one or two persons. The set consists of a square, circular or oval tray with matching teapot, jug, sugar basin, slop basin and tea cups and saucers.

Carpet bowls: earthenware balls about four inches in diameter

80. Cabaret set, in Swansea porcelain, consisting of tray, teapot, jug, sugar bowl, slop basin, cup and saucer.

used for the early Victorian game of carpet bowls. Examples are found decorated in all colours and in white, marbled or painted with conventionally patterned foliage or starry designs in green, red and black. Made by the Sunderland Pottery, Portobello and elsewhere.

Caudle cups: two-handled vessels of porcelain with covers and saucers, elaborately painted with brilliant enamels. These superseded spout cups for the service of caudle in the early 1750s and might match the tea service. It became customary for the well-to-do, on congratulatory visits to a mother on the birth of a child, to present her with a pair of porcelain caudle cups. The catalogue of a sale of Chelsea porcelain held in March, 1756 records twelve pairs of caudle cups enamelled with 'double landskips'. By 1760 they were made in three sizes, large, standard and small. Thirty-three pairs were sold at the Chelsea-Derby sale in 1771, some handsomely decorated at £12 the pair. Caudle cups in Worcester porcelain sold at Christies in the 1770s were described as 'old rich Mosaic Japan pattern'; 'with twisted double handles and flower ornament in enamels'; and six 'with covers and saucers in fine old Japan fan pattern' were sold for 39s. Chelsea-Derby caudle

81. Caudle cups (for greater clarity some shown without their saucers). TOP: Chelsea, c. 1760s; Derby, 1760s; Worcester, 1770s. SECOND ROW: Worcester, c. 1775; Bristol, c. 1775–80; Caughley, 1790s. BOTTOM, 19th century: Spode, flowers painted against gold; 'crown Derby japan'.

cups were more costly. In 1773 a pair in 'peacock pattern, mazarine blue and gold' cost £3 18s.

Caudle cups continued in production throughout the first half of the 19th century in bone china, their bowls varying considerably in shape, ranging from hemispherical to deep and narrow and to wide-rimmed and shallow. Many, covers and saucers alike, were smothered in bright enamels and burnished gold. Marked examples include the work of Spode, Coalport, Derby, Rockingham and Swansea. By the time of

82. Chamber candlesticks, offering a wide range of design for the collector. TOP: early porcelain of Liverpool and Derby. CENTRE: Wedgwood marbled; Spode marbled; Spode bone china 1820s. BOTTOM: mid-19th-century Coalport and Belleek.

the Great Exhibition, 1851, caudle cups had lost their original purpose, but continued to be made as ornate cabinet cups.

Cauliflower ware: *see* Part III.

Chamber candlesticks: *see* Fig. 82.

Chessmen: Josiah Wedgwood was the first English potter to make chessmen. In 1784 he commissioned John Flaxman to design a set of chessmen for production in blue and white jasper ware. The men were modelled as actors playing Macbeth, each armed with a primitive weapon such as bows and arrows, stones, battle axes and daggers. The Wedgwood chessmen were made with three types of bases; rough mounds indicate the 1784 edition, issued only in blue and white. These were superseded by flat, wafer-like bases, in their turn superseded by short, plainly turned attic plinths. Colours then included grey, mauve, dark biscuit, blue, Flemish green, buff and white. A few in white were on blue dipped jasper bases. Pieces were usually of a single colour, occasionally enlivened with a touch of gold. They sold at five guineas the set. The Wedgwood firm again issued chessmen during the mid-19th century, blue with bases of black and natural boxwood distinguishing the opposing sides. These sold for £3 10s 6d the set. Stoneware chessmen of the same period cost £3 1s 6d. All Wedgwood chessmen are impressed WEDGWOOD; early examples were also incised with model numbers and workmen's marks in the form of single initials or fine lines.

Chessmen have been claimed as Castleford stoneware made between 1795 and 1821. The king and queen represented George III and Queen Charlotte in their state robes and crowned. The pawns were kilted Scots Guards and the rooks were elephants carrying square castellated towers.

Rockingham is no longer credited with china sets made c. 1822 to 1826. These were exact copies of an earlier Meissen (Dresden) set, the figures wearing Tudor dress. The opposing sides were in apple green and periwinkle blue enriched with gilding.

The Minton firm issued chessmen in statuary parian designed by the celebrated sculptor John Bell.

Henry Doulton issued a hand-modelled chess set designed by George Tinworth in 1887. The castle consisted of a brown and white mouse within a barred dungeon.

Cornucopia: a horn-shaped flower holder to hang on the wall with ribbons, in fashion throughout the period 1750–1870. It

83. Cornucopias and quintal flower holder. TOP: two of white salt glazed stoneware; one of tin enamelled earthenware. CENTRE: all Worcester porcelain, ornamented in relief and touched with colour. BOTTOM: quintal flower holder in late 18th-century creamware; symmetrical flower holder, white stoneware; wall bracket, mid-19th-century Copeland bone china.

84. Earthenware cottages. TOP: early 19th-century money-boxes, slotted at the back of the roof. CENTRE: crime pieces, 'A View of the Red Barn at Polestead' with figures of Maria Marten and William Corder, 1828; Potash Farm where James Rush murdered Jermy, 1848. BOTTOM: crude versions of the pastille burners popular in bone china, with lift-off roof (left) and a few large flowers (right).

149

contained scented flowers, mignonette being an early favourite until mid-Victorians changed the fashion to trailing ivy. Such vessels were made in pairs with different but harmonising ornament moulded in relief upon their fronts and their backs flat. The collector will find them in porcelain, white salt glazed stoneware, tortoiseshell ware, cream-coloured earthenware, bone china and English majolica.

Cottages, crime pieces: houses that had been the scenes of murders or the homes of murderers or their victims were reproduced for popular chimney ornaments in the 19th century. The earliest noted example is the Red Barn, Polstead, issued in 1828 following the murder of Maria Marten by William Corder. The most popular of all crime pieces came twenty years later. This was Potash Farm, the home of James Rush, the Cornish murderer of his neighbour Mr Jermy of Stanfield Hall. Several potters made versions of each.

Cottages, night-light shelters: made in the form of cottages with cut-out windows from which came faint—but safe— illumination. These were but a development of the centuries-old mortar light, its wick floating in an open container of whale oil which could be kept burning throughout the night and thus obviate the necessity for laborious flint-striking in the morning. The invention of the self-consuming candlewick in 1799 and the development of the slow-burning non-guttering candle in the early 1830s overcame the need for periodic snuffing and night-light shelters in cottage form were designed by several potters of bone china. In most of these the night-light was inserted through a semi-circular arch at the back of the cottage. In some instances the roof and walls lifted off a closely fitting box-like base; the inner wall could be seen forming a door within the porched doorway but left the windows uncovered. Lithophane night-light shelters were made at Worcester.

Cottages, pastille burners: these were containers for slow-

85. China cottages, mainly for burning pastilles, some with cut-out windows for night lights. TOP: early, on stand with lift-off roof; Flight, Barr & Barr, Worcester, with walls and roof lifting off. CENTRE: still simple designs with small mossy flower ornament, (left) showing vine and birds. BOTTOM: cottage with beehive, etc., sometimes found with red brick walls; church with one large morning-glory flower on roof.

151

smouldering cone-shaped pastilles composed of finely pow-dered willow wood charcoal with gum benzoin, powdered cinnamon, perfumed oils and other aromatics. When burned they emitted a pleasant odour particularly approved by the perfume-conscious late Georgian and early Victorian gentry.

Slipware pastille burners are recorded as early as 1700. Whieldon may have made them in earthenware during the 1750s and later in the form of hand-modelled half-timbered cottages decorated with mingled-colour glazes. Porcelain cot-tages in soft paste are extremely rare; they were described contemporaneously as perfume pots and might be shaped as picturesque castles or as pigeon houses. Cottage pastille burners in thin hard porcelain were made at Bristol between 1773 and 1778, the hard, thinly applied glaze showing an exceptionally high lustre marred by minute bubbles. The walls were decorated with sprays of tiny flowers.

In bone china from about 1820 cottage pastille burners represented old-world dwellings surrounded by gay flower beds with minute coloured flowers encrusting the walls and edging the roofs and with gilt-touched chimneys releasing the scented fumes. Other models represented turretted castle gateways, circular toll-houses with cone-shaped roofs, clock towers and creeper-covered churches, water mills, thatched farms, flowery arbours, Chinese pagodas. The majority were rectangular on plan, but circular, hexagonal and irregular shapes were made also. One of their many charms was the profusion of flowers which in many instances were large blossoms hand modelled in full relief. Grass by the doorway and moss on the roof was given a rough texture with shavings of paste scattered on the glaze before firing and afterwards coloured green. Roofs of china cottages were most frequently picked out in lines of gilt to resemble tiling. Such details as gables, dormer windows, window panes, door knockers and handles were often outlined in black.

86. China cottages cont. TOP: summer house sometimes marked *Spode felspar porcelain*; 'Gothic' cottage with big flowers. CENTRE: lavender coloured in elaborate design; lavender, with Minton date symbol for 1855 (big flowers, and doves in the porch). BOTTOM: all white, with touches of gilt; castle with compartment for a pastille in each of the three towers.

In the majority of cottages the roof and walls were made in a single piece, so that the pastilles could be placed upon the flat plinth and lit before being covered with the cottage. In others the roof lifted from the walls like a lid, but these are less plentiful. Some had a pull-out side giving access to a small bowl-like cavity in which the pastilles were burnt.

Cow milk jugs: adapted by Staffordshire earthenware potters from such cows in silver introduced by John Schüppe in the

87. Cow milk jugs. Dappled tan and black, with shaped plinth to include the milkmaid. Late 18th century with tiny milkmaid.

mid 1750s. The potter's style of modelling cow milk jugs displays a naive crudity. By 1815 such vessels had become inexpensive fairings. The capacity of standard models approximated to a gill, the jug being filled from a service pitcher by pouring through an opening cut across the saddle. The animal's neck was stretched forward with the mouth open, the stance taken when lowing. This acted as a spout through which the milk was dispensed into the tea cups. In early examples the neck tended to stretch upwards so that the open mouth was above the highest level of the milk in the jug, which could be lifted without hazard of spilling.

Frequently the cow shared its plinth with a tiny milkmaid, towering over the figure and her stool and pail. In the design of one firm the flat plinth was extended to the right to accommodate her, but in other models she was seated almost beneath the animal. She was crudely hand-modelled in the solid while her pail might be a hollow vessel or a solid representation. In a few examples the cow's back legs were confined in the kicking straps used to restrain restive animals from kicking the pail.

Every kind of contemporary Staffordshire ceramic was used, ranging from white salt glazed stoneware to inexpensive brown salt glazed stoneware, from dark red earthenware to cream-coloured earthenware, pearl ware and stone china. In addition one may find finely modelled examples in Staffordshire bone china.

Cows were frequently decorated with a distinctive palette of colours unaffected by the high temperature of the glazing oven so that they could be applied under the transparent glaze. Tan dominated and this was dappled with a contrasting colour such as black, green, yellow or a dull blue. Other colours included yellow and brown, dirty orange and drab blue with sepia. Occasionally three colours were combined such as dark red, tan and black. Horns and hooves might be in contrasting colours such as yellow or dull green.

Sunderland, Staffordshire, Yorkshire and South Wales potted hundreds of thousands of cow milk jugs in speckled or mottled pink lustre, described alternatively as gold, purple or ruby lustre. In sunlight some of these appear to have a golden hue: reproductions fail to display this effect. Plinths might be coloured with green enamel.

The Glamorgan Pottery, Swansea, was notable for decorating cow milk jugs with transfer prints in black or occasionally in red or green. The transfers were used in pairs. One side of the body might show, for example, a country mansion in a setting of trees, with two men fishing near a well and the other side a family in a boat on a stream with a footbridge, a barn and a dovecote near by. Small prints of cottages would appear on the flat cover and on the plinth. Examples made between 1815 and 1839, whilst the pottery was operated by Baker, Bevan & Irwin, might be marked OPAQUE CHINA in a scroll above the initials B B & I, all in script lettering.

Cradles: congratulatory visits after the birth of a child were important social functions until Victorian days. The mother's bedroom was specially decorated for the occasion and the baby's cradle covered with an elaborately embroidered quilt: the visitor was offered caudle and cake and in return made a small gift perhaps of pins or a coin made appropriate for the occasion by 'gift wrapping' in a pottery cradle complete with a robed baby carved in alabaster or modelled in earthenware. Until the 1740s such figures in earthenware were crudely modelled by hand rolling, pinching and tooling the clay. These cradles ranged from 4½ inches to a foot in length, the width about one-third of the length.

The earliest cradles were basically constructed from a coarse reddish-burning clay coated with a smooth clay slip which concealed the seams made during construction. The quality of the red earthenware progressively improved. Over this, designs were applied in coloured liquid slip by means of a goose quill. Some of the most interesting include initials or date in the pattern (*see* Fig. 88).

A lead glaze, sometimes stained to a brownish tinge with manganese oxide, was applied before firing. This gave the slip, whatever its colour, an attractive yellow transparency. It is important to note that until the 1750s glazing was accomplished by the use of galena (*see* p. 101). Later liquid lead glaze might be used, but the older method continued with slip ware until

88. Cradles. 17th-century slipware; green glaze with moulded pattern, c. 1800; full colour painting over 'wicker' shaping, with child's head shaped in one with the cradle, 1800s.

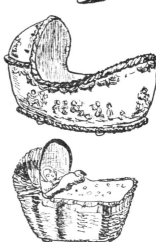

the 19th century. The principal areas in which slip-ware cradles were made include London, North Staffordshire, Kent, Derbyshire, Sussex and Yorkshire.

In the majority of early cradles the vertical sides, ends and base were flat bats of clay. A pair of rockers were added flush with the ends. There were two pairs of turned rocking finials,

157

used also for fastening the coverlet in position, one pair at the sides of the low, rounded hood, the other acting as corner finials at the foot of the cradle.

Cradles enriched with green glaze date from the late 1750s and continued to Victorian times. Moulded cradles are to be found, most of them shaped to resemble wicker. Others, from the 1770s, were encircled with a series of classical figures. Edges were finished with ropework or gadrooning and rockers were less clumsy than formerly. Such cradles were sold complete with 'robed' babies similarly glazed. As cradles rarely bear the potter's trade mark, the type of earthenware used is the main guide to dating which can only be decided within wide limits. Early green-glazed cradles were in dark cream-coloured earthenware; from the late 1770s light-coloured cream ware was general, light in weight; white, hard, heavy pearl ware dates from the 1790s and was used in the 19th century.

White salt glazed cradles containing robed babies were made for nearly half a century from the 1730s. Those made before the 1750s have an 'orange-skin' surface with minute pinholes, a feature rare after 1760. Surfaces were commonly decorated with relief ornament. Cradles of white salt glazed stoneware were revived during the third quarter of the 19th century for displaying in cabinets. These, sold under the generic name of 'Elizabethan ware', were decorated with pseudo-medieval designs in relief.

Cradles of brightly enamelled cream-coloured earthenware date from the 1780s onwards. When a child is included in the design it is made in one with the cradle, consisting of no more than a head and shoulders on a pillow appearing above a coverlet, the features crudely touched in by hand. Most cradles made before the early 19th century were light in weight and thin of section and coloured in various tones of yellow, green, red, blue and black, all capable of maturing at a single firing. Cradles decorated with a miscellany of blue transfer designs were made in the 19th century. In some, a cartouche on the hood contains the name or initials and perhaps the birth date of the child.

Cup plates: date from the 1750s and continued until Victorian days. The *Oxford English Dictionary* defines them as 'little flat saucers in which our grandmothers placed their tea cups when they poured their tea into their deeper saucers to cool'.

89. Cup plate, blue transfer-printed for the American market, with an American view in the oak leaf border used by R. Stevenson.

This involved drinking from the saucer and was in the main a provincial custom dating from early in the 19th century. Tea services have been recorded in Staffordshire blue in which cup plates were included, measuring from three to four inches across. The transferred decoration printed in blue covered the entire surface of the cup plate, with a central picture and a rim border. From about 1840 the printed border might be omitted and the rim embossed in low relief designs which might be touched with underglaze colour.

Few cup plates were marked but SPODE impressed has been noted, and the marks of J. & R. Clews (1818–1834) and J. & W. Ridgway (1814–1830).

Dogs: were made in soft porcelain during the second half of the 18th century, pugs in Meissen style being the most fashionable. They were used chiefly, with other figures, for dressing the dinner table, but are now extremely rare. Dogs were the most popular animal ornaments potted in the 19th century, however, and few breeds were not at some time or other modelled by the Staffordshire potters.

90. Dog figure ornament, familiar early Bow hound.

GREYHOUNDS. Coursing was a national sport and prize-winning dogs were known by name and reputation throughout the country. Many greyhound figures were sold as portraits of celebrated Georgian and early Victorian winners, including McGrath and Pretender. Potters usually coloured their hounds a peculiar salmon-orange with black features, the plinths tinted a rustic green. The three most common of the many poses show the animal sitting upright, standing, or lying prone with crossed paws.

COMFORTER DOGS in earthenware were second in popularity. These dogs, somewhat suggesting a spaniel breed, show little variation of pose or even of facial expression. They were ladies' pets or lap-dogs of a breed now extinct. They were made in five standard sizes, the largest, 18 inches in height, serving as door porters, and summer fireplace ornaments, and ranging down to 6 inch chimney-piece ornaments. The most popular size was 9 inches. Bodies were invariably white-glazed with half a dozen or so spots. The ears were coloured, red being the favourite, although golden ears and spots were

91. Cats and dogs—three cats and two later dogs. The cats: salt glazed agate stoneware; slipware; early 19th-century lustre-painted earthenware. The dogs: poodle made by Minton, Grainger, etc; comforter dog with patches of copper lustre.

little less popular. Black, brown, green, grey and copper lustre may be found. The eyes were pencilled to resemble human eyes and as a final detail one notes a small gold padlock hanging from the collar and a gold chain falling across the chest and disappearing over the back.

POODLES were usually much smaller than comforters and are associated more especially with bone china. They may be found carrying little baskets in their mouths—a trick which many poodles could accomplish. Groups of two or three poodles on the same plinth are now uncommon. Many were carefully modelled with curly hair on neck and head composed

161

of fine threads of china; the mane might be unglazed to produce a more natural effect. The majority, however, display merely a matted surface, quickly achieved.

THE DALMATIAN HOUND or COACH DOG, usually in earthenware, was a late Georgian and early Victorian favourite. These, with pointers and setters, called for great skill in potting.

Very few dogs were marked. Reproductions of all these types are numerous.

Elevators: supports for furniture, shaped to receive castor-ended legs and prevent carpet wear. Ornament may include moulded human masks or lions' heads.

Filters: throughout the 19th century inefficient sanitation produced germ-ridden drinking water and the risk of typhoid and cholera. This prompted a demand for water filters known as filtering machines which are sufficiently handsome to be

92. Filters. By Lipscombe & Co with white applied leaves on a buff ground, the hole at the bottom being for the tap; by Stiff & Sons, Lambeth, in 'Gothic' pattern; by Doulton (*see* Fig. 42).

collected today. Design consisted of a five-gallon cylindrical vessel often in Bristol stoneware, the exterior fitted with a lift-off cover, a pair of lifting handles and a tap and often decorated with attractive designs in white relief such as fruiting vines and other arabesques. Inside was a filter stone, a porous artificial stone which could be cleaned easily and cost 15s. The demand was so considerable that at the Great Exhibition, 1851, there were twenty exhibitors of domestic water filters, several designs being protected by patent. In 1870 an improved filter was marketed by Henry Doulton. This was fitted with a block of manganous carbon. Doulton filters were produced in a range of patterns until the end of the century.

Flower encrustations: applied flowers built from petals cut and shaped from paper-thin paste and applied to such objects as baskets, dishes and so on. The leading exponents were Derby, Minton, Coalport, W. T. Copeland and Chamberlains. Tiny moulded blossoms had been a feature of Chelsea, Bow, Longton Hall, Derby biscuit and elsewhere. But the real development of flower modelling came in the mid-1820s and continued for about forty years in bone china.

Staffordshire made extensive use of naturalistic flower encrustations including convolvulus, carnations, roses and anemones. Bloor's Derby made flower encrustations of a heavier, less translucent paste than Rockingham's with a harder glaze more thickly applied than elsewhere, and now often crazed and discoloured. Scented flowers were an exclusive production. A tiny nosegay would be designed to secrete a fragment of sponge soaked in one of the newly invented 'artificial essences' or perfumes. An alternative was a standing bouquet with green stalks tied by pink or blue ribbons to form the stem and base supporting a variety of flowers which could conceal a perfumed sponge. Vast numbers of encrusted scent bottles in bone china were made at Derby and elsewhere, those of Derby often resembling bottles produced in soft-paste porcelain at Chelsea

93. Flower encrustations. TOP: 18th-century porcelain Bow candle-stick and Worcester basket for roast chestnuts. CENTRE: Chamberlain, Worcester, painted view surrounded by naturally coloured seashells, and Derby standing bouquet of carefully exact flowers. BOTTOM: Rockingham potpourri vase and Minton platter of naturally coloured flowers and fruit.

164

in the 1750s and 1760s and probably shaped in the same moulds which had come into the possession of Derby.

From the early 1830s handsome pot-pourri bowls were made at Rockingham, Coalport, Minton and Derby in many forms, the most frequent being (a) shallow saucer-shaped dishes raised on three or four scroll feet; (b) shaped vases on short stems and domed feet; (c) bucket-shaped vessels with foot rings. They were fitted with low-domed pierced covers ornamented with flower sprays in relief. The cover design included a short central handle topped by a finial in the form of a flower spray or a single bloom. Dishes bearing expertly modelled garden flowers, full size and in their natural colours, date from the mid-1830s. These were superb of their kind, combining fine modelling, harmonious colours and pleasing arrangement.

The collector looks also for flower-encrustations on candle-sticks, inkstands, pastille burners shaped as cottages and other buildings, chestnut dishes, twig baskets.

Food warmers: defined by Josiah Wedgwood in 1774 as 'Night Lamps to keep liquid warm all night'. English specimens may be grouped into three classes: (a) the night lamp which kept warm a cup of posset, caudle, pap or other bedside drink; (b) the toddy warmer with a socket rising from the lid in which a tobacco taper burned, dating from the 1780s to the 1830s; (c) the tea warmer in bone china, 1810–1840s.

The basic design consists of several units. There is the hollow, flat-based pedestal, usually cylindrical. Into the top of this fits the lidded, two-handled pot for warming the liquid, and inside, on the floor of the pedestal, stands the heating unit. The opening required to insert the heating unit, extending from the base to as much as half-way up the pedestal, has a shaped outline. A boldly fashioned human mask may be introduced over the opening to conceal an air vent, and other vents may be sheltered by ornamental shells or leaves. Two

94. Food warmers. LEFT: a complete set in tin enamelled earthenware with a candle holder in the lid. CENTRE AND RIGHT: the pieces that compose a typical warmer—lid, central cylinder, lamp, vessel for the hot drink, vessel for hot water—all in creamcoloured earthenware.

solid scrolls may be placed about half-way up the pedestal to serve as handles. After about 1790 handles were usually loops extending almost the full length of the pedestal; less commonly they were of the double intertwined design held to the pedestal by flower reliefs.

Heat and light were supplied from a small open-flame lamp burning in a pottery font. At first this stood loose on the pedestal floor. By 1790 it was held in a socket which might be a short vertical ring rising from the floor of the pedestal, or a recess sunk into the base which itself was recessed on its underside to lift it slightly above the tray when in use. Early lamps were of the float-wick type, burning a round wick made from four threads of cotton yarn which did not require snuffing. The wick was carried on a floating disc of cork, the centre protected by a covering of copper plate. An oil burning lamp in the 19th century was covered with a loose lid pierced with a central hole and three circular vents to ensure correct capillary action. More costly to burn were candle mortars: a suitable mortar was developed in 1799 by William Bolts. This so increased burning efficiency that night-light mortars would burn steadily throughout the night without guttering.

Into the top of the pedestal, above the heating unit, fits a cylindrical bowl and cover, with one or two flat handles extending laterally. Until about 1820 the cup was supported

95. Food warmer, another design, this by Flaxman for Wedgwood in queensware. A lamp would stand in the base cavity.

in the pedestal by a flat, wide-spreading flange encircling it a short distance below the rim. The body of the cup fitted loosely within the pedestal, providing a space for trapped heat between the inner wall of the pedestal and the outer surface of the cup. After the early 1820s a loose bowl of hot water was inserted into the pedestal top, so designed that its flat base reached to about half an inch above the top of the flame. The cup was placed in this container, protecting its contents from direct contact with the heat.

In some instances the cup and cover were replaced by a teapot. These tea warmers were not associated with illumination and thus could be heated by means of a spirit lamp in the same way as a silver tea kettle.

Frog mugs: popular during Georgian and early Victorian days. A crudely modelled frog or toad was usually placed as though

96. Potters' jokes, for the convivial. The frog has an open mouth to eject liquid into the drinker's face. Above are two versions of the puzzle jug with pierced work to confuse the drinker who must obtain the liquor through one of the nozzles. The lidless pot is a variant of the cadogan teapot (q.v.) made in Devonshire slipware, filled on the inkwell principle through a hole in the base.

climbing the near side of the mug when lifted by the right hand. They were hand-modelled until about 1800. Then the industrial potters cast the bodies of their frogs: the legs were hand-worked and applied. From about 1830 the body might be cast hollow so that the frog spurted a stream of liquid into the drinker's face.

Colour variations were numerous: they are found in dark grey with pink spots, eye rims and mouths in sienna or white, in the glossy brown tone known as Rockingham glaze, and so on. The industrial potters tended to colour their frogs with light beige enamel and black spots. The frog, when not placed climbing the near side of the interior, might rest on the base of the mug, preferably in the leaping position. Two frogs may be found climbing opposite sides of the mug with the handle between them. A quart mug may contain three frogs, one on the base and two climbing the sides.

The majority of remaining frog mugs by industrial potters are in white earthenware, ranging from light-weight cream-coloured earthenware, made from about 1780, through the white pearl wares of the early 19th century and the stone chinas made from 1820 to the heavy, white granite ware of early and mid-Victorian days. These are the mugs most usually found today, distinguished by the different styles of their decoration—transfer-printed, lustred, painted in the colour-range known as Pratt ware or gaudily coloured with japan patterns (*see* Fig. 17).

Fuddling cup: a vessel composed of three to six—occasionally nine—conjoined cups with internal communication through bodies or handles so that, to empty one, the entire set must be emptied. Made of coarse earthenware and slip-decorated (*see* Fig. 1).

Gallipot: defined by the *Oxford English Dictionary* as 'a small earthen pot, especially one used by apothecaries for ointments and medicines'. The earliest reference given is taken from some

97. Porcelain jugs, chronological series. TOP: Chelsea goat-and-bee jug and another somewhat similar design, c. 1745–50; simpler Chelsea pattern used also by Derby etc. CENTRE: variants of this 1750s style from Longton Hall, early Bristol and early Worcester. BOTTOM: main standard style of 1760s–1770s—Bow, Lowestoft, Caughley.

domestic expenses of 1465: 'Item, the same day my mastire paid for a galy pot, 111d.'. A potter's advertisement in the *Bristol Gazette*, 1773, refers to 'Gally pots for Apothecaries'.

170

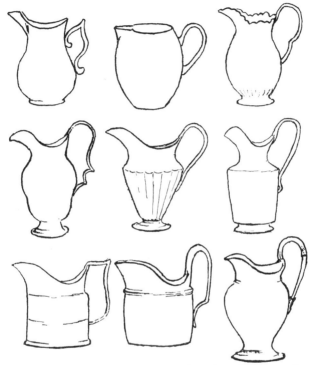

98. Porcelain cream jugs cont. TOP: three from Worcester, late 1750s, 1760s, 1770s. CENTRE: Bristol, 1770s; Lowestoft, c. 1780s; Pinxton, 1790s. BOTTOM: Pinxton, 1800s; Worcester, c. 1810; Swansea, c. 1815–20.

Lady Fermanagh, writing to her husband in 1721 (*Verney Letters*), refers to a consignment of anchovies which she had 'ordered in stone potts, and hath sent them in pittiful galley

171

pots'. Gallipots are here differentiated from the much stronger, salt glazed stoneware impervious to liquids. Earthenware was glazed with galena: liquid lead glaze was introduced in the early 1750s. Gallipots were, then, earthenware vessels covered with galena glaze. It is possible that gallipot is a corruption of galena-pot.

Goat-and-bee jugs: first made at Chelsea in its earliest days. The design, moulded in relief, consisted of two reclining goats lying head to tail supporting the body of the jug which was decorated with raised flowers and a bee, which might be ascending or descending. The handle was shaped as a twig. Some of these jugs were white glazed: on others the flowers were lightly touched with colour. They are known with considerable variations suggesting the use of several moulds. The design was adapted from a silver jug by Edward Wood, struck with the London hallmarks for 1737. The earliest authenticated piece of English soft-paste porcelain is a goat and bee jug incised CHELSEA with a triangle (*see* Fig. 186). Examples may be marked with the triangle alone; with a triangle and CHELSEA; with these and the year 1745; or may be unmarked. The beginner-collector must realise that goat-and-bee jugs were made at Coalport in the mid-19th century, but in bone china, and that reproductions have been made in the present century.

Hot water and hot milk jugs: William Ridgway's introduction in the early 1830s of near-white stonewares having improved heat resistance and capable of being modelled with all-over designs in high relief brought decorative hot water jugs to the fashionable tea table. The vessel might be rimmed and covered with a hinged lid that extended to cover the spout. At first this was in sterling silver, then in Sheffield plate and finally in Britannia metal, a hard form of pewter which when new was polished to a lustre closely resembling that of sterling silver. Such lids were made and fitted to the jugs by Thomas Law,

99. Early hot water and hot milk jugs. TOP: agate ware with Chinese lion knop, 1750s; white salt glazed stoneware, incised ornament, 1740s–50s; tortoiseshell glaze earthenware, 1750s. BOTTOM: around 1770s—Lowestoft; Worcester scale blue; Worcester finely fluted.

Sheffield. Those of silver were struck with hallmarks incorporating the maker's mark T.L. and the monarch's head duty mark. The Sheffield plate fittings were struck with the name THOS LAW & CO., with a symbol of a stemmed and covered cup, a mark entered at the Sheffield Assay Office.

Then Thomas Booth, High Street, Hanley, produced jug

100. Hot water jugs, hot milk jugs, cont. TOP: Wedgwood jasper, 1783; Wedgwood cream ware, resembling a Leeds catalogue item where it is listed as coffee pot or milk pot with snip; Castleford. BOTTOM: Liverpool, Herculaneum, with mask, end of 18th century; two designs by Cork & Edge for the Paris Exhibition 1855 (entitled Bouquet and Vine) *(see also* Fig. 121).

rims and covers in Britannia metal. In the late 1840s he moved to larger premises in Lichfield Street and traded as 'T. Booth & Co., Britannia metal smiths'. The mark T. BOOTH/HANLEY dates earlier than 1850.

A self-acting lid for hot water jugs was patented by Charles Toft in 1854, the manufacturing rights being secured by John Ridgway, Shelton. The lid swung on pivots fitted into notches cut into each side of the rim of the jug so that, being lightly hung and properly balanced, it opened when the jug was tilted for pouring and closed when set down upright. After the expiry of the patent Henry Hall, Hanley, set up as a metal mounter of jugs. He was so successful that in 1872 he acquired the entire front part of the old New Hall Works. His best Britannia metal lids were impressed HENRY HALL/HANLEY.

Jelly Moulds: until the mid-1770s jelly moulds were made only for individual portions. Moulds to turn out jellies large enough to serve at table into individual helpings were introduced by Josiah Wedgwood in cream-coloured earthenware. Hartshorn jelly formed the basis of most Georgian dessert

101. Jelly moulds. TOP LEFT: exterior and interior of outer case. BELOW LEFT: the pyramid that appeared on the table encased in the jelly to support, enlarge and brighten it. CENTRE AND RIGHT: two alternative shapes for the ornamental centre support. Holes in the base allow the jelly to be poured into the mould with this support in position—upside-down—to ensure that the right amount of jelly is used.

175

jellies and could be 'clear, white or tinctured red with saffron'. Flavourings were added as required.

WHITE SALT GLAZED STONEWARE jelly moulds date from the 1730s to 1770s with a depth of about $1\frac{1}{2}$ inches and a pronounced outward slope, with fluted sides, so that the base might be in the shape of a pointed star.

WEDGWOOD MOULDS were fashionable as dessert table decorations for half a century. The mould was composed of two units. The mould proper was undecorated, its glazed interior cast with vertically fluted intaglio designs. With this was used a centre-piece consisting of a column rising from a base pierced with four or more holes. When the liquid jelly was poured into the mould the pillar centre-piece was inserted into it. This was left in position when the jelly was turned out of the mould, serving to support it. For greater decorative effect it was painted with colourful enatmel designs of flowers and foliage or fruit which were visible hrough the clear jelly. By the 19th century, conical and wedge-shaped centre-pieces appeared. The base was now given a deep encircling flange, an inner ring preventing the jelly from slipping, and the outer channel being shaped to fit firmly over the outer mould whilst the jelly set. In most instances the surface of the centre-piece base is decorated to match the column. Other potters reproduced Wedgwood's basic pattern in strong pearl ware with blue transfer-printed ornament.

BRISTOL WARE: from about 1840 stoneware jelly moulds appeared, catalogued as 'moulds for puddings, jellies, and blancmange, of great beauty and artistic design'. They were heavy, thick of section, durable and inexpensive. Ornate examples from the 1850s are found impressed with the names of BOURNE & SON of Denby and OLDFIELD of Bramoton, Derbyshire.

FLINT ENAMEL EARTHENWARE was used for jelly moulds from about 1850. The top decoration was less meticulously modelled than contemporary metal moulds which cost ten times as much.

Knife rests: *see* Fig. 102.

102. Knife rests, small items that can be collected, intended to receive the carving knife at table. A curiously similar shape is shown in the Leeds Pottery catalogue (right) as an asparagus shell.

Leech jar: a vase-shaped jar of earthenware with two handles and a perforated cover. In lead-glazed cream ware they were usually decorated and inscribed LEECHES. They are now largely reproduced.

Lions: modelled from the celebrated lions carved in marble at the entrance to the Loggia dei Lanzi, Florence, were popular during the late Georgian and early Victorian periods. In a typical example the lion, head turned to the left, with left

103. Lion, typical model found in a wide range of cheap wares.

front paw upon a large ball, stands squarely upon a flat oblong plinth, the edge encircled with olive leaves in relief. They were made by Thomas Rathbone, Portobello, coloured greyish blue under a glaze of exceptional brilliance; and also by John Walton, Burslem (*see* William Ball, Sunderland).

Lithophanes: decoration made from a thin, glassy species of hard porcelain impressed with a shallow design in which precise variations in the thickness, and consequent opacity, of the material produced the effect of a detailed mezzotint engraving when held against transmitted light. In shadowed parts of the picture the porcelain was thick enough to resist the passage of light in degrees varying with the volume of shade required: thin areas produced contrasting translucency. Viewed directly, the sharply irregular surface of the porcelain is barely suggestive of any pictorial effect at all.

The process was invented by Baron de Burgoing, Paris, who was granted patent rights in 1827 and licensed the formula and methods in England, Holland and Germany. The English purchaser was Robert Griffiths Jones, Brewer Street, London, who disposed of the manufacturing rights to Grainger, Lee & Co., Worcester. Their name has been recorded impressed on panels, lanterns, night-light shelters, lamp shades and hand fire screens. A teacup apparently decorated in the ordinary way with coloured enamels and gilding might surprise the tea-time visitor when a picture became visible at the bottom as the cup was tilted against the light. Jones termed his patent (No. 5626, March 3rd, 1828) 'lithophanic translucid' and referred to the pictures as 'shadowed drawings'. To potters, however, the patent was known as 'Jones's method of ornamenting china'.

The work involved in producing lithophanes was highly skilled. The patent specifies the process in great detail which, briefly, consisted of preparing a model of the ornamental design, first in wax, then in plaster of paris, and finally in pewter. Each was carefully hand-finished so that the final picture was displayed in surprising photographic vividness. From this the lithophanes were produced by normal porcelain casting methods.

The introduction of colour into such work tended to confuse

the clarity of the picture, but a few examples are known in which the lithophanes were tinted before glazing. After the mid-1850s lithophanes might be tinted throughout their texture by incorporating high temperature metallic oxides into the porcelain.

When the patent expired early in 1842 lithophanes were produced by a few other English potters including Herbert Minton, W. T. Copeland, Adderley & Lawson of Burslem, and the South Wales Pottery. The original patent was acquired in Germany by the Meissen factory and in France by the Baron A. du Tremblay, whose lithophanes are impressed A du T. Those impressed PPM followed by a serial number were made by the Plane-on-Havel Porzellan Manufactory, Thuringia, after 1842.

Mansion House dwarfs: made at Derby from the mid-1780s. These were adapted from a pair of grotesque dwarfs depicted in a book of caricatures, *Il Calotto resuscitato*, published at

104. Mansion House dwarfs, by Derby.

Amsterdam in 1716. The announcements on their hats were inspired by two dwarfs who stood outside the Mansion House in 1780 displaying advertisements in their hats. The hats of the Derby models were painted with a variety of announcements such as sales by auction and theatrical performances. More than twenty different inscriptions have been recorded.

These dwarfs were made in pairs and measured 6½ inches in height. They were catalogued as a 'Pair of Grotesque Punches' and priced 18s a pair. The model No. 227 is usually incised on the base. One wears a wide-brimmed hat, the other a chimney-pot shape. Poorer versions in bone china were made early in the 19th century.

Reproductions have been made. The Royal Crown Derby Porcelain Company issued larger and somewhat finer copies with buckled shoes and standing on smooth plinths. They have also been made in Staffordshire.

Monkey orchestra: an assemblage of more than twenty separate figures of monkeys dressed as musicians. These were originally modelled at Meissen in 1747 and have continued in

105. Monkey orchestra figure, well modelled by Derby. **106. Monkey fairground musician,** with drum and comb by Copeland & Garrett.

production there ever since. They were caricatures of the court jester, Joseph Frohlich, and were designed in ridicule of Count Bruhl's court orchestra at Dresden. They are in hard porcelain and have rococo bases.

Copies and adaptations were made at Chelsea and are recorded in the catalogue of 1756 and at Derby in the 1760s and onwards. These are in soft porcelain. From about 1835 they were made in bone china, notably by Copeland & Garrett (1833–47) and later by W. T. Copeland. They were brilliantly decorated in enamel colours, red, blue, orange and green. Groups of monkeys on rectangular bases were also made. These were marked COPELAND & GARRETT surmounted by a crown in green.

Nappy plates: used in the service of nappy ales in the home. Nappy is defined in the *Oxford English Dictionary* as 'foaming, heady, strong'. Any froth from the head of the ale that spilled

107. Nappy plates or nappy dishes. By Bow and by Leeds where the vessel is catalogued as an escalloped nappy.

down the side of the drinking glass was caught in the shallow nappy plate instead of disfiguring the table.

In March 1756 Bow sold '24 octagonal nappy plates'. The Leeds catalogue of 1814 illustrates an 'escallop'd nappy' in cream-coloured earthenware.

Ocarina: an egg-shaped musical instrument with whistle-shaped mouth piece and finger holes, the name first noted in 1877. This may be found in terracotta, often coated with engobe, decorated in blue under the glaze.

Pew groups: figure groups representing one or two men and a woman seated on a high-backed settle to which no religious significance was attached. They may be considered in three classes: salt glazed; lead glazed; and reproductions. Details of technique show that salt glazed pew groups were made in the late 1730s and early 1740s. They were hand-modelled in white earthenware containing calcined and ground flint instead of sand, introduced in the late 1730s probably by Robert Astbury.

So many reproductions have been made that the collector should be familiar with the constructional technique of the early Georgian pew group potters. The rigidly posed figures were modelled by rolling, cutting and pinching, their clothing being fitted over skeleton cores. A female figure, from the

108. Pew group.

waist up, consisted of an almost plain solid cylinder, the upper end shaped as a neck. A small sphere was modelled into a head; arms of rolled clay were attached to the body, their flattened ends being tooled to represent hands and fingers. The figure was then dressed with paste rolled flat to a thickness of about one-sixteenth of an inch. No legs were concealed beneath the widely billowing skirt, which was composed of alternating strips of black and white clay, the surfaces of the white stripes being decorated with milled lines. Over this was placed a long white apron. A tight bodice and ruffled cap were added and eyes, necklace and other embellishments applied in black slip. The men were more completely modelled than the women, their dress less thoroughly disguising their figures. Their clothing fitted over skeleton cores in the same way, with skirted coats over frogged and buttoned waistcoats. Their heads were bewigged with tightly twisted, rolled curls. Dark clay was used for hat, neck ribbons, cuffs and shoes. The men were often supplied with musical instruments such as fiddle or bagpipes.

A series of lead glazed pew groups was issued. In these, two crudely modelled figures are seated on a circular bench and coloured with touches of manganese purple and brown; they are impressed on the base with the name WEDGWOOD. This is not the mark of Josiah Wedgwood but of one of his several relatives engaged in the pottery trade. An example in the British Museum shows two youths, one reading a book, the other holding a scroll.

Pie-crust ware: great pies of standing crust pastry filled with meat or pieces of game appeared in every well-to-do household until banished from the table by the flour tax levied during the Napoleonic wars. Josiah Wedgwood then potted substitutes for the pastry case in fine-grained vitrified stoneware which ranged in colour from pale cream to pie-crust brown, a ceramic that had been named caneware (*see* p. 50). Known as crock pies they reproduced the standing pie-crust

109. Pie-crust ware. Flat dish for fruit pie, and Wedgwood game pie dish made from the 1790s.

at its most elaborate. The finely modelled walls carried relief ornament sprigged to the sides, the lid had an expansive pheasant or duck finial and crimping was introduced around top and lower edges. The interior was glazed. Each pattern was made in several sizes. Other Staffordshire potters whose names are found impressed into pie-crust ware are John & William Turner, Lakin & Poole, Elijah Mayer and William Adams & Son.

John Davenport issued a series of well-potted pie-crusts encircled with designs in hand-worked cording and with appropriate cover finials. These were impressed DAVENPORT after 1805. Pie-crusts in a buff-brown stoneware were made at Swansea: these are encircled with fruiting ivy in two arrangements.

A caneware capable of being moulded in relief was developed in the mid-1830s by several potters. These pie-crusts lack the sharp undercut lines of the sprigged ornament and were a step further from the pastry originals. Ironstone caneware capable of withstanding oven temperature was developed in Chesterfield. This ceramic was so strong that these vessels really could take the place of pastry as their contents simmered in the oven. A mid-Victorian series is of unknown origin. The vessels are encircled with pheasants, rabbits and ferns and have pheasant lid finials. Their only marks are impressed date symbols such as $5\frac{2}{68}$ for February, 1868.

The Wedgwood firm met the challenge of this oven-resistant ware by making pies in a lighter buff-toned terracotta with moulded decoration on the top and sides. Groups of hanging dead game in relief cover the sides, linked by swags of fruiting vine and on top is a hare or duck moulded in deep relief. This terracotta was not fireproof, but Wedgwood introduced glazed stoneware in which meat or game could be oven-cooked: vessel and all could then be placed inside the pie-crust to come to the table. These are to be found in four sizes and in the 1850s were supplied in quantity to university colleges.

Pill-slabs: flat slabs of tin enamelled earthenware used by apothecaries. These were commonly painted with blue ornament and were used by members of the Society of Apothecaries for displaying their Company arms.

Pot-lid pictures: *see* Part IV.

Punch pot: a gigantic vessel of teapot shape for serving hot punch, measuring about nine inches across its globular body with its cover rounded to continue the curve. The spout was usually of the crabstock variety, a design matched by handle and cover finial. An alternative was a plain swan-neck spout balanced by a loop handle and a turned knob to the cover. An important distinctive detail was the omission of a strainer from the inner entrance of the spout.

Early Georgian examples were in white salt glazed stoneware decorated with enamels: like punch bowls they received all manner of personal inscriptions and political and social propaganda.

Punch pots were also made in soft-paste porcelain when this was fortified by the inclusion of bone ash or soapstone in its composition. They were of smaller capacity than those of white salt glazed stoneware. A Derby example in the Victoria and Albert Museum has a baluster-shaped body painted with exotic birds and its cover topped with a naturalistic lemon and foliage.

Punch kettles in engine-turned red stoneware date from the late 1760s. Here the design includes a fixed arching handle and the vessel stands upon a bowl-shaped brazier of the same material, copper lined and containing a spirit lamp. Marks show that punch kettles continued into the 19th century (*see* Fig. 43).

Quintals: flower holders with five sockets placed fanwise and rising from a square base. These were catalogued by Leeds as flower horns and by the Staffordshire potters as flower tubes (*see* Fig. 83).

Sauce and pickle plates: accessories to the dinner table are particularly interesting to collect as potters could experiment

110. Pickle dish, Bow porcelain (*see also* Fig. 21).

with techniques unsuited to the general run of flatware and hollow-ware. Strong flavourings for individual service at table were essential when much food had to be preserved by drying and salting and the range of such vessels is limitless.

Spirit flasks: in brown and buff stoneware these were first made by Joseph Bourne, Denby, Derbyshire, in the late 1820s and continued until the late 1840s. The flat-faced bottles, varying in height between seven and eleven inches, were surmounted by highly individualistic bust and figure portraits in full relief, including royalty and political celebrities. Early in William IV's reign the long series of reform flasks were issued, culminating in an issue of many thousands when the Reform Bill was under discussion.

Appreciating the popularity of these flasks other potters also developed them, retaining the basic simplicity, cheapness of materials and limited range of colours. Each manufacturer issued his own version of a jolly sailor seated on a barrel, impressed with the name of the liquor concerned, such as 'Old Tom' found on flasks made by Oldfield of Brampton, near Chesterfield. Figures representing 'Smoking' and 'Snuffing' came from the Vauxhall Pottery; mermaid-shaped flasks were made by Stephen Green, Lambeth, whose marine subjects included large fish. Green also made flasks in designs ranging from pistols, pocket books and powder horns to pigs and grandfather clocks, as well as a series shaped as tipstaffs, during the early 1840s (*see* Fig. 42).

Spout pots: originally termed skinkers, in capacities ranging from two quarts to a pint, were used for the service of wine from the early 17th century until the mid-18th century, when they were superseded by cream coloured earthenware. Spout cups of small capacity were also made for the individual service of posset and caudle. The typical cup was lidded and had a loop handle on each side and stood upon a trencher.

The earliest were in silver, followed by tin glazed earthenware. Existing examples have out-curved sides and domed covers. The slender tubular spout rises from the base close to

111. Spout pot, in tin enamelled earthenware blue painted in the Chinese manner.

the body, making it less liable to be broken off. Many were painted in cobalt blue, often displaying symbolic motifs adapted from oriental porcelain. They were also made in white salt glazed stoneware during the period 1730–1760, but because the spout was rough to the lips these were unpopular. Derby, Worcester and Chelsea made porcelain spout cups from the 1750s, accompanied by stand and cover. By now caudle was fashionably served in two-handled spoutless cups, although spout pots continued in the provinces.

Spout pots made excellent feeding cups for invalids: early in the 19th century these were outmoded by the introduction of spout pots resembling diminutive teapots, but with handle and spout at right angles. These are found in bone china (often marked); cream ware; stone china and ironstone china of various qualities.

Stirrup cups: earthenware examples dating from about 1770 in the shape of fox masks are attributed to Whieldon, boldly modelled and splashed with green. Later Whieldon stirrup

112. Stirrup cups. TOP: fist in Egyptian black; fox in Wedgwood basaltes; bull terrier in coloured earthenware. BOTTOM: fish and hare in bone china.

cups were less deeply moulded and were enamelled in naturalistic colours; a green collar would encircle the neck rim. Whieldon designs included the earless fox-head of creamy-white earthenware with olive green markings. A wide variety of fox-head stirrup cups were made by the Staffordshire potters during the next seventy or eighty years, but rarely is an example marked and it is impossible to attribute specimens to individual potters.

Hound-heads ran a close second in popularity to fox-heads. Ralph Wood II, Burslem, made them in earthenware with a light olive-green translucent glaze. John Turner of Green Dock modelled some very life-like examples in earthenware, including an unglazed cane-coloured series with glazed interiors. At least thirty Staffordshire potters made hound-heads. Until 1820 they were skilfully modelled with ears laid flat, and with delicately tinted muzzles. Tones of reddish-brown and black, with gold and black collars, are found, brown markings being a common variant.

SOFT-PASTE PORCELAIN fox-head stirrup cups were made during the fourth quarter of the 18th century. The Chelsea-Derby sale catalogue of 1780 shows them to have been sold in pairs, large size fox-heads at 8s 6d the pair; 'one pair foxes heads for drinking cups 6s', and 'one pair hares heads enamelled and gilt'. Derby fox-heads in porcelain were skilfully modelled, sometimes enamelled in tawny-red tones with gilt collars.

BONE CHINA fox-heads frequently had yellow ears and pink collars; others were glazed in a pearly white; others again were in a single colour throughout, such as brown or yellow, matt on the exterior and glazed within. Later Derby fox-heads were less efficiently modelled, without collars, and highly glazed, the glaze now displaying hair-line crazing. Minton, Coalport, Rockingham and Spode issued hound-heads in natural colourings. From Staffordshire came the bone china hounds in a dull, white biscuit and a well-modelled series in tones of black and grey, reddish-brown or grey-brown. Black ears and a light maroon muzzle distinguished another extensive series.

Other naturalistic heads of dogs and game may also be noted among stirrup cups. These include the heads of deer or stag (without antlers), trout, hare, bear, cock, bull-dog, setter, bull-terrier, dalmatian, and the boxer's clenched fist.

Teapots, Cadogan: a lidless vessel of the puzzle variety adapted for the English tea table from the oriental peach-shaped wine-pot. It was constructed on the principle of the well inkpot, a hole in the centre of the base forming the entrance to a taper-ing tube spiralling within the pot to about an inch below the top. By inverting the pot, tea strained clear of its leaves could

113. Cadogan teapot: the usual Spode design and, right, a view of the base showing the central hole for filling on the inkwell principle.

be poured into the hole which was bevelled off so that it could receive a funnel. The tea passed through the tube into the body of the pot, whereupon the vessel could be righted safely. It was then only possible to empty the pot through the spout.

At first these teapots were made in a hard pearl ware, but from about 1800 the majority were in a heavier red earthen-ware. The body was decorated with peach foliage, flowers and fruit in relief and the whole covered with characteristic pur-plish brown glaze (*see* Rockingham glaze). The relief work might be gilded. A series of later cadogan teapots in pearl ware were given an apple-green ground: these date to the 1830s or later and are unmarked.

Traditionally the first cadogan teapots were made in about 1790 by Thomas Bingley & Co., Swinton (later Brameld's Rockingham Works) to the commission of the Hon. Mrs Cadogan, who lent an example in Indian green ware as a model. These teapots were in small quantity production when Brameld acquired the Swinton pottery in 1806. Sales continued negligible until the Prince Regent visited the Earl Fitzwilliam where he observed these teapots in use for serving rum toddy. He thereupon ordered a large number to give away as presents. In the following season Mortlock, the Oxford Street china seller, sold £900 worth of Brameld's cadogan teapots (*see* Fig. 96).

Teapots, double-spouted: a Victorian vogue from the 1840s to about 1880. One spout extended from the bottom of the pot, its opening covered with a strainer in the usual way, and the other matching spout opened directly from the top of the pot. At this time it had not proved possible to clear tea of its dust which floated on the surface of the liquid in what were termed 'motes'. Formerly a spoon with an almost flat strainer bowl and spear handle, known as a mote skimmer, had cleared the dust floating on the surface of the tea. The secondary spout enabled the server to remove motes much more efficiently by pouring the surface tea into a basin. The tea was then served through the lower spout.

Tea urns: T., J. & J. Mayer, Dale Hall, potted the first in 1850. These were ornately designed and made from a highly vitreous stoneware specially prepared to withstand temperature variations similar to those expected with metal tea urns. The vase-shaped hexagonal body, enamelled with a different design on each side, rose from a spreading dome supported by four sphinx-like feet. A pair of demi-figure handles rose from expansive acanthus leaves and the highly domed cover was topped by a double-mask finial. The brass tap was fitted with a pull-down handle. The Mayers made very few of these, but their successors, Bates, Elliot & Co. and Bates, Walker & Co., from 1870 reproduced them in considerable numbers. Examples have been noted with the mark of a naked boy kneeling before a tall ewer on a plinth inscribed 1790 (Fig. 202).

An unknown potter made tea urns in a vase shape, the body enamelled with an encircling scene in full colours, with a

114. Tea urn, a mid-19th-century design by Mayer.

pedestal foot and domed cover in the rich brown tone known as Rockingham glaze.

Twiffler: a pudding plate. Twiffler making was a specialised branch of the flatware trade until plates began to be machine-made from the 1870s.

Tyg: a name formerly given to porringers by Staffordshire potters. This is now applied by collectors to a drinking cup with two or more handles so that several people might drink in turn, each from a different point on the rim by using a different handle. Sometimes a two-handled design shows the handles set near each other instead of diametrically opposite, for the greater convenience of a couple with the vessel set before them at the fireside (*see* Fig. 1).

Watch stand: *see* Fig. 115.

Wine-bin labels: the earliest were in tin enamelled earthenware and date from the time of James I. The standard shape was triangular with the lower corners clipped vertically and the

115. Watch stands are 19th century flat-back ornaments not always immediately recognised. By placing a working watch in the central hole the owner had a usable bedside or mantel clock.

apex rounded and pierced with a circular hole, size approximating 6 inches wide and 3 inches high at the centre. Others have ogee sides with the apex rounded and slots for hanging. Early bin labels measure about $\frac{3}{8}$-inch thick. This was later reduced to $\frac{5}{16}$-inch and finally to $\frac{1}{4}$-inch.

A typical bin label of the early period has its basic earthenware pale brown or yellowish in colour, the tin enamel flawed

116. Wine bin label. Typical shape in painted earthenware.

with many surface pittings, numerous wear and tear scratches and some chips at the edge. The cobalt used for lettering is richly blue. The tin enamel is tinged faintly blue on late examples.

By 1790 Josiah Wedgwood was making them in pearl ware and the size standardised to 5¾ inches wide by 3¼ inches high. Some were sold in the biscuit, an inked or pencilled inscription being added. The majority were white glazed and the names of the wines painted in black, the upper portion remaining in the biscuit to enable pencil notes to be made. The Wedgwood pattern book of the mid-1790s lists seventy-seven names of liquors which were stocked. They were priced 'plain bin labels, 2d each; labelled, 4d each'.

Josiah Spode made bin labels in ordinary earthenware and in pearl ware, with ogee sides and rounded apex, with the name of the wine transfer-printed under the glaze. Minton's bin labels from 1800 followed the Spode shape with the name enamelled in black and the upper part unglazed. From 1836 the triangular shape came into production. John Davenport's labels have deeply cut-away sides and rounded shoulders. They are smaller than standard, measuring about 4¼ inches wide by 3 inches high.

PART VI

Potters, Their Products and Their Dates of Working

Below are details of prominent potters and their wares. It must be remembered that in many instances they were rivalled or copied by many nameless potters and that a great deal of work must be grouped according to its own inherent qualities rather than for any proved association with a famous maker. In connection with this summary the reader is referred to the illustrations of marks and lists of initials, date letters, etc., that follow in Part VII.

Absolon, William, Yarmouth, Norfolk: an independent enameller who operated in premises known as 'The Ovens' from the mid-1780s to 1815. He painted botanical flowers, landscapes, monograms and other fashionable motifs. His mark, painted in brown script, was ABSOLON YARM, sometimes followed by N 25 in reference to his address.

Adams family: land owners at Tunstall from the time of Edward I and recorded as master potters there early in the 17th century. Descendants now direct the firm of William Adams & Sons Ltd. at Tunstall and Stoke.

JOHN ADAMS (1624–1687) inherited from his father in 1657 a small pottery known as the Brick House at Burslem, where he potted black, mottled and slip wares. His descendants worked the Brick House until 1763 when the premises were leased to Josiah Wedgwood.

WILLIAM ADAMS (1746–1805) one of three cousins so-named, inherited a pot bank from his father, but in 1779 he established the Greengates Pottery where he made dry stonewares and became particularly celebrated for his jasper which ranged from an opaque, dead white to an ivory-like translucency with a surface almost velvety to the touch. His blue jasper is distinguished from Wedgwood's blue by its faintly violet shade. Its quality was equal to Wedgwood's, as examples in the Stoke-on-Trent City Museum testify. Joseph Mongenot was employed as chief designer from 1785. His influence is

117. Adams jasper ware vase with classic white reliefs, 1787–1805.

seen in classical bas reliefs and border decorations for vases, plaques, medallions, teapots and coffee pots, cups and saucers, candelabra drums and so on. In addition, Adams made other fine stonewares, hand-painted cream-coloured earthenware and introduced a pale, stone-coloured earthenware, which might be salt glazed and was favoured for hollow-ware such as jugs, mugs, bowls and wine coolers. These were encircled with sporting scenes or bacchanalian dances in high relief, with characteristic engine-turned borders of interlaced circles. William Adams was early in the field of blue transfer-printing underglaze. His blue-printing on pearl ware from the 1780s is notable for the detailed clarity of its pattern and the exceptionally lovely blue. His caneware might be decorated with green or blue enamel.

William Adams's solid blue jasper, 1779–1790, and his cream-coloured earthenware, 1770–1805, were impressed ADAMS & CO; dipped jasper, other dry stonewares and blue-

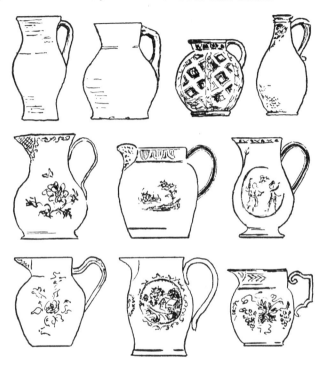

118. Serving jugs, in chronological sequence—one of the most interesting fields for the collector. TOP: primitive shapes, 13th to 14th century; 15th to 16th century; 17th century slipware; 17th century stoneware. CENTRE: white salt glazed stoneware, enamel painted, c. mid-18th century; Wedgwood transfer-printed, 1770; Wedgwood transfer-printed, 1786. BOTTOM: Leeds pearlware, c. 1800; Liverpool, printed, in barrel shape, c. 1800; silver resist lustre, early 19th century.

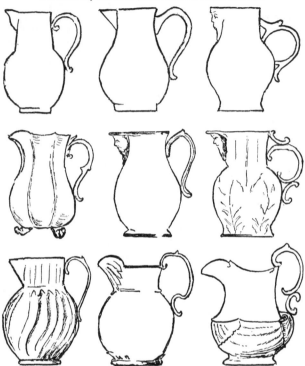

119. Serving jugs cont. Porcelain and china. TOP: Derby, 1760s
Lowestoft, c. 1765; Plymouth, c. 1770. CENTRE: three of Worcester,
c. 1755, c. 1765, c. 1765 with leaf moulding. BOTTOM: New Hall,
c. 1790; two in Davenport bone china, c. 1830, 1840.

printed ware were impressed ADAMS from 1787 to 1805.
W. ADAMS & CO was occasionally impressed on jasper.

BENJAMIN ADAMS (b. 1783) at the age of twenty-two suc-

120. Serving jugs concluded. Nineteenth century. TOP: 1810s–1820s, increasing lip, simple handle; 1820s, Mason waisted type; 1830s, lower waist, wider, flaring, shaped rim. CENTRE: three of 1851 with fancy handles, elongated necks, high lips; 1855, receding lip, taller handle. BOTTOM: 1851 but foreshadowing rising waist and squarer shape; 1862, high, slighter waist, smaller lip; 1865 square top, small lip; 1871 nearly cylindrical.

ceeded to his father's potteries in 1805. Eventually ill-health caused him to lessen his responsibilities and he sold the Greengates Pottery to John Meir in 1820. Adams produced some exceptionally fine transfer-printed work in a delicate tone of blue on pearl ware, heavier than formerly, but more smoothly glazed and on stone china. Patterns included an adaptation of a painting by Claude Lorraine within a border associated with the main picture. The mark is B. ADAMS impressed.

WILLIAM ADAMS (1772–1829) established the Upper Cliff Bank Works, Stoke-upon-Trent, in 1804, and potted blue transfer-printed table wares, hand-painted earthenwares, figures and busts. He bought the main Cliff Bank Pottery in 1810 for the manufacture of bone china. This was elaborately enamelled and lavishly gilded with flowers and cupids in the style of contemporaneous Meissen and Sèvres. By 1818 he was owner of five potteries at Stoke. His son was William Adams, 1798–1865. He chiefly produced blue-printed table ware, his scenes of London and stately homes achieving great popularity. Vast quantities were exported to America; his 'Landing of Columbus' series of twelve views in borders of medallions, animals and flowers being favourites. So successful was this venture that Adams operated his own barges for carrying consignments to Liverpool by canal.

The mark from 1804 was always ADAMS impressed, although blue-printed ware for the United States of America was impressed with variations of the American eagle accompanied by the blue transfer-printed name of the subject on a foliated cartouche. In 1819 William Adams was joined in partnership by his son and the trade mark changed to ADAMS & SON and W. A. & S. Five years later he was joined by another son and the trade mark changed to W. ADAMS & SONS/ STOKE-UPON-TRENT.

WILLIAM ADAMS (1748–1831) of Cobridge and Burslem established himself at Brick House in 1769, specialising in red stoneware and enamelled cream-coloured earthenware. In 1775 he began experimenting with blue printing under the glaze on cream-coloured earthenware and became a prosperous specialist in this work, none of which is known to have been marked. In 1813 he ceased earthenware potting and rented his potteries to tenants. With Philip Eaton as partner he entered the bone china trade, a project which ended disastrously in 1819. Although William Adams had thirteen children none married and this branch of the Adams family became extinct.

WILLIAM ADAMS (1798–1865) of Greenfield: after the death of his father he withdrew from his partnership in William Adams & Sons to direct potteries owned by his wife at Greenfield. Productions included inexpensive enamelled dessert services enriched with liquid gold from the mid-1850s, Egyptian black tea services, green glazed ware and, late in the period, sponge decorated granite ware. The mark was ADAMS impressed.

JOHN ADAMS & CO., Hanley: made jasper, English majolica, ordinary earthenware and parian statuary from 1864 to 1873. Parian busts of celebrities, registered at Stationers' Hall, include Gladstone in 1866, John Bright in 1867, Lord Derby and Tennyson. The marks impressed were J. ADAMS & CO. and ADAMS & CO.

ADAMS & BROMLEY, Hanley: succeeded John Adams & Co. in 1873 and continued until 1886, potting a similar range of goods. The marks, impressed and printed, were ADAMS & BROMLEY and A & B.

Alcock, Samuel & Co., Hill Pottery, Burslem and Cobridge, 1828–1859, manufactured bone china, parian ware, stone china and earthenware. Some very popular jugs decorated with designs in relief were issued, including 'Naomi and her Daughters-in-law', registered at the Patent Office, 27th April, 1847, 'Daniel in the Lion's Den', 1859, and the Distin jug, showing three-quarter length relief portraits of the instrumentalists John Distin and his four sons, often marked beneath 'The Distin Family: the Saxe Horn Performers'.

The mark SAM^L ALCOCK & CO./COBRIDGE was used until

1853 and SAM^L ALCOCK & CO/BURSLEM from 1830 to 1859. The royal arms above SAM^L ALCOCK & CO./PATENT or S. A. & CO., PATENT, dates from 1842.

When the Alcock firm closed the models and moulds were

121. Pictorial jugs. TOP: Walley's Diana; Alcock's Distin family of sax horn players (another version was made by Cork & Edge); Walley's boy and eagle. BOTTOM: by Till & Son, registered 1854; babes in the wood by T. & R. Boote, also by Cork & Edge; lily pattern by Cork & Edge. Such hot water jugs became general when Ridgways developed an improved heat-resistant stoneware.

probably used by their successors Sir James Duke & Nephews whose wares were seldom marked.

Aller Vale Pottery, Newton Abbott, Devon: established 1865 as a common brown earthenware pottery until 1868. It was then acquired by John Phillips & Co., who specialised in fire clay ware such as garden vases and ornamental bricks. The mark during this period was a horse's head, couped, with the proprietor's name in Greek. A fire destroyed the premises in 1887. After reconstruction the firm traded as Aller Vale Art Potteries, using local red clay, usually covered with yellow slip and decorated with graffito designs and mottoes. Bowls, mugs and jugs were glazed brown inside. Bold conventional designs in dark greens and browns were also used in association with proverbs and mottoes. Aller Vale made the popular crocus vases with dark blue ground, bulb, leaves and stem in

122. Crocus vase in Aller Vale ware, late 19th century.

greens and creams extending vertically, the flowers in gold. The pottery closed in 1901. The mark was ALLER VALE impressed.

The good will and plant were taken over by the Watcombe Pottery Co., the combined firms trading as Royal Aller Vale & Watcombe Pottery Co., Torquay. The local red clay was used, a popular green glazed ware being the main production. White slip ware decorated with graffito patterns and proverbs. The marks were ROYAL ALLER VALE and ROYAL TORQUAY POTTERY. The factory closed in 1962.

Baker, Bevan & Irwin, The Glamorgan Pottery, Swansea: established 1813 by William Baker who was joined by William Bevan and Thomas Irwin. Good quality domestic earthenware was made resembling that of the nearby Cambrian Pottery. Closed in 1838 when plant, moulds and copper plates were sold to the South Wales Pottery. The printed marks consisted of various cartouches containing the name of the pattern and the initials B B & I.

Belleek, Fermanagh, Northern Ireland: established in 1857 by M'Birney & Armstrong. They began as potters of domestic table ware in stone china containing felspar from near-by deposits. Soon parian statuary was in production and later on white glazed parian porcelain, usually with decorations enamelled in green and pastel pink which could be fired together in a muffle kiln. The glaze overcame the criticism that its surface was easily soiled and difficult to clean.

Belleek, however, became celebrated for its parian ware glazed with a smooth, nacreous lustre displaying some of the iridescence of mother of pearl. Its use was protected by a patent granted on 1st January, 1858, by J. J. H. Brianchon, Paris. M'Birney & Armstrong acquired the manufacturing rights. This was applied to parian of exceptional thinness— sometimes no thicker than heavy brown paper. Parian glazed with mother-of-pearl lustre obviously inspired a style expressed by ornately modelled forms associated with marine life, sea shells being characteristic with mermaids, tritons, sea horses, dolphins, coral and marine plants.

Following the lead of the Staffordshire potters who were combining parian statuary with units of enamelled and gilded bone china, Belleek contrasted parian statuary with lustred parian, a combination not known to have been copied elsewhere. Stemmed centre pieces, fruit dishes and compotiers for dessert services were made in large numbers, their stems covered with seaweed and shells. Typically the base would be encircled with a group composed of a mermaid, a sea horse and two fish-tailed mer-babies placed between cardium shells which served as sweetmeat or comfit dishes.

123. Belleek wares. TOP: sweetmeat shell on coral stand; sea urchin teapot set on coral. BOTTOM: cobweb plate with raised prunus flowers; muffin dish with lily of the valley ornament; shell vase.

A Belleek speciality was the nacreous glazed basket work, almost unbelievably light in weight and enriched with hand-modelled flowers and foliage, the most usual being posies of roses, shamrocks and thistles, all of gossamer-like fragility, but chrysanthemums, dahlias, honeysuckles, picotees and carnations are found. These were perfected with iridescent lustre. Oval and round, in sizes ranging to 18 inches in length, these baskets usually have D-handles, rarely tall bail handles.

Early parian statuary was impressed BELLEEK POTTERY. Introduced in 1863 and more common is a transfer-printed design of a round tower with an Irish harp to the right and an Irish wolfhound to the left above the name BELLEEK in a ribbon, with three shamrock leaves at each end. This may be in red, brown or blue.

124. Twig work. Wedgwood basket of interwoven strands of earthenware. Belleek basket with flowers in relief, the strands of parian overlaid and not interwoven.

Less common, and used from 1863 to about 1880, was an Irish harp surmounted by a crown, either impressed or printed. When the name IRELAND is present the piece was potted after 1891.

Belle Vue Pottery, Hull: established 1802 by Josiah Hipway, James and Jeremiah Smith, all of Hull, and Job Ridgway of Shelton. The Hull partners had resigned by 1806 and Job Ridgway was joined by his brother George. They operated Belle Vue until 1826, when it was taken over by Edwin Bell, who was succeeded by William Bell who closed down in 1841. Productions consisted chiefly of domestic ware, at first in poor quality cream-coloured earthenware, now badly crazed, and blue and brown transfer-printed pearl ware decorated with landscapes and ceremonial scenes. Teapots with bell-shaped covers were characteristic from 1826. The mark, impressed or blue printed, was BELLE VUE POTTERY HULL in a circle, the name of the pottery in script above a cursive scroll-surrounded representation of two bells; or two bells over-lapping, impressed.

Birch, Edmund John, Shelton, 1796–1818: potter of jasper, basaltes and other fine stonewares. Mark impressed BIRCH or E. I. B.

Bow, soft-paste porcelain, 1745–1775. The first porcelain to be produced in England on a commercial scale was potted at Bow in Middlesex and not at the later and more celebrated china works at Stratford-le-Bow in Essex. Bow porcelain may be classified into five main groups, each with radical differences from the productions of contemporaneous porcelain potteries.

1. Until 1749 porcelain was made at Edward Heylyn's Glasshouse at Bow in Middlesex in association with Thomas Frye. They developed a formula for which they were granted a patent in 1744. Their first porcelain was too coarse and too badly potted to compete with imported productions. Gradual improvements were made until eventually a porcelain of cream-tinted translucency was produced, usually displaying a tinge of green if held to the light. This was covered with a glaze that tended to be drab, mushroom-grey and semi-transparent, although an attempt was made to clear it by adding smalt. The venture proved unprofitable and the partners abandoned it. Very few examples of this period are known.

2. Thomas Frye continued his researches until in November, 1749 he was granted a patent for a new formula. This was sponsored by Weatherby & Crowther, who built a pottery at Stratford-le-Bow which they named New Canton. Frye was appointed works superintendent and production began late in 1750. Bone ash, a new and important ingredient, was added to the frit. The new porcelain was cream-coloured, dense-textured and displayed moons or grease spots. The liquid lead glaze was so lavishly applied that it tended to collect in thick drops and obliterate fine relief work. This porcelain was used

125. Inkwells and inkstands. TOP: most famous Bow souvenir inkpot inscribed MADE AT NEW CANTON 1750; typical inscribed Lowestoft; Worcester with scale background to flower reserves. CENTRE: Derby japan pattern 1820s; Rockingham type with small vertical holders for pens. BOTTOM: Coalport and Minton style pots and taper stick on flower-encrusted tray; Spode scale pattern, the inkpot lids containing holes for pens; Wedgwood terracotta, c. 1830.

208

chiefly for domestic table-ware, but the fact that it failed to withstand boiling water made it unsuitable for teapots, although these were made and illustrated on a trade card issued in 1750. After 1753 its use was largely confined to dinner and dessert ware, enamelled blue and white, or white, and to figures and vases; it continued in production until 1775. Much of this porcelain displays brown patches towards the base, and surface decomposition of the excessively leaded glaze has caused many examples of this period to assume a pinkish iridescence.

3. Between 1755 and 1759 fireclay in the formula was replaced by finely ground hard porcelain wasters from a grinding mill in South London. This was used for domestic ware and could withstand testing by boiling water. During this period Bow porcelain became more radiant with enamelling; in sunshine it sparkles with a radiance quite foreign to the reproductions which abound. This is caused by impurities found in the metallic oxides in a manner which could not be reproduced today.

4. An improved porcelain was produced from 1759, closely resembling Chelsea porcelain, and was made when a temporary stoppage at the Chelsea works led a number of its potters and decorators to take work at Bow. The glaze became ivory-tinted, providing a rich background for enamel colours and gilding, particularly the unique maroon purple.

5. Following a second influx of Chelsea workers in 1765 Bow paste became thinner, harshly white and less translucent than formerly. Its more workable texture and its smoother, gleaming glaze led to the large-scale production of figures and other ornamental porcelain, enlivened with rich, deep lustrous colouring. Table ware became more elaborate, decoration including raised vine sprigs, enamelled fruits, painted birds and blue underglaze grounds with white reserves displaying either colourful birds, or paintings in the Boucher and

Fragonard manner. Late in the period the blue ground might be diapered with gold. This paste continued in use until the factory was acquired in 1776 by William Duesbury, who removed plant, materials, models, moulds and stock to Derby. BOW FIGURES may be classified into three main types; the earliest sold 'in the white'; a series decorated in blue under the glaze; and the delightful figures, groups and bocages in colourful enamels.

Figures in plain white and underglaze blue usually stand on rectangular bases and are characterised by elementary though vigorous modelling, full of technical imperfections. Supports are almost crude in their simplicity, sometimes little more than lumps of clay moulded to resemble a stump, a coat or a dress. When overglaze colour was first applied results were florid, a dry red and a yellowish-green being common, with the addition of lesser amounts of blue, yellow and gold.

Copies of Meissen figures became important items of production. Until about 1758 they usually stood upon flat, regular bases, either lacking all ornament, or with almost imperceptible scrolls in low relief. Colours on these figures included puce, in shades varying from pink to crimson and an opaque milky blue. These colours might be merged to produce marbling effects on the bases.

By 1758 a more elaborate stand had been evolved, with scrolls so designed that the corners of the base became small supporting feet. Bow was the first factory to make the footed pedestal, quickly to become characteristic of 18th-century English porcelain figures. Figures were now modelled with greater delicacy, larger examples being supported by elaborately shaped four-footed bases enlivened with touches of purple and other tints. Small figures generally stood upon round, flat-based pedestals. Additional colours that now found a place on the enameller's palette included opaque purple, brick red and pale yellow, all sparingly applied.

The period 1764–1775 is generally considered disappointing with mediocre design although colours were costlier and richer, and decoration verging on the spectacular. Pedestals were designed with graceful, pierced scrolls. Frank Hurlbutt in *Bow Porcelain* described figures of this period as 'with resplendent garments patterned with a brilliant *rose à la Pompadour* or rich cobalt blue, turquoise or copper red ground, having ornately shaped and scrolled white reserves, delicately pencilled with flowers; breeches or waistcoats of a peacock's tail pattern and gorgeous disc patterns. Dresses of female figures were frequently in blue or crimson with small yellow flowers and miniature gold leaves'.

One very pronounced peculiarity may be seen on many Bow figures. Close examination of the surface will often disclose marks under the glaze made by the modeller's flat knife or sharp tool for smoothing the surface and accentuating lines before firing to the biscuit state.

Bretby Art Pottery, Woodville, Derbyshire: established 1883 as Tooth & Ault. From 1887 was directed by Henry Tooth.

126. Henry Tooth's Bretby ware late 19th century.

In addition to making umbrella stands, *jardiniéres*, vases, hanging pots and similar ware he made earthenware to resemble hammered copper, bronze and steel. 'Carved bamboo' ware was made in combination with bronze (*see* also Linthorpe).

Bristol: this long-flourishing seaport is thought to have produced earthenware from the late 13th century. Tygs, jugs and mugs were recorded in the late 16th century, but the trade was not fully established until 1671, when pottery apprentices were first recorded in the Bristol apprentice list begun in 1593 TIN-ENAMELLED EARTHENWARE, often termed delft ware, bears a close resemblance to Lambeth productions, no doubt as a result of attracting skilled potters and artists at the time of its first establishment. Numerous potters of tin-enamelled earthenware are recorded by name, from 1683 when Edward Ward of Brislington established the Temple Back Pottery until the ware was superseded by cream-coloured earthenware late in the 18th century. Ward's pupil, Thomas Frank, established a pottery at Brislington, which he sold to Thomas Dixon in 1706, when he began to operate another pottery at Redcliff Back in Bristol. Bristol tin-enamelled earthenware has a buff-tinted body, harder, denser, slightly more reddish in hue than Dutch delft-ware. The slightly tinted white enamel coating (a lead glaze rendered opaque with oxide of tin) is thicker, muddier and harder than that used elsewhere. Hollow ware tends to show interior wreathing.

Symmetrical flowers are characteristic and colouring includes a slaty blue, 'quaker green', dull yellow, brownish orange, manganese purple and pale turquoise blue, all colours that could be fired with the white enamel background. The tones are softer than London prepared colours. The styles of a few painters have been recognised; the majority of decorators were mere copyists working from master pieces painted by the head decorator. John Bowen, apprenticed 1734, is associated with individualistic painting in blue on white, creating scenes in which stately men and women are seen among tall, misty trees and gaunt houses depicted with great economy of line and colour; on the other hand his ships are meticulously detailed.

The Bristol decorators adapted much from Chinese designs. Many were at hand in the dock warehouses that received imported porcelains from the East, and others were supplied by ships' captains who were commissioned to carry back sample pieces for copying or adapting to speedy reproduction. The early vigorous colours and bold style of painting gave place to softer tones and more delicate lines towards the mid-18th century. Much was in blue and white, and more in the Chinese

127. Tiles. TOP: Bristol, painted, 18th century; Minton & Hollins, mid-19th century. BOTTOM: Campbell & Co., Fenton and Stoke, established 1868 by R. Minton Taylor, a former partner in Minton & Hollins, 1870s; Maw & Co, Broseley, 1860s–70s.

famille verte palette. There was also effective use of the style loosely called *bianco-sopra-bianco*, an imitation of Chinese incised work, the near-white plate rim—starch blue or lavender blue—being painted with a broad band of white flowers in slight relief around a central ornament consisting of landscapes in blue, or bouquets of flowers in purple blue, olive green and brownish-orange.

Among the wide variety of ware made were plates with edges foliated or scalloped. Punch bowls had flattened flaring sides tangential to the curves of the bottoms. A spout cup might have a lid in the form of a royal crown with open bows such as might be found in contemporaneous flint-glass, with handles in the form of snakes or rolls of clay twisted to suggest coiled tendrils. Rectangular flower holders were shaped as hollow bricks fitted with loose grids. Such a grid was pierced with a large square hole at the centre flanked each side by six, nine or twelve holes for flower stems. Tiles were made by the majority of the Bristol delft-ware potters. Brown salt-glazed stoneware was made by several Bristol potters, but none has been noted with a mark.

SOFT-PASTE PORCELAIN was made at Bristol between 1748 and 1752, steatite (*see* Soapstone porcelain) being used as an ingredient. The resulting porcelain has a hard compact texture and is found in two distinct types: (*a*) with a greyish tinge, not very translucent and appearing greenish if held to the light. (*b*) with a creamy-white tinge, of high translucency and showing ivory if held to the light.

The thin glaze, imperfectly opacified, at first displayed tiny bubbles. It quickly improved, but always was flawed with a multiplicity of microscopic pittings. A starchy blue tinge is characteristic of the glaze in association with blue underglaze decoration. In enamel painted ware the glaze has a warm ivory tint; this glaze receded a little from the foot ring when fired. Blue underglaze decoration is usually badly blurred and frequently in poorly executed *chinoiserie* designs. Enamel painted decoration is in the *famille verte* and *famille rose* styles. Sauce boats in designs adapted or copied from silver plate appear to have been a principal production. This factory is sometimes wrongly referred to by collectors as Lowdin's Porcelain Manufactory. Lowdin, the previous occupier of the premises, died in 1745 and his name has been confused with those of the proprietors, Benjamin Lund and William Cookworthy or William Miller. Plant, tools, stock and formulae were acquired in mid-1752 by Wall and his associates at Worcester.

COOKWORTHY'S HARD-PASTE PORCELAIN business (*see* Plymouth) was transferred from Plymouth to Bristol in 1770. There appears to have been little difference between his Bristol ware and that made at Plymouth; it still remained technically imperfect and inclined to show slight warping. The pottery and patent were acquired by Richard Champion in 1773. The mark at Bristol at first continued to be the chemists' symbol for tin, as used at Plymouth; later a cross in blue enamel or gold with a capital B was used on domestic ware.

CHAMPION'S HARD-PASTE PORCELAIN (1773–82) possessed of the exclusive rights to prepare china clay and manufacture hard-paste porcelain Richard Champion envisaged vast profits, foreseeing a yearly royalty of £100,000 for Thomas Pitt, from whose lands the china clay was obtained. He was fully aware that the quality of the porcelain made by Cookworthy left much to be desired and he applied for a 14-year extension of the patent beyond the expiry date of 1782. This caused costly litigation, ending in Champion being granted exclusive rights to use Cornish china clay and stone in the manufacture of translucent porcelain; its use was allowed freely to makers of earthenware. Thus was created a monopoly which effectively prevented the development of the bone china industry until the close of 1796. Financial troubles befell Champion during the next two years, including the capture of his merchant fleet by the French, and active manufacture of porcelain was suspended in the autumn of 1778. Large accumulated stocks of biscuit ware, however, were decorated and sold until 1782.

Champion's hard porcelain is white, faintly tinged with grey, and many examples are warped or firecracked. If held to the light the tint seen varies from a cold white-grey to a faintly yellowish-green, and small tears are noted, reminiscent of Chelsea moons. Translucency varies with thickness and quality, the result of variations and changes in blending. Its surface appearance, however, is fairly constant. The surface is liable to be marred with brownish specks, and grit is often to be noted in a foot ring. Hollow-ware displays distinct wreathing.

On fine quality porcelain the glaze is thin, clear, brilliant and even-surfaced, its colour being almost identical with that of the paste. This glaze, always hard enough to withstand wear and stains, appears to be perfectly fused with the body, rather than as a separate layer in the manner of soft porcelain glazes. Enamels did not sink into it as into frit glazes; rising slightly above the surface they were in danger of peeling off with use. On blue and white and other cheap ware, Champion used a frit glaze, lustrous and faintly blue in tint.

The greater part of Champion's output consisted of tea ware, for which the heat-resisting hard-paste porcelain was eminently suitable. Dishes and other flat ware liable to sink and warp in the kiln were supported beneath by strengthening ribs. On an oval dish the rib resembled a raised pot hook down the centre of the underside: a plate would be given a supporting ring. Such strengtheners were slightly shallower than the outer foot rims.

The majority of Champion's porcelain appears to have been marked, with the notable exception of the figures. On blue underglaze ware the cross is also in underglaze, and an occasional gilt cross has been noted. The letter B in blue underglaze was also used. On copies of Meissen's porcelain the crossed swords, often with a dot between the hafts, might be used in underglaze blue. This might be accompanied by a cross, a letter B, or the artist's name, all in enamel overglaze.

EARTHENWARE. In the mid-1780s enamelled earthenware was being abandoned in Bristol in favour of the cream-coloured earthenware with which potters in other districts were capturing a new market. Joseph Ring from 1785 made a fine quality cream-ware, thin of section, with good edges, but slightly yellower than contemporaneous Wedgwood or Leeds. The latter were cream-coloured throughout their fabric, but Ring's and other Bristol earthenware is characterised by its yellow glaze on a white body. The delft-ware decorators, skilled in blue painting, continued in this medium which was gradually replaced by enamel decoration in colours. Transfer-printing dates from 1797.

Brownfield, William, Albion Works, Cobridge: from 1836 to 1850 held a partnership in Wood & Brownfield, specialists in blue transfer-printed and sponged earthenware. After Wood's death in 1850 Brownfield modernised production processes and extended the range to include bone china. His entry in *White's Staffordshire Directory,* 1851, describes him as a potter of china and earthenware in the white and enamelled. His most successful decorations were adaptations from Mason's ironstone china. Brownfield was a pioneer of the Victorian fashion for surfaces in relief basket work; he registered a jug so ornamented in 1855.

Brownfield's exhibit at the International Exhibition, 1862, won him a gold medal. The catalogue praised his earthenware and noted that it was superior to much of the porcelain exhibited and its cost considerably lower. At this time he commissioned Hablot K. Browne, the well-known humorous engraver who signed his work Phiz, to design and decorate a

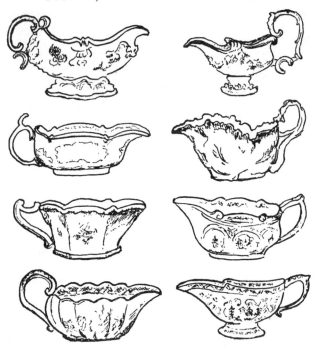

128. Sauce-boats, in chronological sequence, 18th century porcelains (all would have stands or dishes). TOP: Chelsea, early 1750s; Bow, c. 1755. SECOND ROW: early Bristol, early 1750s; leaf form, Longton Hall, c. 1755. THIRD ROW: both Plymouth, c. 1770. BOTTOM: early Derby; Derby.

dinner service which he registered on 14th March, 1862. The cleverly drawn classical figures were transfer-printed and hand-tinted in pinkish-mauve. This service continued in production

129. Sauce-boats sequence cont. TOP: both early Worcester. SECOND ROW: Worcester 1760s–70s; Lowestoft. THIRD ROW: both Lowestoft. BOTTOM: Liverpool, Chaffers, 1760s; Derby, early 19th century.

until the early 1870s. Parian statuary and figures in enamelled bone china were also made, some modelled by Albert Carrier de Belleuse. Experiments were made in aventurine effects.

130. Sauce vessels in useful wares (all would have stands or dishes). TOP: white salt glazed stoneware with surface moulding (one with two feet at front, a style later changed to two feet at the back). CENTRE: Leeds creamware, late 18th century; Spode blue-printed, early 19th century. BOTTOM: duck with head handle (for apple sauce?); fish with tail handle (for a thin sauce, e.g. hot butter or lemon juice).

In 1871, when Brownfield employed about five hundred people, he was joined by his son William Etches Brownfield, the firm then traded as William Brownfield & Son. During the early 1870s pairs of vases were richly painted with pairs of Etty-like subjects such as 'Morning' and 'Midday', acclaimed contemporaneously as 'the highest achievement of modern art'. A curious Brownfield vase of this period was recorded by Jewitt: 'the body is true to nature—that of a sea-bird's egg; the handles are formed of the heads and the bird's legs and feet form the stand'.

After the retirement of William Etches Brownfield in 1890 the business was reorganised on a co-operative basis and, according to J. P. Cushion, traded as the Brownfield Guild Pottery until 1900.

Brownfield trade marks, which might be impressed, but were usually printed, until 1871 included w. b. within the bows of a Staffordshire knot, w. b. and the name of the pattern in an acorn and oak leaf border, w. b. COBRIDGE ALBION on the outer rim of a circle inscribed REG. MARK. From 1871, BROWNFIELD & SON, COBRIDGE STAFFS upon a scroll enclosing two hemispheres, from 1876 SON was changed to SONS (*see* Fig. 149).

Castleford, Yorkshire: operated from the mid-1790s until 1821 by David Dunderdale, who made a moderately fine cream-coloured earthenware. This resembled Leeds ware, but was less brilliantly glazed and often bore enamelled decorations adapted from similar ware produced by Wedgwood. He also made black basaltes, table services and candlesticks in a fine, white half-glossy vitrified stoneware with relief patterns often outlined in bright blue enamel. Some stoneware teapots had sliding covers; another design had a hinged cover swinging on a metal pin but few are marked and there were other makers. The marks were impressed: until 1803, D D CASTLE, FORD; then, when he was joined by John Plowes as partner-

D D & CO CASTLEFORD or D D & CO CASTLEFORD POTTERY.
Caughley (1775–99). The Salopian China Manufactory was
established by Thomas Turner, formerly of Worcester, who
controlled the works until 1799. It was then acquired by
John Rose of Coalport, who operated the pottery until 1814,
when the plant was transferred to Coalport.

PASTE: steatitic (*see* Soapstone porcelain, Part II) as at
Worcester and capable of withstanding boiling water. Until

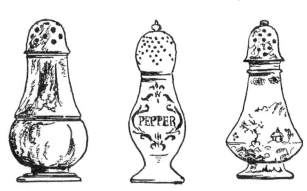

131. Pepper casters in contrasting materials: tortoiseshell glaze on
common earthenware; black enamelled name on pattern-pierced
Leeds creamware; Chinese style blue painting on Caughley
porcelain.

the early 1780s it was white with a cloudy orange or straw-
coloured tinge when held to the light. The paste afterwards
displayed a greyish appearance with an orange-skin surface,
retaining the straw-coloured tint.

GLAZE: clear and brilliant with a faintly blue tint, and lavishly
applied.

DECORATION: Turner specialised in transfer-printing, at first in black, sepia and blue over the glaze. By 1780 he had perfected blue printing under glaze including much pseudo-Oriental pattern. Blues varied from a greyish blue, through a dull purple to a peculiarly vivid violet-blue in the 1790s, not found on any other English printed ware.

Much ware was painted in blue, some of it enriched with gilding. Characteristic are vertical stripes of blue separated by white bands of equal width, with delicate gilded ornament. The popular fisherman or pleasure boat pattern transfer-printed in underglaze blue (p. 36) is very similar to the Worcester version. Gilding also accented lines and edge bandings associated with Chinese patterns in blue. Sprays of foliage in blue and gold were popular, including the Chantilly sprig.

Much fine Caughley overglaze decoration came from Robert Chamberlain after he had left the Worcester porcelain factory where he had been in charge of decorating, the wares being supplied in the white or with underglaze blue for gilding.

MARKS: The letter s in numerous shapes and sizes, painted or printed in blue was used throughout the period. It might be accompanied by SALOPIAN impressed, or the letter c printed underglaze. Earthenware marked SALOPIAN was made by the Salopian Art Pottery Co., c. 1880–1912.

Chamberlain: see Worcester.

Chelsea Porcelain Manufactory, soft-paste porcelain, 1745–69. Its origins are controversial. A goat-and-bee jug (see Fig. 97 and p. 172) is thought to be the earliest authenticated piece of English porcelain. It was Nicholas Sprimont (1716–71) who became the dominant personality at Chelsea with which he became directly associated in the late 1740s; soon more experienced earthenware potters were being attracted from Staffordshire by the lure of high wages. Advertisements of the period suggest that production consisted mainly of table ware. There was a temporary cessation of production from 1756 to 1758. When the factory re-started the paste was

132. Chelsea and other vegetable tureens. TOP: cauliflower; sunflower with leaf handle to lid; apple. CENTRE: asparagus; cos lettuce on a dish of everlapping leaves. BOTTOM: two contrasting melons, in Leeds creamware with painted flowers and by Wedgwood in green and yellow glaze.

strengthened by the addition of bone ash to the frit. The use of bone ash as an ingredient was monopolised until 1763 by Thomas Frye's patent of 1749 (*see* Bow, p. 207). It must be assumed, therefore, that Frye licensed his process to Chelsea.

The project did not flourish financially and from 1764 production 'gradually declined and the Porcelain became scarce'.

In February, 1770, the plant and stock-in-trade were acquired by William Duesbury of Derby, who continued manufacture at Chelsea until December, 1783. Moulds and materials were then sent to Derby and Christies sold 'all the remaining finished and unfinished stock of the Chelsea Porcelain Manufactory with all the remaining buildings and fixtures'.

Chelsea porcelain is briefly classified according to the five major changes made in the paste during the factory's existence. Each may be distinguished by a different group of marks, but it is essential for the beginner-collector to appreciate that Chelsea marks have been reproduced on all manner of fakes and imitations. Each of the groups detailed below may be sub-divided by experts.

INCISED TRIANGLE PERIOD, 1745–49: the paste is creamy in colour and flawed with microscopic specks and has a satin-like texture. If held to the light, irregularly placed small round flecks, more translucent than the rest of the paste, are revealed in the milky-white body. These, known as pinholes, look like floating grease spots and are the fore-runners of the celebrated 'moons' of the two following periods. The glaze was thickly applied, soft and glossy, and age has often given it a yellowish tinge.

Chelsea at this time was devoted almost entirely to the production of table ware, such as moulded cream jugs, salt cellars, coffee pots, and teapots. Embossed reliefs such as prunus blossom were frequent. Some of the early pieces were adapted from silver models—in fact, the term 'silver shape' was later used in various Chelsea catalogues. The triangle was incised beneath the glaze and might be accompanied by CHELSEA in script. Incised and impressed triangles were used by some 19th-century potters, such as the Minton date symbol for 1843.

RAISED ANCHOR PERIOD, 1749–53: the paste now displayed a faintly greyish tone and pinholes were fewer and larger, now known to collectors as moons. After 1750 the porcelain was somewhat whiter than formerly. This improved body was gradually cleared and whitened. A creamy glaze was used, thick, like candle-grease, and inclined to choke the modelling. A characteristic of this glaze was its tendency to shrink, leaving a dry edge. Owing to its exceptional thickness, small pools of glaze were liable to accumulate in the centre of flat areas.

Table ware constituted the main productions. A few figures were made, including some fine birds. Design and decoration were influenced by Meissen and adaptations of Japanese Kakiemon porcelain were made, continuing into the red anchor period. Tea services were made in variety, enamelled in delightful pale shades.

The mark was an anchor in relief impressed on a small oval applied pad. From about 1751 the anchor might be picked out in red over the glaze. Occasionally an elaborate blue anchor was painted under the glaze. Less common is a crown and trident, also in underglaze blue.

RED ANCHOR PERIOD, 1753–56: the paste was now thinner than formerly, of finer grain and more translucent, although still exhibiting moons and exterior blemishes. The evenly applied glaze was smooth, slightly blue against the white of the body, and was seldom crazed. An almost constant feature of pieces of this paste is the appearance of three or four round spur marks on the base.

Soft pastel colours were used to emphasise the delicacy of the sharp modelling. Much table ware was decorated in the oriental manner, the work of highly skilled artists. The earlier Chinese patterns painted in blue under the glaze gave way to dainty decorations in red and gold. Leaves were now painted in light and yellowish greens, side by side, and veined in black. Applied flowers in full relief were introduced.

Excellent reproductions of the Japanese brocade patterns were made, and border patterns in raised work were copied from Meissen. Sprays of painted flowers and fruit in low relief were sparingly applied. Hard-paste porcelain in the white was imported from the East and decorated by Chelsea artists in this style during the period of temporary closure between 1756 and 1759.

The mark was a plain red anchor painted over the glaze in

133. Butter-boats, for fish sauce, or for cream. TOP: Chelsea; early Bristol. CENTRE: early and later Worcester (right with lamprey handle). BOTTOM: Longton Hall; Liverpool, 1760s.

varying forms and sizes, usually small and in a bright hue, but sometimes with a brownish tinge. The Chelsea anchor of this period is also noted in purple over the glaze and blue under the glaze. The anchor with a cable is found painted in red and incised; interlocked anchors, one inverted, were also used.

GOLD ANCHOR PERIOD, 1758–69: the paste differs entirely from earlier periods. It was now strengthened by the addition of bone ash to the frit as a strengthening ingredient, and was therefore denser of texture, harder, chalky white, more translucent, but tended to suffer from fire cracks which are visible beneath the glaze. Warping in the kiln and mooning were overcome. The limpid glassy glaze was liable to craze and gathered in angles and hollows, where it showed a faintly green tinge. It was no less soft than formerly, colours sinking into it with rich effect. Sèvres was the main influence.

Modelling of figures became more meticulous and enamels in pastel shades were replaced by a blaze of vivid colour enriched with gilding. Gilded scroll work was introduced around the decorated panels on the white which formed the central motifs on sets of vases and tea and dessert services, whose magnificence largely depended upon their rich and deservedly celebrated ground colours. The beautiful *gros bleu* or mazarine blue ground appeared in 1759, pea green in the same year, claret and turquoise in 1760, and the rare yellow in 1761. These grounds, too, might be heavily enriched with gold and chased.

The reserves were filled with bouquets, fruit, figure subjects and pastoral scenes copied from engravings after paintings by such artists as Watteau and Teniers. Exotic birds of brilliant plumage were favourite decorations. More often than not they were large crested pheasants with sweeping tail feathers and might be accompanied by other equally colourful birds and insects. Yet another distinctively French style was a feature of Chelsea work from about 1765; large elaborate vases were made with pierced necks and covers and wildly interlacing handles.

Gold anchor marks were in the same designs as the red. A pair of anchors in gold, one inverted, but not interlocked, was an occesional mark. The smaller the anchor, either red or gold, the finer the quality of the piece. These marks are sometimes hidden in crevices, and may be so insignificant as to be discovered only after careful search.

CHELSEA-DERBY, 1770–84: a term applied to Chelsea productions while under the control of William Duesbury. Seldom were more than a dozen workers employed. Oriental and continental porcelain was lent to Duesbury for copying by the Duke of Newcastle and the Countess Spencer. When George III visited the factory in 1773 he granted Duesbury his patronage with permission to incorporate the royal crown in his trade mark. The porcelain of this period is more waxy in appearance than earlier work by Chelsea. Surface smoothness almost equals that of glass.

Table ware followed the forms made fashionable by Sèvres, and decoration consisted chiefly of centrally placed urns, flower sprays or cupids, with festoons and swags. The former costly ground colours were discarded in favour of a beautiful, though inexpensive, red. Edges might be gilt-lined or dotted and foot rims were usually encircled with single gold lines.

Marks were in gold: a Chelsea anchor traversing the downstroke of a script D. A jewelled crown appeared above the anchor from 1773.

FIGURES: early examples might recline directly upon the table, or stand erect upon separate thin, flat square plinths, cut at the corners and bevelled more widely at the top than at the bottom. The later method was to make the stand as part of the figure and not as a separate piece. Early examples of these might be made to suggest rock work and painted pale

134. Coffee cups, in chronological sequence. TOP: Bow with white relief ornament; Chelsea, fluted and painted; Chelsea gold anchor, painted on coloured ground. SECOND ROW: Chelsea-Derby; Derby, late 18th century; Lowestoft, painted in colours. THIRD ROW: Worcester, flower painted, painted and leaf moulded, spiral queen's pattern. FOURTH ROW: Worcester, scale blue ground, 1770s; Bristol, c. 1775; Bristol with development of more formal treatment.

green; various rococo styles of scroll stands were made during the gold anchor period. A characteristic of early Chelsea figures is the distinct painting of leaf veins in fine lines. They were coloured naturalistically with some attempt at realism. At this time decorative sets were made, gracefully modelled, gaily dressed and masked. The most charming sets of figures made during the red anchor period represented characters from the Italian Comedy, after the celebrated Meissen models. Later there were elaborate shepherds and gallants with their companions, but it was not until the end of the period that the figures beceme more highly coloured and given gold enrichment. Flat washes of colour, large areas of white, touches of gold and omission of gilding are typical of early red anchor figures. Figure subjects were copied from paintings by Rubens,

135. Coffee cups, cont. TOP: New Hall and two of Swansea. BOTTOM: Spode, 1820s; Coalport, 1851; W. A. Adderley, 'Shansi' Japanese pattern, registered 1882.

136. Cans for coffee. TOP: rose-painted Swansea, and two of Derby (end of 18th century). CENTRE: Derby, 1800s; Derby with later japan ornament; gilded and flower-painted Worcester, c. 1810. BOTTOM: Spode; Pinxton; Wedgwood, all 1800s.

Teniers, Van Loo, Watteau, Boucher and others. Models of parrots were fashionable, in blue, purple and green.

Figure modelling improved during the gold anchor period and background bocages of flattened hawthorn leaves and flowers and apple blossom came into use behind figures and groups. The theatrical figures differed entirely from those of the previous period. Placed side by side, they hardly appear to be the products of the same factory. Those of the gold anchor period are known to collectors as the Vauxhall Masqueraders, a riotous blaze of colour and gold. Some indication of the renown Chelsea figures achieved at the time, and their resemblance in colour and design to continental models, is the fact that during the years around 1760 various French and German potters petitioned their governments to prohibit the importation of English porcelain figures such as were being made at Chelsea and Bow.

Chelsea-Derby figures are notable for their interpretation of Louis XVI sentimental groups, after the manner of paintings by Boucher, Fragonard and others. Their scroll bases were more symmetrical than those of Chelsea. Colours were smoothly bright and included a pale turquoise, brilliant crimson, purple, green, orange and chocolate. GIRL-IN-A-SWING FIGURES: small group of unmarked primitive figures ascribed to a Chelsea factory, c. 1751.

Clews, James and **Ralph,** Cobridge, Staffordshire (1819–34). These brothers rented a pottery from William Adams in 1817 and manufactured blue and white transfer-printed ware, chiefly for the American market. During the last three or four years of their partnership they printed also in red, brown and black. The Clews were responsible for three very popular series of transfer prints; the 'Three Tours of Doctor Syntax', 'Don Quixote', and the 'Pictures of Sir David Wilkie'. There were some thirty Syntax designs adapted from Thomas Rowlandson's illustrations to William Combe's books of verse published between 1815 and 1821. Borders were composed of large roses and other flowers interspersed with small scrolls. Each piece was marked in blue with the title of the picture in script enclosed in a decorated rectangle.

There were about twenty Don Quixote subjects with borders composed of various flowers with reserves containing small prints from the same series. There were seven Wilkie pictures. The Clews' English views, totalling nearly two hundred, were issued in three series: 'English Views', with borders of bell-flowers and leaves, or of foliage and intricate scrollwork; 'Select Views', with borders of large aster-like flowers and bell-flowers; and 'Picturesque Views', a late series, most examples being found in colours other than blue. 'American Views' have borders of scallops bearing the names of fifteen states with stars between, and another American series may be found with borders of scrolls, flowers and birds. These pictures carried title imprints incorporating the name CLEWS on their backs as well as the impressed name of the firm— CLEWS WARRANTED/STAFFORDSHIRE below a crown. The monarch's initials G R have been noted flanking the crown. The firm became bankrupt in 1835. Some of the copper plates were acquired and used by one of the Adams potters. The Clews' billheads announced that they were 'Potters to Her Imperial Majesty the Empress of Russia'.

Coalport, Colebrook Dale, Shropshire: established in 1795 by John Rose, who had been an apprentice at Caughley until 1785, when he started a small pottery at Jackfield on his own account. In 1795 he moved to Coalport and built premises on the canal bank opposite Caughley, which he acquired in 1799, and absorbed in 1814. By 1798 Rose was making bone china and until the late 1820s was largely engaged in supplying this in the white to London and provincial dealers and enamellers, although much decorated ware was sold. After the death of John Rose in 1841 he was succeeded by his nephew William F. Rose and William Pugh, the latter becoming sole proprietor in 1862.

Rose's pioneer efforts produced characterless china of poor translucency and flawed with black specks, but whiter, stronger and less expensive than the soft porcelains of the 1750s and 1760s. Soon after 1810 Coalport china was distinguished by its soft, white tone, clear surface and creamy translucency. Further technical improvements in the early 1820s made it yet more purely white, finer textured, with a high white trans-

137. Candlesticks, offered many opportunities for typical Coalport ornament (*see* Fig. 138). Here is some indication of earlier treatments in a far-ranging subject ideal for the collector. TOP: exceptional elegance in early slipware, mid-17th century; figure and blossom with a candlestick to give them support, Bow, 1760s; contemporary cream-coloured earthenware. BOTTOM: two of cream-coloured earthenware flanking Wedgwood 'rustic' jasper ware, all in the style of silver, 1770–90.

lucency. Felspar porcelain (*see* p. 46) was in production from 1822 until the mid-19th century.

A soft, smooth lead glaze was used until 1820 when Rose

138. Candlesticks, 19th century. TOP: all-over silver lustre and three unmarked in Coalport style showing the course of the 'revived rococo' manner, clumsy, then semi-formal and finally overwhelmed with naturalistic flowers. BOTTOM: three designs of mixed quality dating to the 1850s, by Meigh, Bell and Coalport; end of 19th-century design by Booth with scale-blue treatment suggesting old Worcester.

introduced his celebrated leadless glaze, hard, transparent and highly lustrous. The presence of lead in the glaze had an adverse effect on the brilliance of enamels laid over it, particularly the delicate tints and those prepared from gold oxide.

During the Coalport-Caughley period decoration in the factory was confined chiefly to painting and printing in underglaze blue, with a small amount of enamelling. The outstanding designs followed Caughley and included the willow pattern (Figs. 77 and 78), and the Broseley dragon printed in two blues—a pure cobalt and lavender—touched with gold. Painted decoration was sparse on the ordinary table ware that always formed the greater part of Coalport's output. Flower painting was mannered and gilding was usually light in hue. Transfer-printed outlines in pink or purple were filled in with

139. Broseley dragon, on a blue-printed dish showing the 19th century's more realistic approach in contrast to earlier adaptations of Oriental monsters: Chelsea (right), and Worcester and Bow below.

brushwork, portions of the transfer remaining undecorated. Although gilding was generous it was never so lavishly applied as on the fine bone chinas of Spode and Derby.

In 1821 Samuel Walker introduced a maroon ground which became a Coalport characteristic. Coalport decoration became

140. Coalport flower-encrusted clock, early 19th century.

richer and more varied during the reign of George IV; splendid dinner, dessert and tea services were issued in brilliant colours with highly burnished gilding.

From the early 1830s Coalport bone china became yet more varied in form and lavishly ornamented, rococo shapes and flower-encrustations being characteristic features until the late 1840s. Vases, clock cases, inkstands, baskets, jugs, pastille burners and night light shelters were overlaid with masses of tiny flowers modelled in the round. These flower-encrusted wares are generally known as Coalbrookdale and may be so marked in blue. Much early ware was unmarked and has been attributed to various other factories.

There is no typical Coalport style, although unmarked pieces may be recognised by their characteristically clear painting in bright, fresh colouring. A series of wide-mouthed jugs in various sizes was a Coalport speciality, painted with large pink roses or bouquets and inscribed beneath the lip. These belong to the period between 1828 and the early 1840s, but are often assumed to date from much earlier. From about 1840 flat slabs of porcelain painted with groups of naturalistic flowers and fruit were fashionable. Coalport made some particularly handsome examples in the form of trays and wall pictures with burnished gilt frames. Egg-shell china was made from 1845.

F. W. Rose considered the firm's felspar porcelain so exquisite that he engaged in the project of copying the more magnificent pieces of Sèvres, Meissen and Chelsea, reproducing the decorations, colours and marks of the 18th century. From 1802 until about 1825 John Mortlock (*see* p. 283) advertised himself as London agent for 'Colebrook Dale China'. He was succeeded by A. B. & R. P. Daniell of Wigmore Street, who undertook to sell all that could be made and even succeeded in borrowing examples of Sèvres from the royal collection for copying. No expense was spared in emulating the rich colours of Sèvres, especially the turquoise. Coalport had used a pale, feeble imitation known as celeste until the early 1840s when an improved version was evolved. But even this never equalled the original Sèvres tone. Coalport was the first English pottery to reproduce the famous *rose pompadour*, for which a gold medal was awarded at the Great Exhibition, 1851. The claret of Chelsea, and the deep, velvety mazarine of old Derby were among the successful efforts in ground colour work. So accurately were they reproduced that it is difficult to distinguish them from originals. These handsome examples of English china, in production for more than a quarter century, are now frequently presented as genuine early work, although paste, glaze and enamels differ entirely and the thinly applied Coalport gilding is distinctive.

Skilfully modelled parian statuary was made from the late

1840s, but the output was small. Collectors should note that a vast quantity of unfinished, unglazed ware, the accumulation of more than half-a-century, was taken from stock after the death of William Pugh in 1875 and decorated in late-Victorian style, although paste qualities and shapes were those of early periods. Such pieces are marked COALPORT/A.D. 1750.

Early Coalport bone china was unmarked, as were the wares of the nearby rival factory run by Rose's brother Thomas and partners, bought by Rose in 1814. From 1815 to 1828 the name COALPORT was painted in blue script underglaze. Felspar porcelain at first was marked J R F S CO. printed in red, suggesting that Rose formed a separate company for its development. More usually the mark was a circle measuring two inches in diameter inscribed in various types COALPORT/ IMPROVED/FELTSPAR/PORCELAIN within a laurel wreath encircled with the words PATRONISED BY THE SOCIETY OF ARTS. THE GOLD MEDAL AWARDED MAY 30th 1820. This was printed in red and in some instances included the name J. ROSE. Marks on bone china from 1828 until about 1850 included: JOHN ROSE & CO., COLEBROOK DALE; C D; C DALE; C.B.D., in blue script and various forms. A monogram CBD in blue or gold was used from 1851 to 1861. From then until 1875 an ampersand was used, the three loops containing the letters CSN. This was in gold, occasionally in red or blue enamel. Between 1875 and 1881 the mark was COALPORT AD 1750; between 1881 and 1891 the same with the addition of a crown; from 1891 the word ENGLAND was placed above the crown, and MADE IN ENGLAND from about 1920.

Cocker, George: a modeller of biscuit figures at Derby in the early-19th century. In 1826, with John Whitaker as partner, he established a china factory at Friar Gate, Derby. Here they produced figures in pearl pottery, a dry body with a finely-textured unglazed surface suitable for figures and busts. The partnership was a failure and ended within the year.

Cocker continued on his own until 1840, making small portrait statuettes and busts of celebrities, and ornamental figures, rustic in character, such as his 'boys' series—boy with hurdy-gurdy, boy with bird cage, boy with pitcher at a well and so on. He produced small animals and birds, too, and baskets filled with exquisitely modelled flowers in the round. Some work was incised COCKER or G. COCKER/DERBY.

Cocker removed to London in 1840 and established a pottery in Chenies Street, Tottenham Court Road, and retail premises in Regent's Quadrant. His London figures might be incised with his nephew's name D. COCKER. In 1851 Cocker removed to Stoke-upon-Trent where he was employed as a modeller of parian figures by Minton until his death in 1868. The marks of Sampson Hancock have been noted on some figures identical with those of Cocker, suggesting that he acquired Cocker's original moulds.

Commondale Pottery, near Stokesley, Yorkshire: made art pottery, terracotta and domestic earthenware from 1872 to 1884. Bacchus and hunting jugs were a popular production. The mark impressed was CROSSLEY/COMMONDALE.

Copeland: *see* Spode.

Crown Staffordshire Porcelain Co. Ltd, Fenton, Staffordshire. This pottery was established in 1830 by Henry Green and continued after his death in 1859 as M. Green & Co. The present title dates from about 1890. The Green firm specialised in toy tea and dinner services and miniature ornaments. From 1876 they made full-size services in bone china with high quality decorations. The firm was also responsible for many notable reproductions of 18th-century porcelain. J. F. Blacker wrote of these productions in 1911: 'By long and careful experiments their chemists have discovered the exact shades of the marvellous enamels which the Chinese brought to perfection . . . the powder blue on the vases made by the Crown Staffordshire Porcelain Company is the result of some thousands of trials extending over ten years. Each piece is what it professes to be, a copy, which is marked with a conventional crown over STAFFS in script or a crown over STAFFORDSHIRE surmounting two Gs, one reversed, in a monogram'. In 1948 the firm was retitled Crown Staffordshire China Co. Ltd.

Davenport, Longport (1793–c. 1885): fine quality earthenware, moulded stoneware and ornate Derby-style bone china.

Denaby Pottery, Yorkshire: operated 1864 to 1870, manufacturing sponged and printed earthenware, including granite. Until 1866 the firm traded as Wilkinson & Wardle, and thereafter as John Wardle & Co. Marks, printed or impressed, were a Staffordshire knot above WILKINSON & WARDLE/ DENABY POTTERIES, and from 1866 the Staffordshire knot with JOHN WARDLE & CO. above and NEAR ROTHERHAM/ DENABY POTTERY below.

Denholme Pottery, Yorkshire, established early 1790s by Samuel Catherall, whose family operated the pottery until 1893. Coarse earthenware was the mainstay, but collectors will find puzzle jugs with a slight brown or almost black glaze, and slip decorated ware which may be impressed DENHOLME.

Nicholas Taylor potted similar ware from 1893 to 1909, the mark incised in script letters being N TAYLOR/DENHOLME (or TAYLER).

Derby: porcelain from 1749 and bone china from 1805.

DERBY PORCELAIN MANUFACTORY, 1749–1755. André Planché, financed by John Heath, a Derby banker, made porcelain figures in a newly developed department of the Cockpit Hill Pot Manufactory. Some of these figures were decorated in London by the independent enameller William Duesbury, whose account book for 1751–53 records that he decorated 'Darby Figars' and noted dancers and seasons. Extremely rare remaining specimens suggest a heavy, glassy non-phosphatic paste, difficult to fire and with an uneven glaze.

141. Derby figures—typical of innumerable minor Derby figures, cow and calf with flower support and flowered plinth, 1760s.

It was sold in the white and might be incised DERBY in script, with or without a script D.

DERBY PORCELAIN COMPANY, Nottingham Road, Derby, 1755–86: directed by William Duesbury and supported financially by John Heath. An advertisement of 1756 showed productions to include 'fine figures, jars, sauceboats, services for desserts and a great variety of useful and ornamental porcelain *after* the finest Dresden. Models are all exquisitely painted in enamel with flowers, insects, India plants . . .'. By 1757 the factory had been enlarged and the number of employees doubled. The art of figure making was carried to a high degree of excellence; some five hundred models in constant production were inventoried in 1795. Many other short-term figures are recorded.

Duesbury's figures were modelled with a sharpness of outline not found on contemporaneous work; garment folds are almost knife-edged. The pedestals, often flat plinths, usually have three or four dark unglazed patches caused by pads of clay which served as rests for the figures when the glaze was fired. These patches are present on both enamelled and biscuit figures of a later period. Colouring on early figures is pale, the glaze over-blued, in contrast to later brilliance in the Chelsea style. As regards Derby bocages, the petals and the light

142. Sequence of teapot outlines (Figs 142–145). TOP: Chelsea, late 1740s; typical of Chelsea, Bow, etc., 1750s. SECOND ROW: Longton Hall, 1750s; Chelsea, 1760s. THIRD ROW: Derby, 1760s; Lowestoft, 1770s. BOTTOM: Plymouth and Bristol, 1770s.

244

yellow leaves are appreciably thinner than those of competitors. Gilding is sparse, normally enriching only garment edges and buttons. An important development in 1770 was the purchase of the Chelsea factory resulting in finer colours and glaze (*see* p. 229). It appears that Chelsea continued to make seals, scent bottles, tooth pick cases, tiny plaques for inserting in brooches, breast pins and buttons.

Derby paste was improved with bone ash introduced from 1770 and continued in use until about 1805. The porcelain then became close-grained with a creamy translucency. Enamels penetrated deeply into the soft lustrous glaze, which is free from crazing and easily scratched. Enamels were applied less thickly than those of Chelsea and Bow, so thinly indeed that brush marks were unable to float out and remain visible. A characteristic Derby feature on figures of this period was a reddish brown ringing a dark spot to represent the eye pupil; eyebrows and eyelashes were often in the same tint.

Duesbury's famous white figure groups in unglazed biscuit porcelain were advertised from 1771. The translucent paste, velvety to the touch, was easily flawed in firing. Subjects were mainly from classical mythology.

Colours include a beautiful apple green, canary yellow, pale lavender, deep claret, brilliant orange, coral, rose and pink of the crushed strawberry tint, a popular Derby colour. Until 1782 an exclusive semi-matt enamel blue was used, described contemporaneously as lapis lazuli. This can be felt slightly raised above the glaze, showing it to have been laid on thickly. It was abandoned in favour of an underglaze cobalt blue.

WILLIAM DUESBURY & SON, 1786–96: carried on the factory on lines little different from those of the first William Duesbury, who died in 1786. At about this time William Billingsley initiated a new technique in flower painting, abandoning sharp outline in favour of colours applied in soft washes.

143. Porcelain teapot outlines, cont. TOP: Caughley and New Hall, late 18th century. CENTRE: two more from New Hall showing change in style from late 18th century to early 19th. BOTTOM: two in silver-style, Pinxton.

Instead of leaving the ground for high lights Billingsley swept the whole field with a single colour, obtaining contrasts by removing surplus colour with a cotton wool stipple or clean brush. The effect was more delicate than anything previously seen on ceramics. Few table-wares pre-date c. 1770 as the soft porcelain could not withstand hot liquids, although a considerable trade was carried on in cabinet cups and saucers.

A few months before his death in 1796 Duesbury II was joined in partnership by Michael Kean, a London miniaturist.

DUESBURY & KEAN, 1796–1811: during this period the Derby factory was directed by Michael Kean. It was he who abandoned soft-paste porcelain in favour of the harder, whiter bone china. John Haslem, a Derby decorator, inferred that non-frit bone china was in full production by 1805. This was more opaque than the frit porcelain formerly made and displayed a greenish translucency when held to the light. Its thin, hard glaze failed to absorb the enamels, thus losing the former blending of enamel with glaze. Kean retired in 1811, selling his share to William Sheffield, father-in-law of Duesbury III.

DUESBURY & SHEFFIELD, 1811–1815: during this period the quality of the ceramic deteriorated and craftsmanship in modelling and decorating was less efficient. Moulds formerly used at Chelsea and Bow were brought into use, but the finished goods were of a lesser quality than the soft-paste originals.

ROBERT BLOOR, 1815–48: the bone china of this period suffered from experiments. For the most part the rather heavy paste lacks transparency and the hard thick glaze has tended to craze and discolour. Bloor specialised in inexpensive ware and utilised the large accumulated stocks of porcelain in the white by decorating them cheaply and gaudily. Much of this is now attributed to 18th-century Derby. Under Bloor's management Derby lost its former reputation for fine ware. In about 1820 muffle stoves were abandoned in favour of large enamelling kilns. Enamels fired by this method eventually tended to flake, leaving white spots in the pattern. The works closed in 1848, models and moulds, including those from Chelsea and Bow, being bought by Samuel Boyle, who later sold them to W. T. Copeland, Stoke-upon-Trent.

LOCKER & CO., 1848–59: a group of Bloor's employees acquired part of the old Derby premises and began to manu-

144. Teapots, cont.: early 19th century. TOP: Spode, black stoneware, engine turned and painted with a framed view. SECOND ROW: Wedgwood with spreading view, 1815, and Davenport, ditto. THIRD ROW: Minton in pattern no. 678, with flower reserves in leaf ground, c. 1825; Spode with flower reserves, bone china, 1820s. BOTTOM: Mason's ironstone with blue willow pattern; Spode felspar porcelain with formal patterns and rose posy.

145. Teapots up to mid-19th century. TOP: Castleford, c. 1820; Rockingham, late 1820s. SECOND ROW: two in revived rococo style of 1830s–40s often wrongly attributed to Rockingham. THIRD ROW: cheap but decorative methods of the 1830s–40s—(left) shaped in low relief and touched with colour by hand, and (right) all-over transfer printed in blue with scenes and borders. BOTTOM: mid-19th-century signs of returning restraint in designs by Cork & Edge and by Copeland.

facture bone china under the direction of William Locker, formerly a clerk with Bloor. Their productions were marked in red transfer, LOCKER & CO., late BLOOR on a band encircling DERBY.

STEVENSON, SHARP & CO., 1859–61: succeeded Locker & Co., the transferred trade mark being a crowned garter containing the name in full.

STEVENSON & HANCOCK, 1861–1866: Sampson Hancock joined Stevenson after the death of Sharp in 1861. The mark reverted to the old Derby jewelled crown and the script D with two batons and six dots, the batons being transformed into swords with hilts flanked by the initials S and H in large capitals. The same mark was used by Sampson Hancock when he became sole proprietor in 1866. The firm was absorbed by the Royal Crown Derby Porcelain Co. in 1935.

DERBY CROWN PORCELAIN COMPANY was an entirely new factory established in 1876 to specialise in high quality bone china and earthenware. Following a visit by Queen Victoria in 1890 the firm traded as Royal Crown Derby Porcelain Co. Ltd.

Don Pottery, Swinton, Yorkshire, when established in about 1790 was very small, earthenware being sent out for decoration to Newton, an independent enameller of Swinton, who worked also for other small potters. In 1800 John Green, a partner in the Leeds and Rockingham potteries, bought the business and rebuilt the premises. In 1807 other members of his family joined him in partnership, the firm then trading as Greens, Clarke & Co. and from 1822 as John & William Green & Co. In 1834 the business was sold to Samuel Barker of the Mexborough Old Pottery, which ten years later was amalgamated with the Don Pottery. In 1851 the firm was acquired by Henry and Edward Barker, who traded as Samuel Barker & Son. In 1882 the pottery was again under its old name until it closed in 1893.

Greens, Clarke & Co. (1807–1833) made earthenwares—white, cream-coloured, brown-glazed, blue-glazed, and green-glazed, marbled, black on-glaze, black printed, painted and enamelled, as well as fine stonewares, such as Egyptian black and cane ware. An uncommon feature was pearl ware covered with buff engobe and painted with designs in black.

A pattern book was issued, identical with that of Leeds, the copper plates, inscribed DON POTTERY in a small label, probably being taken over when the Leeds Pottery closed in 1820. The final edition of the Leeds catalogue illustrated 269 items, whereas the Don version shows 292. On the title page the names and place were changed to 'Greens, Clarke & Co., at Don Pottery, near Doncaster' and it also stated that articles could be 'ornamented with gold and silver to any pattern'.

Many of the patterns and shapes were inspired by Wedgwood cream ware, the same pierced-rim plates and dishes, spoons and ladles, tea and dessert services, and vases. Much ware was sold undecorated, as was then customary, but there was also some excellent enamel painting such as landscapes, coats of arms, and flowers with their names inscribed beneath. At this time eight large kilns were in operation, three for biscuit and five for glazing; nearly three hundred workers were employed. Don earthenware lacked the finish of Leeds and obviously sold at lower prices. Trade was mainly with London, the Continent and Turkey. Jewitt has recorded that good quality bone china was made between 1810 and 1812.

The mark preceding 1807 was DON/POTTERY impressed or pencilled in red. The marks from 1807 were DON POTTERY; GREEN/DON POTTERY. From about 1820 a demi-lion rampant holding a pennon inscribed DON and rising from a plinth inscribed POTTERY was the usual mark. Hunting jugs have been noted with a pad impressed DON. The demi-lion, slightly modified in shape and mane, was blue-printed with the name BARKER above the pennon. From 1851 until the factory closed in 1893 the demi-lion was enclosed within a garter, sometimes with DON POTTERY above and S B & S below. An uncommon mark at about the time of the Great Exhibition in 1851 was a blue-printed shield containing an eagle rising out of a ducal coronet. This has been observed on blue-printed ware with the initials S B & S below and IRONSTONE above.

Doulton & Co.: John Doulton partner in a small pottery from 1815, launched his renowned Lambeth factory in 1826. At first little more than industrial salt-glazed stoneware was made and some decorated brown stoneware, such as tankards, spirit bottles, bellarmines and motto and puzzle jugs, their colourings restricted to the tints of the clays with, usually, broad bands of rich brown at top and bottom.

By 1870 the firm had become celebrated for ornamental salt-glazed stoneware, including incised or graffito work upon ordinary salt-glazed brown stoneware. In 1872 underglaze painting of fine earthenware was introduced and became celebrated as Lambeth faience (page 60). At about the same time Doulton's silicon ware was issued—a vitrified unglazed stoneware decorated with coloured clays, bronze, green, brown, blue, chocolate, grey, white and black. This was followed by marqueterie ware, marbled clays in checker work, obtained by cutting and compressing in various ways, being used for moulding the forms, subsequently glazed and perhaps finished in gold. Regarding art ware, every piece is impressed with the name, monogram or mark of the artist. The name Royal Doulton found on many marks dates from 1902. Doulton & Co., Burslem, was established 1882.

Dublin, Ireland: in 1752 Henry Delamain established the 'Irish Delft Ware Manufactory' and introduced the use of coal for firing his kilns. The pottery was continued by his widow after his death in 1757, and her executors carried on until 1763. The wares resembled French faience in shape, but

146. Character mugs and jugs, popular and cheap in Doulton stoneware, but offer other possibilities too to the collector. TOP: many pieces were made commemorating Lord Rodney's victory, such as Derby porcelain jugs with Rodney masks, often dated 1782, and the museum rarity mug in Ralph Wood style. Nelson (top right) is by Doulton & Watts, dating to 1837. BOTTOM: typical earthenware satyr, about 1800; jug commemorating Wellington; Doulton brown stoneware Napoleon.

decoration followed those of Liverpool and Bristol delft ware and were painted in bright blue or manganese purple. Presumed marks in blue include DUBLIN with a crowned harp above, H D in monogram, and H DUBLIN with the H and D conjoined.

Dudson, James, Hanley, 1838–1888: a potter of fine stonewares, ornamental figures, domestic earthenware and mosaic ware. From the outset he made ornamental figures, including comforter dogs; a selection were exhibited at the Great Exhibition, 1851. His finest productions were white and coloured dry stonewares—drab, blue, sage-green and so on, with relief decorations. Many of these were registered at the Patent Office and modelled by experienced potters. In mosaic work, from 1856, Dudson produced some attractive patterns. Marked pieces are uncommon, but DUDSON impressed together with various registration marks has been noted on jugs. Stoneware teapots might be marked JAMES DUDSON, HAN-LEY/LICENSED BY THE PATENTEES.

Duke, Sir James & Nephews, Hill Pottery, Burslem: were successors of Samuel Alcock in 1859 and operated until 1863. Bone china table ware, English majolica, terracotta and jet vases, stoneware jugs and parian statuary were made. In 1861 they produced, in parian, a full-length portrait statuette of *Lord Elcho* in the uniform of the London Scottish from a marble by William Beattie. In 1862 they exhibited *Innocence Protected*, also after Beattie. This firm used the impressed mark of an open hand.

Eccleshill, Yorkshire: operated by J. Woodhead from 1835 to 1867. Chief production was salt-glazed stoneware similar to that of Brampton. Bristol stoneware was made from the 1840s. Earthenware included busts and statuettes of celebrities, ranging in height from a few inches to several feet, jugs, cradles, knife boxes, salt kits and puzzle jugs encircled with lively scenes in high relief. The mark was ECCLESHILL, impressed.

Fremington, Devon: a pottery was established on the sites of medieval and Elizabethan potteries by George Fishley late in the 18th century. He was succeeded by his son Edmund in 1839 and his grandson Edwin Beer Fishley in 1861. It was he who gave colour to his wares by evolving an iridescent glaze discovered to be ideal for combining with the local clay. This was made in a variety of colours, the most common being a rich dark green splashed and mottled with other colours.

During Edwin's period pottery was reproduced in 17th- and 18th-century forms and is now often mistaken for early work. These were in red earthenware glazed in mustard-yellow. Puzzle jugs were inscribed with lines of mis-spelled doggerel

147. Fishley, Fremington, example of simple coiled ware (*see* Part III) in a cheap, asymmetrical candlestick, 19th century.

verse. Tygs were made with three or four loop handles, the yellow glaze marked with mottled green and painted with birds and stylised tulips and pseudo-Georgian inscriptions such as: 'Of liquer good both neete and fine to fill mee full is your desine 1774.' Edwin Fishley also made graffito vases in the Etruscan style fashionable in mid-Victorian days. Beer jugs in white pottery were made in a range of 18th-century styles, hand-painted with red ornament and known by such names as 'Galley Mouths', 'Long Toms' and 'Thirty Tales'.

Throughout its period of operation Fremington was celebrated for clay ovens for the home-baking of bread. Constructed of hard, compact clay, the oven was covered with raised brickwork, the mouth at the front being covered with a cast iron door. They were heated from within by furze of which only a small quantity was needed, twopennyworth being considered ample to bake seven or eight shillingsworth of flour.

The mark incised from 1861 to 1906 was E. B. FISHLEY/ FREMINGTON/N.DEVON in detached script letters, or the name FISHLEY painted in red.

Goss, W. H., Falcon Pottery, Stoke: established in 1858 to specialise in paper-thin parian hollow-ware. His particular aim, however, became jewellery for the lady's dressing table and boudoir and her costume needs in brooches, shawl pins, bracelets, necklaces and pendants. Many of these trinkets were ornamented with delicate floral work. Goss's pendant crosses achieved great popularity. In 1872 he patented a process by which his jewellery could be modelled with even greater delicacy. The glistening iridescence of this mother-of-pearl ware was sometimes tinted primrose yellow with flowers in their natural colours. Goss made jewelled porcelain in the style of Sèvres, but of finer quality; his jewels never fall out, having been set in specially prepared hollows.

In the early 1890s Goss introduced his ivory tinted porcelain with a seemingly waxen surface, a variety of parian. This is best known as the basis for coats of arms enamelled in full colour over the glaze. This was an idea conceived by his son Adolphus, who invented the brilliant enamels for the purpose. As souvenirs for holiday makers the project was highly successful.

From about 1860 Goss used the mark of a rising falcon with W. H. GOSS below; from 1891 the name ENGLAND appeared below the name. W. H. GOSS and W. H. G. are also found printed or impressed.

Grainger of Worcester: Thomas Grainger, a nephew of Humphrey Chamberlain and a former decorator at the Chamberlain factory, established decorating workshops in 1801 with a decorator named Wood as partner. They began by buying Caughley bone china in the white and decorating it in the Chamberlain style. In 1812, with a partner named Lee, he began to manufacture bone china, the firm being styled

148. Serving jugs. The development of serving jugs in imaginative designs was largely of the 19th century, but readers may be reminded of the early slipware owls, Nottingham ware bears, white stoneware curiosities of jug and teapot. Here are shown later 18th-century notions and the full flowering of the 1840s. TOP: Voyez's familiar 'Fair Hebe' jug in tree-trunk shape with figures, bearing the date 1788; typical cheap jug of around 1800 with popular low-relief figure of Britannia, frequently found in heavy 'high temperature' colouring; hunting jug in stoneware with partly coloured background, in the tradition of 17th-century brown stoneware hunting jugs and showing a design used by Spode, Wedgwood, Davenport and so on, well into the 19th century. BOTTOM: heavy moulded reliefs entirely covered with silver lustre; familiar 'Silenus' jug by Minton, also found in Doulton brown stoneware; tree-stump with oak leaves by Ridgway & Abington, registered 1846.

Grainger, Lee & Co., Royal China Works, Worcester. Among popular products was table ware embossed with birds and sprays of wild flowers enriched with polychrome enamelling. In 1828 they acquired the sole manufacturing rights for lithophanes.

Thomas Grainger was succeeded by his son George in 1839, the firm then trading as George Grainger & Co., 'inventors, designers and manufacturers'. By 1848 they had evolved 'a new ware called semi-porcelain', and stone china which was a great success when exhibited at the Great Exhibition, 1851. In the late 1840s they entered the parian ware trade. In the naturalistic style of the mid-19th century they devised jugs shaped to suggest that they were formed of leaves and flowers —of lilies of the valley, for instance, and of water lilies

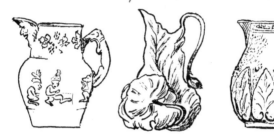

149. Serving jugs. Brown Chesterfield ware, 19th century, continuing earlier traditions including greyhound handle; Grainger's water lily design, 1851, for a water jug; simpler style of 1864, with low reliefs in formal pattern, registered by William Brownfield in parian ware.

intended for serving water. Their display at the 1851 Exhibition included a coffee service covered in an open honeycomb pattern showing a rich blue ground through the perforations, noted at the time as being 'manufactured at a comparatively small cost'. The firm was acquired by the Worcester Royal Porcelain Company in 1889, continuing to operate independently until 1902.

Greatbatch, William (1735–1813), Lane Delf, Fenton Low: a former Whieldon apprentice and modeller who established his own pottery in 1759. He worked under an arrangement by which Josiah Wedgwood, also just starting in business, agreed to take his entire output in the biscuit state for glazing and decoration. Greatbach excelled in cream wares of unusual design, such as pineapple and cauliflower teapots. Later he decorated teapots with black transfer-printed designs over the glaze. An example in the British Museum is marked PUB-LISHED AS THE/ACT DIRECTS JANY/4, 1778 BY W/GREAT-BACH/LANE DELF/STAFFORDSHIRE. Such a mark was a legal obligation regarding direct printed engravings for sale; apparently Greatbach was unaware that this did not apply to transfer printing, which suggests that this was his first essay in this work. Other printed teapots by Greatbach are recorded. A bad debt caused him to fail in 1787. He was then employed as a modeller by Wedgwood until 1807 at five shillings a day and a free house.

Grosvenor, Frederick, Eagle Pottery, Glasgow: established 1869 and continued into the present century, potting Bristol ware and salt-glazed stonewares. Marks: impressed and printed, an eagle erect with outstretched wings, also GROS-VENOR & SON.

Hadley, James (1837–1903): Worcester Porcelain Co.'s most important 19th-century modeller. In 1896 with three sons he launched his own art pottery, absorbed by the Company in 1905.

Herculaneum: *see page 269.*

Isleworth, Middlesex: established by Joseph Shore in 1760, making earthenware in a small way and specialising in Welsh ware which continued in production until the pottery was closed in 1820. When Richard Goulding joined the firm in 1795, the mark was an impressed S & G or S & G ISLEWORTH. Similar wares impressed FG and WS & S are considered by W. B. Honey to be of German origin. In the early 19th century Isleworth made hunting jugs in brown stoneware decorated with sporting subjects in high relief and with greyhound handles.

Kishere, Joseph, Mortlake, Surrey (1800–early 1840s) made ordinary drab brown stoneware spirit flasks, jugs and mugs ornamented in low relief with sporting and drinking scenes. These were impressed: I K, KISHERE MORTLAKE, KISHERE, or KISHERE'S POTTERY MORTLAKE SURREY.

Lakin & Poole, Burslem: Wedgwood and Ormsby record that this pottery was established in 1770 by John Lakin to make cream-coloured earthenware and black basaltes. In c. 1791, Thomas Lakin was joined by J. E. Poole and they began to specialise in blue transfer-printed ware, notably landscapes. They also achieved a reputation for figures and groups reflecting contemporary social life. One of their most spectacular pieces was the 'Assassination of Marat by Charlotte Cordé of Caen, in Normandy, 1793'. They were among the several potters who issued the ever-popular 'Tithe Pig' made in several sizes. Lakin & Poole figures were usually on high square plinths with colours discreetly applied. Toby jugs were made. The marks impressed were LAKIN, LAKIN & POOLE, and R. POOLE. The firm went bankrupt in 1797.

Leeds Pottery, Yorkshire (1760–1878): was chief among the potteries that made cream-coloured earthenware. This was made from a fine light clay, yellowish in tone, covered with a rich glassy glaze that had a tendency to run and in crevices showed a faintly green tinge. The best Leeds glaze has the appearance of having been floated on and spread without bubbling or crazing; it scratches less easily than the glazes on most contemporaneous earthenware. Being lighter in weight than the ware of its rivals, Leeds cream ware was more economical to export to continental countries which imposed import taxes.

Leeds drew upon the three main styles of ornament, Chinese, rococo and classic. The debt to Chinese porcelains is important; the firm made gourd and melon shaped sugar boxes and sauce boats derived from naturalistic Chinese design.

From China, too, came the typical handle for tea and coffee pots, consisting of two intertwined strips ending in such motifs as flowers, leaves and berries. The Staffordshire potters had used such handles much earlier, but the design became established as a Leeds feature on the squat low teapots with their curved spouts and flower finials.

Pierced decoration was a Leeds characteristic, patterns being cut with hand punches, hole by hole. Diamonds, hearts,

150. Chestnut dishes— contrasting treatments in dishes for serving hot roast chestnuts which were spoiled by close covering. ABOVE: Worcester, with pierced lid and stand; delicately pierced Leeds creamware. RIGHT: Minton's English majolica with sweet chestnuts and their leaves shaped in relief.

circles and other motifs were so cleverly combined as to suggest patterns of lace. This form of decoration was used to edge tea and dessert plates; it was the basis of the intricate pierced baskets, shell dishes and candlesticks; in some of the elaborate centrepieces and urns it took on the quality of fine silverwork. Basket-work was also made, built up from extruded strips of clay. The majority of cream-ware was issued undecorated, but fine black transfer-printing was produced, and in the 19th century blue-printed ware. Other pieces might be painted with enamels, in shades of red, violet and green.

Leeds also made other types of earthenware, including fine-grained agate, pearl, tortoiseshell and lustre wares. A thriving business was carried on in engine-turned basaltes, red stone-ware and small figures in the Ralph Wood style.

The marks changed but little. The first of importance, dating from 1783, was LEEDS * POTTERY sometimes impressed twice and crossed on blue-printed ware of the early 19th century. Instead of an asterisk a dot or hyphen might be used and all are sometimes found following the Y instead of

151. Leeds Pottery: two designs of typical double-twist handles with shaped finials, used also by other potters of the period; the rough gnarled handle termed crabstock, from crabapple wood.

being placed centrally. Another mark is HARTLEY · GREENS & CO/LEEDS POTTERY, sometimes impressed in the form of a double horse-shoe. After bankruptcy in 1820 different managers tried to keep the pottery working until 1878.

W. B. Honey has pointed out that in genuine old Leeds the letters composing the mark were usually somewhat irregularly set. Marked black basaltes medallions and cream-ware with silver lustred reliefs are modern.

Lessore, Emile, decorator: a pupil of Ingres, joining the Minton firm in 1858 from Sèvres, where in 1851 he had introduced a new technique in porcelain decoration, enamelling with the freedom of the artist's brush. Previously, figure painting on ceramics, as distinct from commercial enamelling, had been stippled in the same way as miniature painting on ivory. Lessore worked in subdued, delicate colours. After a few months he moved to the firm of Josiah Wedgwood & Sons, where he remained until 1863. He was acknowledged as the outstanding figure painter of his day. His work is signed in script E. LESSORE or E L.

Linthorpe, near Middlesbrough: this pottery was established in 1879 by John Harrison and flourished for ten years under the management of Henry Tooth. Extravagantly designed art

152. Art pottery, typical of the designs used by Henry Tooth at Linthorpe in claywares under brilliant glazes.

pottery was produced and the factory was celebrated for the brilliance of its rich flown and speckled colour glazes and, later, also for its flowers in coloured slips.

Liverpool: earthenware jugs and mugs were in considerable production by the 'earth potters' of Liverpool early in the reign of Charles II. A century later so prosperous was the trade in ceramics that more than eighty master potters were established in the town.

TIN-ENAMELLED EARTHENWARE: made from a light buff clay was in production by 1710 and included 'fine white and painted pots and other vessels and tiles'. Liverpool became celebrated for blue-painted tin-enamelled punch bowls. The principal makers were Seth and James Pennington, Richard Chaffers, Zachariah Barnes and S. & T. Shaw.

153. Typical of innumerable everyday jugs produced at Liverpool in squat barrel shape with rising spout that tended to become larger and taller.

CREAM-COLOURED EARTHENWARE: noticeably light in weight, this displaced the tin-enamelled ware during the 1780s, being decorated with painting in cobalt blue and enamel colours, or in blue or black transfer-printing.

SOFT PASTE PORCELAINS: characteristics of these varied with the different potters, making it impossible to give hard and fast rules regarding classification, for rarely indeed are 18th-century marks to be found and ten firms produced porcelain during the half century. Compared with other soft paste porcelains Liverpool work has a distinctly greyish hue. The basic clay of local origin appears to have contained impurities which the primitive methods of refining failed to remove.

SOAPSTONE PORCELAIN: this was manufactured by 1756. Already, four years earlier, Richard Chaffers had established a pottery on Shaw's Brow for the manufacture of tin-enamelled earthenware. In December 1756 he was advertising that his 'Porcelain or China Ware . . . is proved with boiling water before being exposed for sale'. This heat-resistant soapstone

154. Mugs. TOP: 17th century, in early clayware; mid-century slip-ware; later slipware; mid-century tin enamelled earthenware or delft ware. SECOND ROW: two in unglazed red stoneware (so-called Elers ware); Dwight's marbled stoneware; brown and buff stone-ware with relief ornament, 18th century. THIRD ROW: Liverpool tin enamelled earthenware, early 18th century; Whieldon-Wedgwood red earthenware, 1750s; Whieldon-Wedgwood marbled, 1750s; white salt glazed stoneware with cast ornament. BOTTOM: Notting-ham ware, c. 1750; white stoneware with enamel painting; Liverpool barrel, transfer printed, later 18th century; quick painting and gilding towards end of 18th century.

155. Mugs cont. Porcelain. TOP: Chelsea; Bow; two of Longton Hall. SECOND ROW: early Bristol, c. 1755; Liverpool, c. 1760; two of Worcester, c. 1760 and c. 1770. THIRD ROW: Derby, c. 1760; Plymouth, c. 1770; two of Lowestoft, c. 1780 and c. 1790. BOTTOM: Caughley, 1780s; Derby, 1790s; Swansea, c. 1815; Coalport, 1820s.

has a clean, hard-looking, very slightly grey body with a faintly bluish milky glaze. When held to the light it shows a greenish translucency varying in intensity according to thickness of section. The glaze, which is marred by tiny bubbles, was brush-applied, leaving bare patches on the foot-rim; a thunder-cloud effect is often present.

Some of Chaffers's porcelain is decorated with moulding in low relief, forming reserves for blue decoration under the

156. Later mugs. TOP: late 18th-century styles in Wedgwood basaltes; creamware; Bristol earthenware; Mason early 19th-century ironstone. CENTRE: early 19th century in artist-painted Derby china; copper lustre; two of Mason's octagonal designs. BOTTOM: Wedgwood basaltes, rush-weave design; gilded bone china, so-called Sunderland lustre; sponged ware.

glaze, or in enamels over the glaze. High-lights in relief work may be accentuated with colour. Chaffers's blue and white is cleanly painted, the blue itself inclining towards a slaty tinge. Designs were copied and adapted from Chinese porcelains. Enamels, too, were applied in the Chinese style, motifs including rocks, flowering plants, birds and robed figures, most frequently coloured pale yellow, brick red, emerald green and blue. A red border encircling the rim of a piece of hollow-ware is characteristic, as are also several simple diaper borders. Some black and red transfer prints were used, the majority of lines being coarse and blurred because of some defect in the glaze. The bases of Chaffers's hollow-ware are invariably glazed, and handles shaped in the Worcester style, but thinner. His jugs were the first in which the lip was raised slightly above the level of the rim, a style continued by later potters (Fig. 153). He also began the vogue for barrel-shaped mugs with everted rims and grooved base rings. Foot-rings are triangular in section and slightly undercut.

Following the death of Chaffers in 1765 the firm came under the control of Philip Christian, a potter of tin-enamelled earthenware who continued the soapstone formula until the early 1770s. He then made excellent table ware and vases of highly translucent, finely glazed porcelain. The quality of his enamelled decoration surpasses that of any other Liverpool potter.

Seth Pennington, established by the late 1770s, was outstanding among Liverpool potters for the consistent high quality of his productions. These, when held to the light, show a green translucency. There is a distinct tinge of colour in the glaze, resulting in a duck-egg green appearance. Table-ware is exceptionally heavy and thick, particularly at the base, and may be decorated with relief ornament beneath the rim—blue flowers and designs of a mythological or symbolical character. His blue enamel is of an exceptionally light hue. His brother James, established as a potter in 1768, became a specialist in porcelain punch bowls decorated with a brilliant blue, applied so lavishly that it stands out from the surface. He also advertised 'elegant, cheap and serviceable china ware'.

Zachariah Barnes, merchant, has been associated with porcelains made late in the Liverpool story. Knowles Boney states in *Liverpool Porcelain of the 18th Century* that 'there is no evidence that he ever potted anything in his life.'

BONE CHINA: this was made from about 1800 by the firm of Worthington, Humble & Holland who, in 1796, had taken over a factory specialising in finely transfer-printed earthenware jugs, but without commercial success. The new proprietors abandoned the traditional methods of Liverpool and introduced modern methods, employing forty experienced hands from Staffordshire. They named the works Herculaneum and manufactured cream-coloured earthenware. By 1800 they were also making bone china of heavy, almost opaque paste; potting and glaze are excellent. All kinds of table-ware were made, bat-printed tea and coffee services, decorated in various colours, showing views of country seats and spas, or stippled figures of men and women. Urn shaped vases in garnitures of three were enamelled in brilliant colours, the body usually being in a red, blue or orange ground colour; handles are in the form of conventionalised dolphins, birds, winged heads and so on. Herculaneum closed in 1841.

Longton Hall, Staffordshire (1749–60): under manager William Littler made soft paste porcelain including thickly glazed 'snowman' figures and decorative domestic wares.

Lowestoft, Suffolk (c. 1757–1802): made soft paste porcelain useful wares, dated commemorative souvenirs, 'trifles', ornaments, occasional figures. 'Oriental Lowestoft' is misnomer for Chinese export porcelain.

Madeley, Shropshire: a pottery was established in 1825 by Thomas Randall, who had established himself as an independent decorator in London in 1812 and by 1815 was employing more than forty decorators. George IV as regent and king was an avid collector of Sèvres porcelain; the resulting nation-wide collecting vogue for this ware caused examples to fetch fabulous prices. Dealers searched in vain for a potter willing to make soft-paste porcelain of the Sèvres type and capable of decorating it in the early styles. Randall was the man who most nearly met their requirements, but he would never give his expensive copies of early Sèvres the double-L mark.

Characteristic Madeley porcelain was of the Nantgarw type, but much thicker of section and only dimly translucent, easily abraded with a file and with a glaze faintly tinged with green.

157. Teapot, attributed to Madeley.

Moulding in relief was sometimes used. By 1828 the paste had a mellow, creamy hue closely resembling that of old Sèvres, with a thin, hard glaze. Much Madeley porcelain was decorated with ground colours having the slightly granular appearance of powdered enamel applied over the glaze. Flaws in the body, and there were many, such as fine hair cracks, were concealed beneath this ground colour, which might be in dark blue, light blue, turquoise, apple green or soft pink. *Bleu de roi* was seldom used without a delicate covering of gold tracery in patterns of network, meander lines or *oeil de perdrix*.

In the late 1830s the demand for old Sèvres reproductions ceased and Randall turned to bone china, decorating it in Coalport styles. Much of this was table ware. In 1840 he abandoned manufacture and set up as a decorator at Shelton, near Hanley. Very rarely is a mark found upon a genuine example of Randall's porcelain or bone china.

Martin Bros, Southall, Middlesex: operated 1873 to 1915, specialising in fine salt-glazed stoneware in a wide range of designs. At first they produced table ware and clock cases, but the majority of their productions were purely ornamental, thrown, decorated and glazed vases, bowls, dishes, bottles and hollow-ware grotesques. Colour effects were unusual. Early blues were strong and crude; later, some attractive low-toned blues were evolved. Greens, browns, yellows and blacks were consistently of fine quality. White in various tones formed excellent grounds for applied ornament. Tortoiseshell and

158. The Martin brothers, two examples of their work. Many versions were made of the bird with detachable head, some thought to be caricatures of Gladstone.

cherry red were frequently used. The palette was limited to colours capable of maturing at a single firing. Inlay work, such as honeycomb patterns, was produced by Edwin Martin who delighted in ornamenting his pieces with fish, crabs, jellyfish and floating sea anemones as well as dragons, flying birds, insects.

Masons of Lane Delf: after the retirement of Miles Mason in 1813 his son Charles James Mason was granted a patent for the manufacture of 'English porcelain'. With his brother George Miles he exploited this as 'patent ironstone china'. Success was immediate and after two years they were able to expand their premises into a long row of four-storied workshops with mills and kilns at the rear known as the **Patent Ironstone China Manufactory.**

271

Decorations were carried out in bright, high temperature colours with sometimes the addition of enamel colours over the glaze. The basic metallic oxides were mechanically ground by a method newly introduced to the pottery trade, superseding laborious and costly hand-grinding. These colours were applied quickly and lavishly in flat washes over transfer-printed outline patterns, consisting chiefly of reds, blues and greens, but including also yellow, puce, brown, jet and gold, fired individually. Some of the finer ware was smothered in brilliant colours and gilding. Many types of quickly painted polychromatic designs were used in quaint jumbled patterns. Motifs to be expected include the following, either singly or in combinations: large flowers resembling a peony and a full-blown rose, sprigs of prunus, daisies, birds of paradise, waterfowl on the wing, butterflies, gnats and other flying insects.

The now celebrated Mason jugs, octagonal on plan and with the well-known reptilian handles, were given a heavy, faintly blue glaze, and the base usually has a 'wiped' appearance. They were sold singly and in sets ranging from three to fourteen, measuring $2\frac{1}{2}$ inches to 12 inches in height. Blue-printed earthenware was also made.

After the retirement of George Mason in 1829 to devote himself to politics, the firm traded as C. J. Mason & Co. until 1845. The range of productions was extended beyond the table ware for which ironstone was primarily intended and included fireplaces, garden seats, vases 4 to 5 feet in height, large 'fish pond bowls' painted with Anglo-Chinese patterns, even bedposts.

After Charles Mason's partner withdrew in 1845 he carried on alone until 1848, when he was declared bankrupt. He started again at Longton in 1851, but finally closed in 1854 when he sold the moulds and copper plates to Francis Morley, who in 1862 was succeeded by G. L. Ashworth & Bros.

The earliest trade mark was MASON'S PATENT IRONSTONE

CHINA, in a single line when convenient, otherwise in a circle. Before 1820 this had been succeeded by a black transfer-printed mark composed of a crown with the name MASON'S above and PATENT IRONSTONE CHINA below. This mark continued throughout the period of C. J. Mason & Co., but from 1840 the word PATENT had been replaced by IMPROVED. A printed mark of this period illustrates the front elevation of the factory above an escutcheon inscribed FENTON/STONE WORKS/CMJ & CO with STAFFORDSHIRE POTTERIES below. Both Morley and Ashworth continued the original Mason mark in black (*see* Fig. 33).

Mayer, Elijah, Hanley (1770–1830): until about 1790 worked as an enameller to the trade. He then became a manufacturer and was celebrated for the excellence of his enamelled cream-coloured earthenware, black basaltes and bamboo wares decorated with lines and foliage in blue and green enamel. The basaltes were noted for their fine texture and blue-black colour, the relief decoration being sprigged and hand-finished. Many commemorative pieces were issued in this ware, such as jugs embossed with a portrait of the Prince of Wales when he was appointed Prince Regent in 1811, and coronation pieces made ten years later. Until 1805 the name E MAYER was impressed; afterwards E MAYER & SON.

Meigh, Job and his successors, Old Hall Works, Hanley: cream-coloured earthenware and red pottery were made at the Old Hall Works from 1790. By the end of the century blue-printed ware was in production, reaching a very high standard by 1810 with bright, clear-cut linework. Egyptian black was made, decorated with burnished and matt gilding and coloured enamelling. By 1812 the firm was styled Job Meigh & Son and in 1823 was awarded the Society of Arts gold medal for a leadless glaze suitable for use on a coarse red pottery. In the mid-1830s Job's son, operating as Charles Meigh, began to make a stone china which was sold under the name of white enamel ware, although it was given the semi-matt finish of smear-glazing and, with its vitrified texture, bore some resemblance to the later parian ware. Appreciating the classic restraint of its marble whiteness, Meigh introduced the ware in neo-Gothic designs and a considerable range was evolved. By the mid-1840s more than seven hundred workers were employed. The firm became the Old Hall Earthenware Co. in 1861 and was succeeded by the Old Hall Porcelain Co. in 1886. Marks included J M & S from 1812 to 1834 on blue

159. Pictorial jugs, popular designs in early Victorian pictorial jugs. TOP: Ridgway jousting knights, 'published', 1840; Meigh's early Gothic design, 1842 and his 'York Minster' version, registered in 1846. BOTTOM: Minton's 'Coach and Railway' jug, 1847; Victorian bacchante, surrounded by grape vines; Jones & Walley's fortune-teller, 1842.

printed ware, the name MEIGH, and from the 1830s ENAMEL PORCELAIN, OPAQUE PORCELAIN, INDIAN STONE CHINA.

Meli, Giovanni: (early 1840s–1864) an independent modeller of Little Fenton who established a parian pottery in 1852. Exhibited at the International Exhibition, 1862. Mark G. MELI impressed. In 1864 he sold goodwill, plant and moulds to Robinson & Leadbeater. Later he established a successful terracotta pottery in Chicago.

Mexborough Old Pottery, Yorkshire: established in the mid-1790s by Sowter & Bromley, who specialised in blue transfer-printed earthenware until 1804. The mark, impressed, was SOWTER & CO/MEXBRO. Under other owners to 1840s.

Middlesbrough Pottery: established 1831, concentrating on good quality cream-coloured earthenware, mainly for the

160. Middlesbrough Pottery, attractively painted plate bearing its mark.

continental market. Marks were impressed, an anchor with or without a cable and surrounded by MIDDLESBRO' POTTERY in horse shoe form, and MIDDLESBRO' POTTERY CO.

From 1852 Isaac Wilson & Co. operated the pottery until its closure in 1887. The range of goods included exceptionally well-painted enamelled ware, opaque white stone china and lustre. Impressed marks are I. W & CO/MIDDLESBRO, and a crown on stone china. Transfer-printed marks include the pattern name with MIDDLESBRO POTTERY. An expansive mark in green or brown transfer depicts a view of the pottery and its five kilns.

Mintons, Stoke-upon-Trent, established 1789: in that year Thomas Minton set up as a master designer and engraver of copper plates to the pottery trade and also supplied stock transfers to minor potters. In 1793 he built a pottery and manufactured blue transfer-printed cream-coloured earthenware and pearl ware. In 1796 he began the production of bone china decorated with blue transfers, in imitation of painted Nankin porcelain. Orders were heavy and within two years more than fifty people were employed. He had obtained the assistance of William Pownall and the technical knowledge of Joseph Poulson, making them partners and trading as Minton, Poulson & Pownall. In 1797 they founded the Hendra Company at St Denis, Cornwall, to work and purify china clay deposits. This company operated until the 1850s. By 1808 Thomas Minton was once again sole proprietor until he was joined in 1817 by his son Herbert who, after the death of his father in 1836, raised the status of the Minton firm until it ranked as the most influential in the country. Mr Geoffrey Bemrose has described the Minton firm as 'a veritable branch of the Sèvres manufactory in matters of taste'.

Early Minton bone china was faintly greyish in tint and inclined to be flawed with black specks. After John Turner joined the firm as managing potter in 1803 he made outstanding improvements in paste and glaze. Decoration until 1820 was simple. Thomas Minton's original pattern books showing bone china tea ware in full colour are still in existence, dating from 1796 to 1836. Each design is numbered and this reference was painted on the china beneath Thomas Minton's trade mark, a blue enamel imitation of the Sèvres double-L mark, but incorporating the letter M. Mark and pattern number considered together may determine the approximate age of Thomas Minton's bone china. Decorative wares in revived rococo style marked only with pattern numbers are particularly liable to be ascribed to other factories.

161. The development of tea cups (Figs 160–163). TOP: four by Chelsea. SECOND ROW: three by Chelsea-Derby, c. 1770–1780. THIRD ROW: two from early Derby pattern pattern bock, late 18th century. BOTTOM: Derby, early 19th century.

The dates of fashionable designs may be traced progressively. The first pattern is a handleless cup and saucer decorated with roses and foliage in pink and green enamels with touches of blue, the rims encircled with bands of roses. The capacities of both were equal, a feature continued throughout Thomas

Minton's period. The saucer has a wide, flat base without either a central depression for the cup or a foot ring beneath. Until 1800 blue patterns predominated. Minton's tenth cup saucer, for example, was edged with plain blue and sparsely enamelled with cornflower posies, lilies of the valley and small six-petalled flowers all in dark cobalt. The key pattern border associated with Regency design appears in 1798 and the well-known Bourbon sprig during the following year. This decoration appears for the first time on the flat of the saucer. Until 1800 decoration was very sparse; then richly coloured patterns became popular. At first borders were extended to reach half-way down the cup and over the outer half of the saucer, but still leaving bands of white around the rims. By 1805 rims were covered too, so that saucers were ornamented from bouge to rim.

All-over patterns incorporating exotic birds and peonies in blue, red, green and brown appeared at about the same time, usually with gilded rims. From this period it is possible to trace increased use of gilding, such as the fruiting vine with gold foliage and grapes and tendrils in blue. There was a short-lived vogue for delicate line work in masses of fine tendrils. Detailed line work, including grounds of intricate scrollwork, were set with oval reserves containing views; two on the cup and four on the saucer. A print-like clarity was ensured by painting them entirely in black enamel. When black ornament had a renewed vogue around 1830 a cup might be encircled with a single view. Japan patterns were introduced in 1805 in deep borders on a cup and flat-centred saucer. Stronger japan colours were introduced by 1808, when the pattern included blue and pink peonies with foliage in various tints of green.

The third pattern book was started in 1823. Exterior ornament was repeated on the inside of cups, the whole being lavishly gilded. A small matching posy might be painted in the

162. More early porcelain tea cups. TOP: three from Lowestoft with more or less Oriental painting. SECOND ROW: Longton Hall; New Hall hard paste; Bristol, 1770s. THIRD ROW: Bristol, with handle, c. 1775–80; Nantgarw; Swansea. BOTTOM: Swansea at their most delightful including (left) ornate cabinet cup.

base of the cup. A year later elaborately designed stars in black or black and gold might be substituted for colourful flowers. Wavy rims first appear in the mid-1820s. A long range

163. Tea cups, later porcelain and bone china. TOP: three of Worcester, 1760s–1770s. CENTRE: two of Worcester, c. 1780s; Worcester, c. 1810. BOTTOM: Chamberlain japan pattern on Nelson breakfast cup, 1802–5; Chamberlain perforated honeycomb pattern, 1851; Grainger honeycomb, 1851.

of sprays, lines, dots and rims in jet black superseded gold at this time, but the main vogue was for black patterns entirely dominating the design. The foot ring was introduced to cups in 1829.

The fourth pattern book, 1830–36, illustrates many tea plates. The first is wavy-rimmed, painted with simple sprays in green. This was followed by the fashion for all-over transfer-printed flower backgrounds containing reserves of

164. Tea cups, 19th century. TOP: three by Spode—gold on red ground with white flowers, painted flowers with gold scale on blue ground, painted roses and white reliefs—numbered 879, 1166, 2079 in pattern book of 1804. CENTRE: two by Minton—no. 76 in first pattern book, and no. 638 of about 1825; cup by Davenport, c. 1825. BOTTOM: Rockingham, 1820s; Coalport 1851; Ridgway, Philadelphia Exhibition 1876.

painted decoration with lustred rims. The ground colours are named as mazarine blue, celeste blue, Exeter blue, crimson, pink and straw. In 1833 came the first cups in a design captioned 'French shape', with everted rim and deep foot ring.

Herbert Minton gained control of the factory after his father's death in 1836. By effectively modernising various processes without affecting appearance, he converted formerly expensive table services into everyday commercial wares. He issued blue-printed ware in greatly improved techniques and more brilliant blues than formerly. At this period the quality of competing blue and white tended to decline. During the next decade he created an entirely new style in ceramic ornament, the number of employees increasing to more than 1,500.

After Léon Arnoux was appointed chief designer in 1848, Minton decoration adopted styles from old Sèvres including the production of cabinet porcelains never intended for utilitarian purposes. Minton was the only British potter at the Great Exhibition, 1851, to be awarded a special medal for 'Originality and Beauty of Design'. Parian statuary came into production in the mid-1840s; a catalogue issued in 1852 names 233 subjects (*see* Part III). It was the Minton firm that evolved English majolica in 1850 (q.v.).

Herbert Minton died in 1858 and was succeeded by his nephew Colin Minton Campbell. Under his direction appeared the acid gold process in 1863 (*see* Part IV). Other Minton triumphs during the third quarter of the 19th century were *pâte-sur-pâte* ornament from 1870 (*see* Part IV), and the now scarce reproductions of Palissy ware, Della Robbia and Henri Deux ware (*see* Part III) which were made from a calcareous clay body covered with opaque white enamel; enamel glazes supplied the colour decoration.

Minton trade marks are numerous. Transfer-printed marks were used, composed of elaborate cartouches incorporating the pattern name or type of ceramic, such as 'stone china', or the pattern number with initials in script letters indicating the trading names of various partnerships: M, early 1820s to 1836; M & B during the Minton-Boyle partnership, 1836–1841; M & CO, 1841–1873; M & H during the Minton-Hollins partnership, 1845–1868. Many other marks were used incorporating the name Minton from 1862 to 1873 and Mintons from 1873 to 1950. From 1851 a filled-in ermine mark with three dots above might be impressed or painted underglaze; this identified wares that had been dipped in a soft glaze on which enamelled decoration was to be applied. The printed mark of the terrestrial globe with MINTON inscribed across the equator appeared from 1863 to 1872. The globe was then surmounted by a crown and the name altered to MINTONS. This was again altered to MINTON in 1950. In 1891 ENGLAND was added and the globe flanked with laurel branches from 1911 with EST 1793 below.

Impressed symbols have been used from 1842 to indicate the year of manufacture (*see* Part VII).

Mortlock, John and his successors (1746–about 1930): a celebrated firm of china sellers and decorators established in Oxford Street, London in 1746. At that time London premises were not numbered, displaying only signboards; Mortlock's sign, first hung in 1750, was of a large brown stoneware jug, its shoulder encircled with hops and barley in relief. During the 19th century the Mortlock firm acted at various times as London agents for Coalport, Minton, Worcester, Wedgwood and Derby. Huge quantities of fine porcelain and earthenware passed through their hands, usually bearing the maker's name, and also Mortlock's name and address as china seller. The various changes in the style and address make it possible to attribute pieces very closely according to the records of the London directories.

The founder died in the 18th century, the directory entry for 1802 naming the firm 'John & William Mortlock, 250 Oxford St, Coalbrookdale China Manufacturers'. The contemporaneous meaning of the term manufacturers was that they bought china in the white and decorated it in their own workshops or through independent decorators. By 1811 the firm operated as John Mortlock, suggesting that John's brother William had died. By 1830 the establishment of the next generation is suggested by the entry once again of the firm in the style 'John & William Mortlock, 250, Oxford St, Manufacturers of china, glass and earthenware'. In 1835 the partners separated, John Mortlock remaining at 250, Oxford St, while William established himself at 18, Regent St; both described themselves as 'china and glass dealers'. From 1841 to 1843 John was in partnership with Sturges, trading as Mortlock & Sturges. At the time of the Great Exhibition, 1851, John had removed the decorating department to 58, Park St and William announced that he was 'China-seller by Special Appointment to Her Majesty'. By 1875 the backstamp showed the Regent St firm as 'by special appointment to the Queen and H.R.H. the Prince of Wales. Depôt for Minton's china'. John in 1877 registered as his trade mark a printed garter star with a map of the world superimposed with his name and address (Fig. 203). At this time he moved his workshops to 31 & 32, Orchard St and marked his decorated ware MORTLOCK'S STUDIO LONDON. In the 1880s and later, his mark incorporated the name of the potter surrounded by a ribbon bearing his name and address. By 1890 the trading name was John Mortlock & Co. 'by special appointment to H.M. the Queen, H.R.H. the Prince of Wales, H.R.H. the Duke of Edinburgh, &c. Principal London depôt for Mintons, Worcester, Wedgwood' and the addresses 466–470, Oxford St, 31–32, Orchard St and 2b, Granville Place, Portman Square. The trade mark was then a stoneware jug copied from the original shop sign. By 1899 the name was Mortlocks Ltd.

Nafferton Pottery, Yorkshire: Charles Longbottom built an earthenware kiln in 1848 and was succeeded by his son Samuel, who continued until 1899. The mark S L impressed has been recorded on large two-handled covered vases, flower-pot stands and bowls with ivy leaves and sprays in relief.

Nantgarw and **Swansea Porcelains,** Wales: in 1813 William Billingsley, with his son-in-law Samuel Walker as partner, and £250 in capital, established the Nantgarw pottery to make soft paste porcelains. Unfortunately distortions and fire cracks were extensive and the venture proved unprofitable. The porcelain, however, was milk-white in colour and of impressive translucency. Productions consisted almost entirely of plates and dishes with wide, heavily moulded rims, their depth low in proportion to diameter. The scroll moulding in relief on plate rims so closely resembled early Sèvres that when decorated by London enamellers it was difficult to distinguish between them. In October 1814 Billingsley and Walker joined L. W. Dillwyn at Swansea, where they stayed until September 1817, then returning to Nantgarw and continuing to make porcelain. The paste now made was very white, notable features being its high translucency, the finer potting and a greater range of shapes. The original glaze was used.

Typical decoration on flat-ware consisted chiefly of conventional flower sprays painted between relief border motifs and a central expansive floral bouquet. Other pieces were decorated with the life-size naturalistic flowers then fashionable. Yet other plates were ornate cabinet pieces meticulously painted with birds, flowers, landscapes, elaborate figures and classical decoration covering the entire field. Grounds and borders were coloured in the fashionable deep green, turquoise, claret and *bleu de roi* and the lavishly applied gilding was highly burnished.

At Swansea in October 1814 Billingsley and Walker were faced with the task of strengthening their porcelain while retaining its whiteness and translucency. Eighteen months of experiments produced many variations of paste, but no standard porcelain emerged from the kiln.

In mid-1816 a change in constituents was made, resulting in a porcelain which proved more tractable in the kilns. Its clear greenish translucency when held against the light has caused collectors to name it duck's-egg porcelain. It was glazed with transparent flint-glass, thickly applied. Close

165. Changing outlines of tea sets. TOP: Worcester, c. 1770s. CENTRE: black basaltes, c. 1780s. BOTTOM: Derby, c. 1790s.

inspection reveals striations, apparent irregular wavy markings associated with flint-glass of the period. Like all glazes on Swansea porcelain it never shows crazing. The quality of the porcelain was such that the London china sellers welcomed it whole-heartedly. This was a commercial failure, however, and production ceased after six months.

Steatite was then added to strengthen the paste and in the spring of 1817 the new porcelain was ready for marketing. This porcelain is less transparent than the duck's egg quality and when held against the light reveals a smoky yellow cloudiness. Its thin glaze is impaired with flaws known as

166. Tea sets cont. TOP: ornate style of Swansea, c. 1815; CENTRE: Spode, c. 1820s. BOTTOM: frequently transfer-printed specimens, 1840s.

pigskin pitting, usually almost invisible, but sometimes very apparent. This porcelain was rejected by the London china-sellers. It is known to collectors as 'trident Swansea' because it bears the impressed mark SWANSEA with one or two tridents.

Relief moulding on flat-ware rims, produced by pressing into plaster moulds, continued at Swansea. The clay was so heavily pressed, however, that the design was outlined on the underside of the rim, a little known Swansea characteristic. Six reserves between the mouldings were painted with flowers. Another Swansea shape is seen in plates with cruciform ribbed embossments. Enamels used by the Swansea decorators were softer-hued than those of the London enamellers whose work is recognised by greater depth of hard brilliance. Swansea gilding was thickly applied and now displays a slightly brassy tone; London gilding lavishly applied to Swansea porcelain still retains its original brilliance.

Swansea shapes included a considerable amount of small hollow-ware adapted from fashionable French porcelain. Insects, landscapes with floral borders, scattered sprays of flowers, as well as flowers and scrolls in low relief decorated this porcelain. A dark green enamel of peculiar tint was a Swansea characteristic.

After production had ceased the remaining stocks of biscuit were eventually glazed and decorated, much by Thomas Pardoe at his enamelling workshops at Bristol. His decoration is recognised by the gritty textures of reds, greens, yellows and blues. All kinds of patterns came easily from his brush, lightly painted sprays of garden flowers, sprigs of foliage, birds, fruit, animals, butterflies, shells, Oriental motifs, and landscapes of local interest. He used a fine underglaze blue for borders and his gilding was lavish and in intricate designs.

New Chelsea Porcelain Co. Ltd, Longton, about 1912–1951: specialists in reproductions in bone china of various early English porcelain shapes and decorations such as Chelsea, Bow, Lowestoft, Plymouth, Bristol and Swansea; also Chinese of the Kang H'si period, Sèvres, Meissen (Dresden) and others. The printed marks from 1919 included the name *New Chelsea*, *Chelsea* or *Royal Chelsea* in script with an anchor.

Plymouth: the first hard-paste porcelain to be made in England was by William Cookworthy, a wholesale chemist of Bristol. He spent about twenty years in prospecting the West

Country for deposits of china clay and china stone—which he finally discovered on the Cornish estates of Thomas Pitt, later Lord Camelford—and in the development of a manufacturing technique from the initial preparation of the materials to the final firing of the decorated ware. He was granted a patent on 14th July, 1768. Cookworthy styled his firm The Plymouth New Invented Porcelain Company and within a few months was employing between fifty and sixty operatives. The factory was transferred to Bristol (q.v.) in 1770, giving Plymouth a life of about two years.

Existing examples show that at first the body was white with a slight tendency towards grey and a translucency also faintly

167. Shells. Many shells are collected. These are from Plymouth and Belleek (*see also* Nautilus ware, Fig. 37).

grey. Fractures had a granular appearance and firecracks, warping, pinholes and other flaws were frequent. Upon a change being made in the formula the porcelain became milky white with a surface suggesting polished ivory. Translucency varied from a faintly yellowish green to a cold white-grey tone. Fractures were smooth. Firecracks were common and wreathing was characteristic of Plymouth porcelain. There were few surface defects apart from occasional dark brown spots with black centres, brought about by the presence of iron particles in the clay. A surface condition known as pigskin pitting may be noticed, however, where imperfect wedging in early stages of manufacture caused minute depressions. A more serious defect was due to an insufficiency of technical knowledge regarding kiln construction. Cookworthy found it impossible to prevent what he referred to as 'those tinging vapours' during firing. Consequently most Plymouth porcelain has a faintly brown or smoky appearance.

Plymouth at first followed the Chinese method of drying the modelled clay to leather consistency, dipping it into glaze and then firing it. Uneven patches brought about by imperfect fusion of paste and glaze eventually caused this method to be abandoned in favour of a glaze separately fired in the soft porcelain manner, consisting almost wholly of china stone. This glaze, brilliant, thin and transparent, incorporated with the paste, causing the porcelain to appear dense and semi-opaque. Where this glaze collected in crevices it displayed tints varying from a pale greenish-yellow to a faint cobalt blue.

Blue painted underglaze was the sole decoration on early Plymouth. The colour was dull and often overfired to a brownish-black. Eventually this was improved and the result was a deep blue-black, so thickly applied that it was inclined to run with streaky effects. Naïve oriental flowers were the usual motifs. Decorations in bright coloured enamels were introduced in the form of Chinese figures, birds, butterflies, foliage and floral sprays. These stood out sharply against the brilliant glaze. Enamels were difficult to fix to the thin, hard glaze, however, and might display a dry effect when some of the flux was lost to the glaze without softening into it. This sometimes caused the colour to flake away, so that the collector finds merely a rough surface to the glaze. Unfortunately, too, some colours were ruined by over-firing. Vase decorations superficially resembled those of Chelsea, particularly in brilliantly plumaged exotic birds. Richly coloured grounds might be used and gilding was frequent. Cookworthy issued many figures, most of them clumsily executed, their clothing decorated with widely spaced motifs and their bases touched with red or brownish-crimson.

The chemist's symbol for tin was the mark used at Plymouth and has been noted in five colours: blue underglaze on blue

168. Bird models for the collector. TOP: enamel-coloured parrot in white salt glazed stoneware; phoenix in Plymouth porcelain, found coloured and in the white. BOTTOM: Derby peacock on flower base, a long-continued favourite; earthenware, typical of much cheap ware, simple outline, gaudy colours, around 1800.

and white porcelain, gold, red, reddish-brown, and blue enamels. It was occasionally incised.

Rockingham, Yorkshire: established 1745 at Swinton, near Rotherham, after the discovery by Edward Butler of a bed of good quality yellow clay. He made nothing more than common brown domestic ware and on his death in 1765 the pottery continued equally uneventfully under Thomas Malpass. None of their productions has been identified.

EARTHENWARE: the pottery was acquired in 1785 by Thomas Bingley in association with John and William Brameld. They modernised and enlarged the plant and premises, increasing the range of their productions, but no marked examples have been recorded. Bingley won repute for his firm by originating the Swinton tea and coffee services, brown, chocolate-coloured and mottled, sometimes lightly gilded with oriental and floral

169. Rockingham. The kind of shapely, elaborate little cream jug expected of this firm to which much unmarked inferior work is attributed; unusual style of vessel attributed to Rockingham as a goats' milk jug, with models of goats at the brim.

designs. From 1787 to 1806 the firm was in partnership with Leeds, trading as Greens, Bingley & Co., Swinton Pottery. Their price list was identical with that of Leeds and stated that they made queen's ware, nankeen blue, tortoiseshell, Egyptian black and brown china. This brown china was pearl ware or cream-coloured earthenware covered with a lead glaze heavily stained with pure oxide of manganese, producing a purple-brown colour (*see* Rockingham glaze).

The Bramelds became sole proprietors in 1807 and the wares, which previously had been unmarked, began to bear the name BRAMELD impressed. In 1813 the pottery passed into the possession of William Brameld's three sons, Thomas, George Frederick and John Wager Brameld.

They continued to make brown china, notably light in weight, and the collector will find jugs with octagonal necks, hot water jugs, teapots, coffee pots and mugs. The handles on mugs are characteristic; the upper part is shaped as the tail of a horse and halfway down the loop changes into a leg with a hoof terminal. Cane-coloured stoneware jugs and mugs, decorated with sprigged relief work in white or blue, date from about 1820. The range of productions included, too, blue transfer-printed pearl ware and green glazed ware, light in weight compared with Staffordshire productions and usually with an iridescent glaze.

The name BRAMELD was impressed on earthenware from 1806 to 1842 in many variants usually followed by a plus sign and a numeral, or a symbol such as a triangle. Cane-coloured stoneware was marked with an oval embossed cartouche bordered with roses, thistles and shamrocks encircling BRAMELD.

BONE CHINA: the brothers Brameld from about 1820 or earlier engaged in experiments which in the spring of 1826 resulted in their setting up as potters of fine bone china, which for sixteen years gave Rockingham a reputation for lavish splendour. This work was technically so perfect that their financial resources proved unequal to the strain and the Bramelds were adjudged bankrupt and the 'Swinton Pottery, late in the occupation of Messrs Brameld' was advertised to be let. The 78 year old Earl Fitzwilliam then agreed to finance the project and the works resumed production, being named Rockingham Works with the Fitzwilliam crest, a griffin *passant*, introduced as the factory trade mark. For much of the next sixteen years nearly 400 people were employed.

Because of its bone ash content Rockingham porcelain had a paste of intense whiteness when compared with frit porcelains and was clearly translucent. Much of the ware was crazed in a very fine network of hair lines indiscernible to the casual eye.

The enamels used at Rockingham were unrivalled during the 1830s. Particularly gorgeous were the ground colours, perhaps the most perfect of their period. Among these the thick, smooth opaque apple green is the most celebrated and was unique to Rockingham; the somewhat harder shade of green sometimes noted resulted from the use of an impure metallic oxide. Rockingham blue grounds, which include a deep *gros bleu* verging on violet, were notable for their rich shadings and variations of tone, the mazarine and *bleu de ciel* being particularly soft and attractive. Reds varied from a deep pink to a maroon, reminiscent of Chelsea's more than half a century earlier. Derby's canary yellow was copied, but the Rockingham version was considerably darker. The delicate peach tint of Rockingham is very rare. A pink ground enriched with a gilded diaper pattern was a favourite decoration.

In an effort to outshine their rivals the Brameld brothers turned to the lavish application of gilding, sometimes in delicate lace patterns never made elsewhere, but usually in areas of solid gold highly burnished. Wide gilt borders with heavy gilt knobs and gilt animals for handles and cover finials were characteristic. With the passing of years Rockingham gilding has tended to acquire a faintly copper tinge.

Dessert services were characterised by relief-moulded edges, usually enriched with delicate gilt scrollwork and handles in the form of moulded leaves with the veins picked out in gold. Dinner services were issued in considerable numbers in shapes adapted from late Georgian silver and enriched with delicate sprays of flowers in natural colours, often against a yellowish background.

Among costly tea table decorations were tea cups painted with well-composed views on the base and sides, the exterior ornamented with patterns of gilding. Rockingham originated the resplendent style of painting a tray or dish centrepiece surrounded by a gilded cartouche containing a skilfully executed miniature in each corner. Rockingham vases, although excellently potted, display little originality in form or decoration, many of them obviously being inspired by Derby and Worcester.

Rockingham figures and statuettes are sometimes as gracefully elegant as any comparable figures in English ceramics. Unfortunately, however, some were coarsely enamelled with broad washes of semi-translucent colour. A very few flat-back figures have been found with a gold-inscribed title on the plinth in the style of earthenware figures. Small shepherdesses, dancers and similar minor figures were made in a rather chalky biscuit and may easily be mistaken for Derby when unmarked.

The patronage of the nobility, essential for the sale of the Bramelds' finest productions, declined after the death of William IV in 1837. The result was financial disaster and closure of the works in 1842.

The Bramelds did not consistently mark their bone china. The usual mark found on productions of the period 1826–1830 was the griffin *passant* printed in red above ROCKINGHAM WORKS/BRAMELD in script. In 1830 the word royal was added to the firm's title and to the griffin mark, the most common inscription being ROCKINGHAM WORKS/BRAMELD /MANUFACTURER TO THE KING in script. ROYAL ROCK^M WORKS/BRAMELD and ROYAL ROCKINGHAM/BRAMELD are also found. These marks are all printed in purple.

Bone china, bought as white biscuit, was still decorated in part of the old factory by Isaac Baguley, formerly manager of the Bramelds' gilding department. For a time he and his son Alfred used the old griffin mark. John Wager Brameld, too, set up as a decorator at 7, Coburg Place, Bayswater, London, and operated from 1844 to 1851. He specialised in finely decorated cabinet ware as splendidly enamelled and as lavishly gilded as before. There was, too, a considerable output of domestic ware and among Brameld's display at the Great Exhibition in 1851 was table-ware painted with flowers including rose, thistle and shamrock in brilliantly coloured enamels.

Royal Lancastrian Pottery, Clifton Junction, Manchester: art pottery from 1903, notable for its lustres.

Ruskin Pottery, Smethwick: founded 1898 by W. Howson Taylor. Notable art pottery specialising in colour glazes.

Sadler & Green, Liverpool: John Sadler and Guy Green established themselves in Harrington Street as transfer-printers on tiles in 1756, and later printed on Staffordshire and Liverpool earthenware and porcelain sent to them for this purpose. Wedgwood sent consignments of cream-coloured earthenware regularly for printing. They were for long wrongly believed to have been the inventors of transfer-printing.

Scottish potteries of note include: (c. 1750–1810) Delftfield, Glasgow; (19th century) J. & M. P. Bell, Port Dundas, Springburn, and Verreville, Glasgow; Airth; Alloa; Greenock; Kirkcaldy; Musselburgh; Paisley; Scott Bros and Rathbone, Portobello. The Scottish Porcelain Co., Prestonpans and Nautilus Porcelain Co., Glasgow, made Goss-style armorial ware.

Spode: Josiah Spode (1733–97) at the age of 29 was appointed manager of Turner & Banks, Stoke-upon-Trent. He acquired the factory on mortgage in 1770 and continued the manufacture of inexpensive domestic earthenware and sporting serving jugs with decorations in relief. He developed the trade to include cream-coloured earthenware decorated with coloured enamels in simple designs. Plates might have perforated rims, and patterns rapidly became more elaborate. He then experimented with all-over transfer printing under the glaze. This process was introduced to Staffordshire by William Adams, Cobridge, but Josiah Spode developed the process

170. Potpourri. Some of the potters' most decorative work went into ornamental vases with perforated covers intended to hold potpourri or perfume. Spode made many particularly handsome specimens. TOP: flower-encrusted porcelain of the 1760s; Wedgwood 'porphyry', 1783; Worcester with painted view, end of 18th century. CENTRE: Derby with painted scene; Swansea; Spode footed style—all early 19th century. BOTTOM: Spode, c. 1810, showing outer pierced lid and inner solid lid for retaining the perfume when not required; Coalport, flower-encrusted, 1830s; Spode in late Regency style.

commercially and brought great prosperity to the Potteries. In 1801 there were more than fifty china sellers in London specialising in Staffordshire blue. For the first few years Spode applied this decoration to cream-coloured earthenware. By the mid-1790s he was printing on white pearl ware, a body which greatly enhanced the beauty of the prints. Spode decorated his ware with a rich luminous blue, more attractive than the so-called 'Staffordshire blue' of his contemporaries. Spode's printed table ware was renowned from its inception in 1785. The printing of the pictorial central panels was always clear and unsmudged; the borders never over-ran the rims and transfer joints were almost imperceptible.

Meanwhile Josiah Spode was experimenting towards a new porcelain paste, stronger, whiter and more translucent than English soft pastes and Oriental and Continental hard pastes. The firm's old pattern books prove conclusively that table ware in his new bone china was in production by 1795. He then installed newly designed kilns and other plant. The first year's profits exceeded £15,000.

Following Spode's death in 1797 the pottery came under the control of his son Josiah Spode II, with William Copeland in charge of sales. Copeland died in 1826 and Josiah II a year later. Both were succeeded by their sons, W. T. Copeland and Josiah Spode III. Within two years the latter died and Copeland became sole proprietor. Under his progressive guidance output rose to immense proportions and in 1833 he took Thomas Garrett into partnership, the firm trading as Copeland & Garrett until 1847. Since then the firm has been controlled by Copeland's direct descendants to the present day, although the name of Spode has been retained in some trade marks.

Spode's early designers of bone china table ware profited largely by decorations used by the established potters of soft paste porcelain. New patterns were continually produced with a wide range of subjects, rich enamels and burnished gold.

Regarding Spode japan patterns, the evidence of the old pattern books proves that such decorations in deep velvety blues, bold patches of scarlet and rich gilding were more imaginative than the later flood of japan patterns from Derby.

Josiah Spode II introduced felspar porcelain in 1800. This was used extensively for table services until 1833. It was

171. Ice pails or ice cream pails. The Swansea vessel on the left shows the assembled pail. CENTRE AND RIGHT: Spode version showing lid and inner compartment to fit over the ice held in the main vessel. As with a jelly mould, a portion of such a specimen may be difficult to recognise.

remarkably translucent, a factor which greatly enhanced the beauty of enamel decoration. By 1805 Spode was marketing stone china, an opaque, extremely hard ceramic superficially resembling hard porcelain (*see* page 73). Spode's version is double the weight of earthenware and displays a blue-grey tint. Spode was the finest imitator of his day, successfully producing close copies of Chelsea ornament. His most ambitious attempt was the claret ground with bird decorations in gold. Copies of Meissen would be difficult to distinguish from originals were it not for the difference in paste. The same was true of his numerous French imitations. His salmon-scale decoration was livelier than that made by Wall's Worcester.

Marks on Spode wares were plain and unmistakable. Although altered frequently they were never cryptic or contrived in any way to resemble the marks of other potters.

172. Miniature watering can, a charming Spode piece which requires lid and recessed dish as shown, but is more often found incomplete. Another of these 'toys' is seen in Fig. 7.

Steele, Edward, Hanley: operated mid-1870s to 1889. Jewitt recorded that in parian Steele made 'some hundreds of different single figures, groups, busts and animals, many of large size'. He also made English majolica dessert services with figure centrepieces, comports, vases, teapots and jugs, all carefully modelled on an excellent body. Majolica was marked with a ring containing ETRUSCAN MAJOLICA, encircling the monogram E S. This is recorded by J. R. Cushion. Parian was unmarked.

Stevenson, Andrew, Cobridge, Staffordshire: from 1816 to 1830 made dark blue transfer-printed earthenware, in which the decoration displayed outstanding technical ability. More than thirty English scenes are known, but the bulk of his ware was intended for the American market. He even sent a young artist named W. G. Wall to sketch views on the spot. Borders were handsomely designed with large flowers, roses and foliage.

His impressed marks were: a crown enclosed in a double circle inscribed A. STEVENSON WARRANTED STAFFORD-

SHIRE, the name A. STEVENSON, and a three-masted ship with the name STEVENSON above. A printed mark attributed to Andrew Stevenson is a ribbon inscribed SEMI-NANKEEN, with a crown, rose, thistle and shamrock above and a sailing ship below.

Sunderland, Co. Durham: made inexpensive domestic earthenware from 1740 and cream-coloured earthenware from about 1780. Decorations in the 19th century were mainly in lustre and by transfer-printing. The vast production of earthenware can be visualised from records of a flint-crushing mill that operated with a weekly output of twenty tons early in the 19th century—and this was but one of several. Collectors look for lustre, frog mugs, chimney ornaments, Sunderland lion ornaments, mugs decorated with portraits of Jack Crawford, a local hero of the battle of Camperdown in 1797, innumerable maritime subjects and verses, sets of matching jugs from cream size to two-and-a-half gallon capacity, and a wide range of gift china. Transfer-printed ware includes many views of Wearmouth Bridge, opened in 1796 and known in twenty-two versions, fourteen of them rare. This is often wrongly termed Sunderland Bridge, fourteen miles distant.

DEPTFORD or BALL'S POTTERY, established by William Ball in 1857, produced purple lustre notable for its distinct orange tinge. Ball later acquired the original moulds for the Sunderland lions; in his productions the vicious-looking fangs of the originals were replaced by a row of even teeth. In 1884 the firm was re-titled Ball Brothers and continued operating until 1918. The impressed mark was BALL BROS/SUNDERLAND.

LOW FORD or DAWSON'S POTTERY: founded by John Dawson in 1800 and continued under his direction until his death in 1848. The firm's style became Thomas Dawson & Co. in 1837 and from about 1840 output exceeded that of any other Sunderland pottery; production ceased in 1864. Productions included lustre wares, canary yellow mugs with the

173. Attractive blotchy lustre, associated with Sunderland. In the flower-painted text the frame is part of the lustre plaque. The jugs at the bottom show views of the Wear Bridge, Sunderland: often printed detail around the view gives a clue to the date.

bridge transfer-printed in black, inkpots shaped as birds' nests, panels to fit into cabinet work, tiles with landscape views in colour or sepia. Marks include: DAWSON, J. DAWSON/LOW FORD, DAWSON & CO, DAWSON & CO/LOW FORD POTTERY.

PHILLIPS, JOHN, NORTH HYLTON POTTERY (1815–64): formerly Phillips & Maling (about 1800–1815). In the first half of the 19th century Phillips was well-known for the quality and range of his domestic and ornamental ware painted with purple lustre. The mark until 1815 was MALING impressed. Afterwards marks were printed and include PHILLIPS & MALING, HYLTON POT WORKS, J PHILLIPS/HYLTON POTTERY, JOHN PHILLIPS/HYLTON POTTERY.

SOUTHWICK POTTERY: established in 1788 by Anthony Scott and continued until 1897. Made a higher quality earthenware than was usual among the Sunderland potters. This pottery produced some of the most clear-cut of the Sunderland lions and mosaic ware in olive grey or brown made by a mechanical process devised in about 1830 by Thomas P. Scott. Jasper ware in the Wedgwood style was made in the mid-19th century. A wide range of transferred work on white earthenware was issued, and enamelled designs on cream-coloured earthenware. Marks were numerous and might be impressed or printed. The earliest, until 1829, were A. SCOTT & CO and SCOTT SOUTHWICK. Scott was joined by his sons in 1829 and marks included ANTHONY SCOTT/& SONS, S & SONS, SCOTT & SONS/SOUTHWICK, A. SCOTT & SONS.

SUNDERLAND or GARRISON POTTERY (1807–67): the range of productions included pink lustre, sponged, printed and painted copper and silver lustre, lively figures, tobacco jars, stands for clocks and watches. John Phillips became owner in 1807; from 1813 to 1819 the firm was styled Phillips & Co. and Dixon & Co.; 1820–26, Dixon, Austin & Co.; 1827–40,

Dixon, Austin, Phillips & Co.; 1840–67, Dixon, Phillips & Co. Marks, impressed and printed, included the name of the various partnerships.

THE WEAR POTTERY: established in 1786 by John Brunton. The name was S. Moore & Co. from 1803 until the pottery was closed in 1874. Productions of interest to collectors include lustre wares and chintz pattern jugs, in addition to the usual Sunderland wares. Marks were: S. MOORE & CO, S. M. & CO, MOORE & CO, MOORE & CO SOUTHWICK.

Sutherland & Sons, Longton: recorded as a maker of parian statuary, majolica, terracotta and stoneware from 1865 to 1875. The mark S & S was impressed or printed.

Swansea: *see* Nantgarw.

Twemlow, John: potted at Shelton during the mid-1790s. Jewitt possessed and quoted from an invoice dated 1797 showing the types of ware made, but unfortunately omitted the prices and the quantities ordered: 'E Black Teapots, capt., fest^d and fig^d [Egyptian black teapots, capped, festooned and figured]: ditto, upright, fest^d and fig^d; Oval E Black Teapots; ditto prest leaf; scallop top, fest^d and fig^d and banded; ditto prest leaf and fest^d and fig^d and banded a tip; ditto creams to match; ditto fluted; ditto coffee pots; octagon teapots, with scallop top, and creams to match; oval plain teapots; blue and enamelled handled cups and saucers, London size, sprig and border and vine pattern; bowls to match.'

Walker & Galley, Tunstall: manufactured 'shiny black and Egyptian black wares' for a few years until November, 1841, when the partnership ended, Thomas Walker continuing on his own account until the mid-1850s. Domestic wares in Egyptian black were potted by normal methods, but commemorative and decorative medallions and similar pieces were cut on the medallion machine. The mark was WALKER impressed.

Walker, William, 112 Minories, London: a retailer described

174. Teapots, in useful wares of the 18th century, now collectors'
treasures. TOP: Elers-type red ware, early 18th century; glazed red
ware, around 1740. SECOND ROW: black, Wedgwood, 1750s, also
found in tortoiseshell mottling; white salt glazed stoneware with
relief ornament, 1750s. THIRD ROW: marbled, found in surface
marbling and in agate ware, 1750s; green and yellow which may be
in pineapple, cabbage or cauliflower shaping. BOTTOM: two typical
shapes of 1760s with crabstock detail in red ware and white
stoneware.

175. Later 18th-century teapots. TOP: two of 1770s (right being a Leeds type). CENTRE: neo-classic shape, Wedgwood jasper, and more usual modified form in Nottingham ware, 1770s. BOTTOM: bamboo forms in caneware with painted leaf detail, Spode and Wedgwood, 1790s.

in the *London Directory*, 1785, as 'Glass and China Seller and Tea man'. By 1790 the business was operating as Walker & Co., and by 1801 the firm was entered only as tea dealers. The firm was styled Walker & Nash, tea dealers, by 1807 and had closed by 1814. A creamware sauce-boat in the Victoria and Albert Museum is impressed WALKER MINORIES.

Walley, Edward, Villa Pottery, Cobridge: established 1841 and operated by Jones & Walley until July, 1843, when Walley became sole proprietor, continuing to make parian, ironstone china and earthenwares until 1856, and specialising in ornamental parian jugs in high relief, often in sets of three. The earliest was entered at the Patent Office in July, 1849, but the registration certificate was not issued until 21st June, 1850. This was the very popular Diana jug, depicting a lively scene of the huntress with horse, hound, two boys and a deer (Fig. 121). Many other relief designs were registered. The trade mark on these incorporates the diamond-shaped registration symbol into a narrow border containing name, registration date and the pattern name, such as 'Ranger', in a label at the base. IRONSTONE/CHINA/E. WALLEY was impressed.

Walley, John, High Street, Burslem, 1850–67: blue and white earthenware teapots and Rockingham glaze. Marks printed or impressed J. WALLEY and J. WALLEYS/WARE.

Walley, William, Marsh Street, Shelton: born 1785, died 1842. Employed eight people potting sporting dogs and simple figures in earthenware for a few years until his death.

Walton, John, Burslem, 1806–1835: a specialist in figures and groups in a brittle earthenware, often with a crudely modelled bocage composed of a few star-shaped branches of oak leaves enamelled in bright green and black, with central acorns and split acorn cups that tend to lose their identity and be coloured as flowers.

His subjects included rustic and Biblical groups and farm animals placed on tall mounds, often roughly rocky. Thus a figure of a sheep may include a lamb sheltering in a rocky recess of the green base. Characteristically a Walton base includes rounded scrolls picked out in blue and often with the name of the subject inscribed on the front. Walton also made

176. Early 19th-century earthenware figures. TOP: ewe and lamb by Salt; fishwife by Walton; more realistic fishwife by Rathbone, Portobello. BOTTOM: details to note in such figures: (left) early and later scrolls by Walton; footed plinth by Obadiah Sherratt; v-topped oak leaf by Walton; casual oak leaf by Sherratt; shapely plinth by Neale.

toby jugs which were marked. The name WALTON impressed on a raised scroll appears on the back of many figures.

Wedgwood, Josiah: the most celebrated of all English potters, and his enduring reputation still influences present-day production. He was son, grandson and great-grandson of potters, apprenticed to his elder brother in 1744 and in 1752 was in partnership with John Harrison at Cliff Bank Works, Stoke-

177. Tea cups, in useful wares. TOP: three by Wedgwood—a V. & A. Museum specimen in red stoneware engine turned, c. 1760s; transfer-printed, c. 1775; and jasper 1785. SECOND ROW: Leeds creamware, c. 1770; Wedgwood cane ware with bamboo handle, 1792; handleless Leeds, with band of marbling. THIRD ROW: transfer-printed by E. J. Phillips & Co., Longport (tomb of Franklin) c. 1820s; black transfer-printed, Liverpool style; banded with lustre, showing typical deep saucer, early 19th century. BOTTOM: Ridgway useful wares shown at Great Exhibition.

upon-Trent, where they made agate ware knife hafts and buttons. Two years later he was in partnership with Thomas Whieldon; they made vast quantities of almost profitless salt-glaze. More profitable were marbled and agate wares, tortoiseshell and Egyptian black. Wedgwood was ceaselessly experimenting with clays and glazes, having sensed the need to bridge the gap between delicate porcelain and coarse earthenware and stoneware. In 1759 he perfected his now celebrated green glaze (page 56), upon which he placed a sufficiently high value to risk parting from Whieldon and establishing his own pottery at Ivy House Works, Burslem, where he made domestic ware until 1773.

It was at Ivy House that he evolved his celebrated cream-coloured earthenware (page 44). Some kind of ornament was almost always present on this ware, such as a rim-band of leaves in relief, enamelling in colours or transfer-printing. In 1763 he moved to Brick House or Bell Works where the cream-ware business was carried on until 1773, when it was transferred to Etruria, which he had founded in 1769 with Thomas Bentley as partner.

Wedgwood was delayed in the production of jasper until 1774. Other fine stoneware bodies perfected here included basaltes, cane ware, etc. (page 46). Pearl ware dated from 1779. Bentley died in 1780, but not until the death of his cousin Thomas did Josiah take into partnership his sons John, Josiah and Thomas, together with his nephew Thomas Byerley. The style of the firm, which had been Wedgwood & Bentley from 1768 to 1780, then Josiah Wedgwood until 1790, thereupon became Wedgwood, Sons & Byerley. In 1793 his sons John and Thomas resigned and the firm's style was Wedgwood, Son & Byerley, until Byerley's death in 1810. Marks, however, always displayed the name Wedgwood.

Josiah Wedgwood never attempted to make porcelain, but his successors ventured into the bone china business from

1812 to 1822. Manufacture of this ware was revived at Etruria in 1878, the printed mark consisting of a representation of the Portland vase with WEDGWOOD below.

Whittington Pottery, Derby: in the early 1800s made bone china decorated with bat-printed transfers.

Wincanton Pottery, Somerset: operated by Nathaniel Ireson. Dated examples prove manufacture of tin-enamelled earthenware from 1737 to 1748. Blue and manganese decorations were used, also a powdered manganese ground, sometimes with reserve medallions, through which lines might be scratched. The mimosa pattern in trellis-work borders, also made at Bristol, has frond-like leaves and each flower consists of a dot within a circle. Some plates are edged by a fine brown line. Marks were painted and might be WINCANTON or NATHANIEL IRESON.

Worcester: porcelain manufacture began here in 1751 by the Worcester Tonquin Manufactory, whose fourteen partners included the celebrated Dr Wall (d. 1776) and William Davis, formerly a Bristol technician. Davis held the position of works manager until his death in 1783. The business was then bought by Thomas Flight, jeweller to the Royal family and the firm's London agent. The word 'Royal' was added to the firm's title in 1788, the works then becoming known as the Royal Worcester Porcelain Company. After Thomas Flight's death in 1791 his son John took Martin Barr into partnership and traded as Flight & Barr. The latter's son Martin Barr II joined the firm in 1807, which was then re-titled Barr, Flight & Barr. In 1813 George Barr joined the business, which then operated as Flight, Barr & Barr until 1840 when the factory was acquired by the firm of Chamberlain.

Robert Chamberlain, formerly a porcelain decorator under Dr Wall, had founded a decorating and enamelling workshop at Worcester in 1783, buying porcelain and earthenware in the white from Caughley and Staffordshire. Following his death

178. Worcester teapots. TOP: c. 1760, painted with Chinese landscape; with partridge or quail pattern, c. 1765. CENTRE: c. 1770; c. 1775—in typical stand such as all would have had when sold. BOTTOM: c. 1780, with background in scale pattern; c. 1800s.

in 1798 his sons Humphrey and Robert launched into the manufacture of bone china, and were responsible for some finely decorated ware. In 1822 the factory came into the possession of Walter Chamberlain and John Lilley. They acquired the business of Flight, Barr & Barr in 1840, abandoning Wall's old premises and transferring plant and moulds to their works at Diglis. The united firms traded as Chamberlain & Company until 1852. W. H. Kerr and R. W. Binns then took over the firm, which ten years later was converted into a limited company known as the Worcester Royal Porcelain Company Ltd.

FIRST PERIOD, 1751–83. Soapstone porcelain was made from 1752 (*see* BRISTOL page 215), varying from a faintly bluish-grey to a creamy white and displaying a faintly bluish-green tinge if held to the light. The early glaze was softly white with a suspicion of green, evenly smooth and glossy rather than brilliant. Late in the period the ware was glazed with a mixture of grog and oxide of tin evenly distributed and faintly opalescent in appearance.

Until c. 1760 production was limited to domestic ware which might be enamelled in colours, but more usually was decorated in underglaze blue. The tint of the blue ranged from a clear bright sapphire to a dark indigo—sometimes almost blue-black. Potting was skilful and finish excellent. A notable change in policy took place in 1763 and Worcester began to cater for a richer clientele. Some of the finest of Worcester porcelain was made between then and 1783. In 1769 the firm advertised porcelain ornamented with 'beautiful Colours of Mazarine blue and gold, Sky-blue, Pea-Green, French-green, Sea-green, Purple, Scarlet and other varieties of Colour' on dinner, dessert, tea and coffee services.

The Worcester decorators modified the vivid complexities of colour and pattern which characterised Japanese porcelain, mingling them with the patterns and colours of Meissen and Sèvres; from the medley issued characteristic oriental Worcester, firmly established by 1770. Every fashionable design of the day was adapted by the Worcester decorators. Binns refers to 'lovely exotic birds, those gorgeous ornithological fantasies of the imaginative painter, impossible but quite beautiful. Quaint posies of old fashioned flowers—chrysanthemums, roses, carnations (generally striped) and picotees,

179. Detail of quail or partridge pattern, familiar on Worcester porcelain and also used by Bow. **180. So-called Lord Coventry or 'Blind Earl' pattern,** often noted on copies of Worcester.

the sweet blue nemophila and the dainty auricula in colours soft and harmonious; curious old landscapes in more than doubtful perspective, generally framed in turquoise husk borders shaded with black and gilt; rich and luscious-looking fruit; butterflies and insects, occasionally animals, and, apart

181. 'Dishevelled bird', a typical Worcester example.

from the Chinese style, rare figures'. The Meissen influence was expressed in colourful birds, pink scale patterns, scattered posies and flower sprays, and bunches of fruit: even Meissen crossed sword marks were imitated.

Queen Charlotte's pattern (Fig. 69) must not be confused with the more familiar queen's pattern (Fig. 70), with its alternating panels, often arranged spirally, of red on white, white on blue, with gilding. This is found also on Derby and Lowestoft porcelain.

The blue grounds of Worcester are celebrated, the best known being salmon-scale blue, powder blue, mazarine or dark blue and overglaze enamel blue. The device of breaking up a blue ground by diapering it with a close scale pattern, known to some collectors as salmon-scale, dated from 1760. On early examples large scales were laboriously outlined and washed in; the later small scales were more speedily produced as an underglaze background around flower or bird ornament. Less frequently scale pattern is found in salmon-pink. Such ground colours enclosed white reserves painted with flowers, fruits, birds, insects, and figures.

Transfer-printing was introduced at Worcester in 1757, a decoration continued there until 1774. All manner of pictures were transferred to the porcelain, following the current vogues for pastoral scenes with shepherds and milkmaids, romantic ruins in classical landscapes, and subjects from sporting prints. Some patterns were adapted from *The Ladies Amusement or Whole Art of Japanning*, 1760. The colours used were generally jet black, deep red, lilac or pale purple over the glaze until 1770, when underglaze transfer-printing in blue and in sepia was introduced. Thereafter, transferred designs might be hand-decorated with bright-coloured washes of enamels, enlivened with touches of gilding. The bat process of transfer-printing was introduced during the Flight period (1783–93).

Marks of the Wall-Davis period were varied, but not more than two may be regarded as true trade marks—the crescent and the cursive capital or script w. The block capital w is found only on blue printed porcelain. The crescent in

182. Pots for plants and bulbs. TOP: Wedgwood, unglazed red stone-ware; Turner stoneware. CENTRE: Wedgwood buff stoneware with white sprigged pattern, 1810; Worcester crocus pot, c. 1765; Spode violet basket, gold over red ground, c. 1810. BOTTOM: two flat-backed designs, Chamberlain, and in style of Bloor Derby.

various sizes is found in outline, with shading lines and in solid colour, the small open crescent in blue underglaze being the most common. A red open crescent is found on some enamelled porcelain from 1770. In varying forms the crescent appears to have continued until the end of the Flight period in 1793. The script w in blue and in several forms was used from 1755, sometimes in association with a blue crescent. The 'Chinese seal' in underglaze blue, a fretted square, appears in five different designs on porcelain printed in underglaze blue. Other varieties of the seal are found on all classes of porcelain. THOMAS FLIGHT (1783–93); FLIGHT & BARR (1793–1807); BARR, FLIGHT & BARR (1807–13); FLIGHT, BARR & BARR (1813–40). Under this regime the soapstone paste and the glaze were at once altered. The new porcelain lacks the translucency of earlier Worcester and shows a faintly yellow tint if held to the light. Commercially, however, the paste was considered an improvement, even though there was no longer a harmonious blending of paste with glaze and decoration. Styles and designs were in the fashionable classical mood and decorators of pictorial panels developed a technique characteristic of Worcester, outlines being perfect and colours applied with precision. Ornament included landscapes, figure subjects, copies of celebrated paintings, allegorical pictures, illustrations of poems and so on. Groups of flowers and finely painted shell patterns were in great demand. Less expensive decoration consisted of blue painted or printed flowers and blue bands, with or without gold decorated sprigs.

Flight & Barr from about 1800 began to manufacture bone china; the paste was hard-looking and faintly grey, less attractive than that being made contemporaneously by Spode and Minton, at Derby and at Coalport. Pure whiteness and high translucency were achieved by about 1820. Meanwhile Thomas Flight's soapstone porcelain continued in production, and shortly after Martin Barr II joined the firm in 1807 a great improvement was recorded in the texture and whiteness of the porcelain. Early in the 19th century decoration became simpler and enamel colours, cruder and harder than formerly, were used for naturalistic, but mechanical flower painting. From about 1810 considerable quantities of flat ware were made, the borders and rims decorated with raised rococo moulding. These might be enamelled in full colours, or in blue and gold. The introduction of Walker's enamelling muffle kiln at this time gave greater brilliance to enamel. The firm concentrated chiefly on table ware and vases, style and flamboyance of decoration resembling that of competitive bone china, but with greater attention given to details.

The earliest of Thomas Flight's marks was the name FLIGHT painted in script, either above, or accompanied by, an open crescent in blue, red or gold. The name might be impressed into the paste. A crown was added to the mark in 1789. From 1793 to 1807 FLIGHT & BARR appeared below a crown. The presence of an incised letter B indicates that the piece was made from one of the experimental pastes initiated by Martin Barr I. From 1807 to 1813 the name BARR FLIGHT & BARR was printed in red or blue underglaze, accompanied by the firm's Worcester and London show room addresses. The impressed initials B F B surmounted by a crown are attributed to this period. From 1813 to 1840 the mark, printed in blue, was FLIGHT, BARR & BARR in script, or F B B impressed.

CHAMBERLAIN'S (1783–1840): Robert Chamberlain was a decorator only until the 1790s, when his sons began to make bone china. This had a slightly grey appearance, but was progressively improved until 1815 when its translucency equalled that of Spode, although the paste was hardly so white. In 1811 they introduced a soft paste, very translucent and with a fine clear surface. Some magnificent matching dinner, dessert and breakfast services were made, known as REGENT CHINA and so marked. This continued in production until about 1820. A Chamberlain characteristic in bone china table ware consisted of borders in a chain or network design with carefully painted bouquets of garden flowers. From about 1821 many services were decorated with paintings of old castles, each piece displaying a different scene, with its title printed or impressed on the underside. Japan patterns in

183. Chamberlain vase with typical encrustations and painted view (*see also* Figs. 53, 93).

red, blue and gold date from about 1820. Vases lavishly gilded and painted with views of eastern towns belonged to the 1830s. The Chamberlain apple-green was celebrated for the beauty of its tint.

Marks on Chamberlain's Worcester always included their name; some early pieces were unmarked. Until 1808 CHAMBERLAINS or CHAMBERLAINS WORCS was painted in red script, often accompanied by a pattern number. The same marks in purple date between 1808 and 1820 and rare examples are found in gold. The first of the printed marks was CHAMBERLAINS/WORCESTER/& 63/PICCADILLY/LONDON in red script, used between 1814 and 1820. The usual marks from then until 1840 read CHAMBERLAINS/WORCESTER/ & 155/NEW BOND STREET/LONDON./ROYAL PORCELAIN MANUFACTORY. This might be surmounted by a version of the royal coat of arms or a jewelled crown.

The two Worcester firms united in 1840 and until 1852 the

Chamberlain section traded as Chamberlain & Co. The factory passed through a period of depression until 1852.

KERR & BINNS (1852–62): quickly revitalised the concern. They enlarged and modernised the factory and engaged first-class designers, potters and decorators, and began a programme of prestige building. By the mid-1850s the number of employees exceed six hundred. The technical and artistic improvements must be credited to R. W. Binns, partner, manager, art director and historian.

By 1853 they were advertising parian statuary, and in the following year began to manufacture adaptations of 16th-century Limoges enamels. Worcester painting *en grisaille* on underglaze royal blue has been classed among the finest porcelain decoration in England. This enamelling differs entirely from ordinary porcelain painting, the white enamel being thick and somewhat translucent, so that effects of light and shade were obtained by varying the number of flat washes applied. Much of this work is decorated with exquisitely chased gilding.

Ivory porcelain was evolved here and introduced in 1856. Groups, figures, busts and ornaments were made in the biscuit state which resembled the natural tint of ivory. Other goods in this porcelain were coated with a soft glaze and from the mid-1860s might be decorated with metallic colours. From about 1897 Sabrina ware introduced new glaze effects.

The mark was a circle containing four cursive Ws, radiating from a centrally placed crescent, with the numeral 51 between its horns. On cabinet pieces a shield was used, bearing the inscription K & B/WORCESTER.

WORCESTER ROYAL PORCELAIN CO. LTD. was formed after Kerr's retirement in 1862. The Raphaelesque style of porcelain was introduced in that year. From ivory porcelain, covered with a soft slip dip, also stemmed several other varieties of ware, including those known as stained ivory, jewelled, pierced and japanesque. The mark was the Kerr & Binns circle of cursive Ws surmounted by a crown (*see also* Grainger of Worcester, p. 256).

Yearsley, Yorkshire: a member of the Wedgwood family was established here late in the 17th century potting useful earthenware of coarse brown texture coated with green lead glaze. A puzzle jug in the Victoria and Albert Museum is incised JOHN WEDGWOOD 1691 in script; he is not to be confused with a 19th-century potter of the same name at Burslem. Jewitt recorded a semi-circular open-topped baking oven with a hollowed ledge around the inner side and a flat bottom, and with handles at the sides. This was excavated on the site and is dated 1712.

York China Manufactory: established 1838 by Haigh Hirstwood, formerly a decorator at Rockingham where he worked on the magnificent table services for William IV and the Duchess of Cumberland. In 1826 he copied about five hundred insects preserved at Wentworth House for the Rockingham firm, to use as decorators' references. Hirstwood bought his ware in the white from Sampson, Bridgwood & Co., Longton. His style obviously resembled that of Rockingham and it is difficult to distinguish between the two. Principal productions were dinner, dessert and tea services, vases and figures. No mark is known.

PART VII

Potters' Symbols, Initials, Date Letters

On many an easily collected piece of old china, such as a piece of blue-printed useful ware, a clue to the maker is offered in a cartouche upon the base. This often gives prominence to the name of the pattern, such as the 'Asiatic Pheasants' used by several 19th-century potters, but as a subsidiary detail the cartouche border may include the maker's initials or the name of the pottery, more rarely the name of the china retailer such as Mortlock or Daniell. The list below is by no means exhaustive but covers most of the initials a beginner-collector is likely to chance upon, covering a period from the 1740s to the end of the 19th century. It results from innumerable enquiries I have received through Country Life. In a number of instances the registration numbers and other details of specimens that have passed through my hands have enabled me to add to the generally accepted information, especially regarding 19th-century manufacturers.

This list is to be consulted together with the illustrations (Figs. 184 to 203) which show the symbols used by many firms either with unobvious initials or none at all. At the same time the beginner-collector should bear in mind several points that may contribute to a more exact elucidation of a mark and its period of use.

1. In many cases more than one potter has used the same initial or initials: B, for example, is found in many styles and this applies, too, to M and D, as well as to such symbols as anchors, crowns and royal coats of arms.

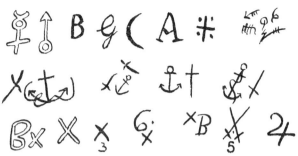

184. Marks. Porcelain, Bow and Bristol, FIRST AND SECOND ROWS: Bow, c. 1747–1776. FIRST ROW: two early incised marks; six marks in underglaze blue. SECOND ROW: typical painted mark, c. 1760–76, which varied considerably; variant in blue and red; two variants in red. (A few early Bow inkwells were inscribed MADE AT NEW CANTON sometimes with a date such as 1751, *see* Fig. 125). THIRD ROW, Bristol porcelain, 1750–2 (when the mark, very rare, was BRISTOL or BRISTOLL) and 1770–81: two incised; five in blue, sometimes including workman's number and the crossed swords imitating Meissen. The final mark in this row (the sign for tin) had been used by Cookworthy also at Plymouth.

2. Sometimes the initial of the town is placed under, after or between the maker's initials, such as in the mark $_F^{J\ R}$ used by James Reeves of Fenton. B (Burslem), C (Cobridge), H (Hanley), L (Longton), S (Stoke), T (Tunstall), may be mentioned.
3. Sometimes a diamond-shaped mark with a central 'Rd' accompanies a mark and gives a definite date between 1842 and 1883 for the introduction of a design, though not the actual year of manufacture of the piece of china so marked (*see* pp. 357–8). Subsequently long registered numbers were used and the dates of these, too, have been verified (*see* p. 359).

4. A firm's name that includes the word LIMITED or its abbreviation indicates a date after limited liability was defined by law in 1860 and the words TRADE MARK on a mark indicate that a piece post-dates the Trade Mark Act of 1862. But it is important to realise that there was a considerable time-lag before such details were incorporated into many potters' marks.

5. In the same way the word ENGLAND was often added to a firm's marks some years after the McKinley Tariff Act of 1891 required it upon the wares exported to America so that

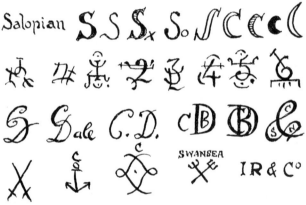

185. Marks. FIRST AND SECOND ROWS: Caughley, Shropshire, porcelain made by Thomas Turner c. 1775–99, who also used SALOPIAN in capitals, and letters s and c variously painted and printed in blue. The shaded crescent and pseudo-Oriental marks of numerals disguised by flourishes, all rare, are attributed by Geoffrey Godden to Worcester. THIRD AND FOURTH ROWS, Coalport, c. 1795–20th century: various marks using the initials C B D (Coalbrookdale); imitations of Meissen, Chelsea, Sèvres, Swansea; initials I. R. & CO for the proprietor from 1814 John Rose. Other marks incorporate the name Rose or Coalport (*see* Fig. 202).

it frequently proved most convenient to include it in the full range of a firm's marks. MADE IN ENGLAND may be recognised as a 20th-century variant.

It is interesting when a collector succeeds in finding marked wares that trace the advancement of a firm from a simple name to the name '& Co', with the subsequent inclusion of '& Sons', perhaps, and the addition of ROYAL and TRADE MARK to the trade name in the manner which became conspicuous in the later 19th century. A still later specimen may show the eventual inclusion of ENGLAND by successors often remote from the firm's founders, but yet anxious to preserve the goodwill of the original name. A mark may draw attention to the foundation date with ESTABLISHED and a date, occasionally a date far earlier than can be associated directly with the firm in question and referring instead to the first establishment of a pottery on the site.

Indeed, for the very beginner the dates on some wares may be the most obvious pitfall, expecially when, as in some 19th-century Coalport marks, for example, the date A.D. 1750 is found without the inclusion of the word ESTABLISHED. In Fig. 202 some interesting examples are shown though these, of course, are confusing only to those who look first to the mark rather than to the general style of a piece. Indeed, in the mark itself one soon comes to note changes of style in typeface and general presentation that offer obvious clues to approximate dating.

Even the beginner is generally aware of the way in which the marks of famous firms were copied by lesser potters, the swords of Meissen and Ls of Sèvres (Fig. 202) being the most obvious examples. Chelsea's gold anchors, small and obscure on genuine pieces, are far more often found on imitations in English bone china or continental hard porcelain. Sometimes it is even possible, by tilting the piece to the right angle for a slanting light, to see where a less desirable mark has been

186. Marks. Porcelain, Chelsea, Chelsea-Derby and Longton Hall.
FIRST ROW, Chelsea Porcelain Co. c. 1745–69 (all genuine marks
are very small, and copies abound): incised triangles, one including
the name; rare underglaze blue crown-and-trident c. 1745–50;
'raised anchor' in an applied relief, c. 1749–52. SECOND ROW,
Chelsea: two painted red anchors, c. 1752–6; typical gold anchor
of c. 1758–69 and also Chelsea-Derby 1770–75; two imitations of
Meissen marks. THIRD ROW: four marks of Chelsea-Derby; two
marks of Longton Hall (c. 1750–60) used early 1750s.

removed, leaving no more than a slight roughness in the glaze.
Stoke-on-Trent: this name on Staffordshire ceramics dates
from 1910 when several of the pottery towns were incorporated into a single city. Its presence in a mark shows the piece
to have been made later than 1910. The name Stoke-upon-
Trent, one of the incorporated towns, was used earlier.
Impressed marks: names and towns impressed into ceramics
often curve slightly upward at the ends. This was caused by
using a curved stamp, pressed into the clay with a circular
movement to prevent adhesion and probable tearing of the
clay which happened when a straight stamp was pressed

downward. Nothing was easier than for the operator to deviate from the straight line, the result being a curved impression.

Initials and Names as marks

A & B, *or* A B   Adams & Bromley, Shelton. Earthenware, jasper, majolica, parian. 1873–94.

A & CO   E. Asbury & Co., Longton. Bone china. c. 1875–1925 (*see* Fig. 190).

A BROS   G. L. Ashworth & Bros, Hanley. Earthenwares, Mason's ironstone. 1862–

A B & CO   Allman, Broughton & Co., Burslem. Earthenwares. c.1860–5.

A B & CO   A. Bullock & Co., Hanley. Earthenwares. 1880–1915.

ADAMS & CO   William Adams and successors, Tunstall and Stoke. Earthenwares, stonewares, etc. (Also used the marks ADAMS, W ADAMS, W A & S, W A & CO.)

A S   A. Stanier, Burslem. Earthenwares. 1895–1930s.

B

A S & CO   Ambrose Smith & Co., Burslem. Earthenwares and china glazed ware painted blue. 1780s.

AULT   William Ault, Swadlincote, Derbyshire. Earthenware. 1887–1923.

B   *See* Bow, Bristol, Derby, Worcester marks, Figs. 184, 188, 189.

B   Thomas Barlow, Longton. Bone china, earthenware. 1850–80.

B (*with anchor*)   British Anchor Pottery Co., Longton. Earthenware. 1865–

B & B   Bates & Bennett, Cobridge. Earthenware. 1868–1890s.

B & B   Bridgett & Bates, Longton. Bone china. 1883–1915.

B & CO, *or* B CO (*in six-pointed star*)   Boulton & Co., Longton. Earthenwares. 1890s.

B B   Barker Bros, Longton. Earthenwares and bone china. 1876–early 1900s (*see* Minton, Fig. 196).

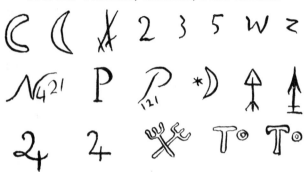

187. Marks. FIRST ROW: eight marks of Lowestoft (1757–c. 1800) including two pseudo-Worcester crescents, Meissen swords and typical workmen's numerals and letters sometimes found inside foot-rims. **SECOND ROW:** New Hall China Manufactory mark, c. 1780–1815; painted P for either James or Seth Pennington, Liverpool, c. 1760s–80s; P for Pinxton (1796–1813) used with or without a number until 1800; rare crescent in purple and late marks after William Billingsley left for Mansfield in 1799 and the factory was run by John Coke. **THIRD ROW:** Plymouth (1768–70), two marks of sign for tin; Swansea impressed tridents (1814–22); two impressed marks noted on porcelain of Plymouth, Bow, Bristol, Worcester during period 1760–75, attributed to modeller Tebo or Thibaud who went to Wedgwood 1775.

BB & I, *or* BB & CO   Baker, Bevan & Irwin, Swansea. Earthenware. 1814–39.

B & C   Bridgwood & Clarke, Burslem. Earthenware. 1858–74.

B & CO   L. A. Birks & Co., Stoke. Earthenware, bone china.
S P   1890s.

B & H   Bednall & Heath, Hanley. Earthenware and bone china. 1879–1901.

B & H, *or* BH & CO (*sometimes with swan*)   Beech & Hancock, Burslem. Earthenwares. 1851–76.

B & H   Blackhurst & Hulme, Longton. Bone china. c.1890–1930s.

B & L   Burgess & Leigh, Burslem. Earthenware. 1851–

B & S   Bishop & Stonier, Hanley. Earthenware and bone
BISTO   china. 1891–1939 (*see* Fig. 191).

BARKER   S. Barker & Son, Don Pottery, Swinton,
DON POTTERY   Yorks. Earthenware. 1834–93.

BARR FLIGHT & BARR   *See* Worcester, p. 318 and Fig. 189.

B C CO   Britannia China Co., Longton. Bone china.
       1895–1906.

BELLEEK (*with Irish wolfhound, etc.*)   D. M'Birney & Co.,
       Belleek, Co. Fermanagh, Ireland. Eggshell porcelain,
       parian etc. 1858–   (*see* Fig. 191).

B F (*monogram*)   Burmantofts, Wilcox & Co., Leeds. Art
       pottery. 1882–1904 (*see* Fig. 192).

B F B   *See* Worcester, Fig. 189.

B G P CO   Brownfield Guild Pottery Co. (*see* mark W B below).

BOURNES   J. Bourne & Son, Denby, Derbyshire. Stonewares.
       c. 1805–   .

B P CO   Brownhills Pottery Co., Burslem. Earthenware,
       stoneware, etc. 1871–96 (Also Blyth Porcelain Co.,
       20th century).

BRAMELD (*often with a figure or symbol, impressed*)   *See*
       Rockingham, Fig. 199.

BRETBY   Tooth & Co., Woodville, Derbyshire. Art pottery.
       1880s–

BRISTOL POTTERY   *See* P & A below.

B W M   Brown-Westhead Moore & Co., Hanley. Earthen-
       wares and bone china. 1862–1904.

C A & SONS   Charles Allerton & Sons, Longton. Bone china,
       earthenware. 1860–1940.

CADOGAN   Noted on Rockingham Cadogan teapots.

CAMBRIA   Swansea Pottery, Wales. Earthenware. c. 1780–
       1810.

188. Marks. Porcelain, Derby. FIRST ROW, early: two incised marks, both very rare (William Duesbury & Co); two with anchor associated with Chelsea-Derby period, c. 1770–84, and c. 1770–80; crown and D without batons, c. 1770–84. SECOND ROW: incised, or painted, or N alone, occasionally on figures, c. 1770s; blue, puce, red or gold, c. 1782–1820; Duesbury & Kean, c. 1795; three imitations of foreign marks—two Oriental and Meissen. THIRD ROW, Bloor period, c. 1815–48: painted roughly in red; three printed in red; imitation of Sèvres in blue. FOURTH ROW: Locker & Co, King St factory, 1848–59; Stevenson & Hancock, and later Sampson Hancock, King St factory, c. 1860–1935; Derby Crown Porcelain Co., 1877–90; Royal Crown Derby Porcelain Co. 1890–
(with ENGLAND added from 1891 and MADE IN ENGLAND from c. 1920).

189. Marks. Porcelain, Worcester. FIRST ROW, Wall period, 1751–83, marks used from c. 1755: in underglaze blue; in red; in blue printed; three typical w marks in underglaze blue; three typical workmen's marks of early years. SECOND ROW, imitations of famous foreign marks: Meissen (Dresden); Sèvres; Fürstenberg; Chantilly; 'Chinese seal'; two sets of marks from early japan ornament. THIRD ROW, periods of Flight (1783–92), Flight & Barr (1792–1807), Barr, Flight & Barr (1807–13), Flight, Barr & Barr (1813–40) and Kerr & Binns (1851–62): two blue painted marks of Flight; incised B of Flight & Barr; impressed mark of Barr, Flight & Barr (a similar mark with the letters F B B was used by Flight, Barr & Barr); two marks of Kerr & Binns, the shield showing the end figures of the year. FOURTH ROW: Worcester Royal Porcelain Co. Ltd, 1862–75; 1876–91 (a similar mark was used after 1891 surrounded by 'Royal Worcester, England'); mark used c. 1889–1902 by firm that began as Grainger Lee & Co. 1812 became George Grainger & Co. 1839 and was absorbed by the Porcelain Co. in 1889 (alternatives including initials G.G.W.); two marks of James Hadley & Sons (1896 and 1897) absorbed by the Porcelain Co. in 1905. The other Worcester firm of Chamberlain & Co (1786–1852) used their full name until they became Kerr & Binns.

331

CAULDON   Brown-Westhead Moore & Co. (*see* BWM above).

C & E   Cartwright & Edwards, Fenton. Earthenware and bone china. 1857–

C & E   Cork & Edge, Burslem. Earthenware, stone china, Egyptian black, etc. 1848–60. Followed by Cork, Edge & Malkin, and Edge & Malkin (E M & CO) to 1900s.

C & G   Copeland & Garrett, Stoke. Earthenware, bone china, parian, etc. 1833–47. And *see* Spode, p. 296.

C & W K H   Charles Harvey & Sons, Longton. Earthenware, granite ware, bone china. 1840–53.

C B D   *See* Coalport, Fig. 185.

C D

C B L   Collingwood Bros, Longton. Bone china. c. 1880–1957 (Some marks claim 'estab. 1796').

CHAMBERLAINS   *See* Worcester, p. 319.

CLEWS   J. & R. Clews, Cobridge. Earthenware, much blue-printed. 1818–34 (*see* p. 233).

C M   Charles Meigh, Old Hall, Hanley. Earthenware, stoneware, cane ware, etc. 1835–49.

C M & S   Charles Meigh & Son, Old Hall, Hanley. As above. 1851–61. Then became Old Hall Earthenware Co. (*see* O H E C).

C M S & P   Charles Meigh, Son & Pankhurst, Hanley. Earthenware, parian, etc. 1850–1 (Then Charles Meigh & Son).

C P CO, *or* G C P CO   Clyde Pottery Co., Greenock. Earthenware. c. 1815–1900s.

C P P C   Crystal Porcelain Pottery Co., Cobridge. Bone china. 1880–1900s.

CYPLES OLD POTTERY 1793, *or* CYPLES RED POTTERY 1793   J. T. Fell & Co., Longton. Earthenware. 20th century.

D   *See* Derby, Figs. 186, 188.

190. Marks. TOP: Adams & Cooper, Longton, 1850–77, bone china, typical of innumerable marks incorporating small initials (*see* pp. 327–352) (many others include the name of the maker or the factory as, e.g., all the marks of the Spodes and their successors Copeland & Garrett, often incorporating a subject title. In this summary only those with no clearly discernible initials are shown: thus the crowned harp (Fig. 191) is a nameless alternative to the more familiar wolfhound, harp and Irish round tower surmounting the name Belleek); eagle mark, one of several used in the 19th century, especially on blue-printed wares for the American market, by the William Adams family of potters of Tunstall and Stoke from c. 1770; printed mark of W. A. Adderley from c. 1876 to 1905 showing typical inclusion of pattern name at the top. BOTTOM: E. Asbury & Co, Longton from c. 1870; G. L. Ashworth & Bros., Hanley from 1862, with indistinct A.BROS and pattern title, successors to Masons; J. & M. P. Bell & Co., Glasgow, often with initials J.B., 1840–1920s.

D   Thomas Dimmock, Shelton. Earthenware. 1828–60.

D & S   Dimmock & Smith, Hanley. Earthenware. 1825–60.

DAVENPORT   John Davenport and his sons Henry and William, Longport. Bone china, earthenware, ironstone china etc. (Many marks incorporating anchor, *see* Fig. 192). c. 1793–1890.

DAWSON (*also* FORD POTTERY)   John Dawson, Sunderland. Earthenware. 1800–64.

D B & CO   Davenport, Banks & Co., Hanley. Copies of antique earthenware, majolica, terracotta, Egyptian black. 1860–73. Continued by D. Beck & Co. to 1880.

D B & CO (*may be with beehive*)   Dunn, Bennett & Co., Hanley and Burslem. Earthenware. 1875–

D D & CO   David Dunderdale & Co., Castleford, Yorks. Earthenware, fine stoneware, etc. 1790–1820.

DILLWYN   Swansea Pottery, Wales. Earthenware. 1780s–1870 (Mark used first half of 19th century).

DON   Don Pottery, Swinton, Yorks. Earthenware. 1790–1893 (*see* Fig. 193).

DOULTON   Doulton & Co., Lambeth. Stoneware etc. c. 1858–1956. Burslem. Bone china, earthenware. 1880s–

DOULTON & WATTS   Doulton & Watts, Lambeth, London. Stoneware, etc. 1815–58.

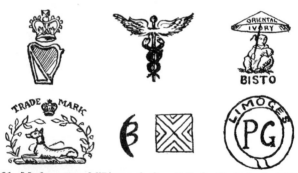

191. Marks. TOP: M'Birney & Co., Belleek, N. Ireland, 1858– (mark used c. 1860–90); two marks of Bishop & Stonier, Hanley, 1891–1939. BOTTOM: T. & R. Boote, Burslem, 1890–1906; two pseudo-Worcester porcelain marks but on earthenware by T. G. & F. Booth, Tunstall, from 1884; misleading mark (impressed) of Sampson Bridgwood & Son, late 19th century.

D P CO   Dresden Porcelain Co., Longton. Bone china. 1896–1904.

E & C C   E. & C. Challinor, Fenton. White granite ware and printed earthenware. 1862–90s.

EASTWOOD (*sometimes misread as Wedgwood*) William Baddeley, Hanley. Wedgwood-type wares. 1802–22.

E C (*in scroll*)   E. Challinor, Tunstall. Earthenware. 1840–67.

E I B, *or* E J B   E. J. Birch, Shelton. Fine stonewares, such as jasper, etc. 1796–1813.

E K & CO, *or* E K B   Elkin, Knight & Co., Fenton. c. 1820–25 and successors Elkin, Knight & Bridgwood. 1825–40. Bone china, earthenware, Egyptian black.

E M CO   *See* entry for C & E.

ENGLAND   Not found on ceramics made before 1891 when it was required on exported wares by American customs regulations known as the McKinley Tariff Act and became a standard detail of most marks although some firms only included it considerably later. MADE IN ENGLAND usually indicates a 20th-century date.

EVANS & CO, *or* EVANS & GLASSON   Cambrian Pottery, Swansea, taken over from Dillwyn & Co. Earthenwares. 1850–70.

E W, *or* E W & S   Enoch Wood from 1780s and Enoch Wood & Son. c. 1820–46. Earthenware, bone china, fine stoneware, etc.

F   *See* Fig. 189.

F (*with anchor*), *or* F & CO   Thomas Fell (& Co.), Newcastle-upon-Tyne. Earthenwares. 1817–20 and 1820–90.

F & R P   F. & R. Pratt & Co., Fenton. Earthenwares. 1818– (*see* pp. 71, 125).

F B B   *See* Worcester, p. 318.

FISHLEY   Several members of the Fishley family made simple slipware, etc., at Fremington, Devonshire, through

192. Marks. TOP: British Anchor Pottery Co. Ltd. from 1885;
typical use of registration diamond on a mark by W. Brownfield,
Cobridge, 1850–92, this showing registration of a pattern (a
moulded parian jug) 29th, April, 1864 (*see* pp. 357, 358); Buckley
Heath & Co., Burslem, c. 1886–1900. CENTRE: Burgess & Leigh Ltd.,
Burslem, from 1867, used also by J. F. Wileman with initials J.F.W.,
1869–92; impressed mark of Burmantofts, Leeds, 1882–1904; Case
& Mort, Herculaneum Pottery, Liverpool (from city crest) 1833–36.
BELOW: anchor mark on bone china attributed to the Davenport
Co., (John and his sons Henry & William), Longport, 1793–1890,
more often found in marks which include the name (uninitialled
anchors also being noted on 18th-century porcelains, 19th-century
earthenwares and 20th-century bone china); Crown Staffordshire
Porcelain Co., Fenton, late 19th century; two marks of T. Dimmock, Shelton, c. 1830–60.

most of the 19th century: these are often ascribed to earlier centuries.

FENTON STONE WORKS   On several marks used by C. J. Mason & Co.

FORD   Dawson & Co., Ford Pottery, Sunderland. Earthenwares, etc. 1799–1864.

F S (*monogram*)   Felix Summerly, pseudonym of Henry Cole whose Summerly's Art Manufactures were commissioned from leading artist-designers. *See* mark on a Minton parian figure of Dorothea after John Bell, (Fig. 200). c. 1846–50.

G (*under crown*)   (Sometimes C under crown) James Neale & Co., Hanley. Wedgwood-type wares. Fourth quarter 18th century.

G & C J M, *or* G M & C J M   The Mason ironstone china firm, Lane Delph: these letters used 1813–29.

G B H   (In black under lion on a jug commemorating death of George IV, 1830, Hopley collection), Goodwin, Bridgwood & Harris, Lane End. Earthenware. 1829–31.

G. BROS   Grimwade Bros, Hanley and Stoke. Bone china, majolica, earthenware. 1886–   (*Grimwades* from 1900).

G C P CO   *See* C P CO above.

G F B (*in Staffordshire knot*)   G. F. Bowers, Tunstall. Bone china and, from 1860, also earthenware. 1842–71.

G G & CO, G & CO W, *or* G W   George Grainger, Worcester. Bone china, parian, etc. Late 1830s–1902. Marks used mainly third quarter of 19th century.

G J (*monogram*), *or* G J & SONS (*sometimes on affixed seal on parian statuary*)   George Jones (& Sons), Stoke. General pottery and parian. 1861–1957.

G L A & BROS   G. L. Ashworth & Bros, Hanley. Earthenwares, Mason's ironstone china, etc. 1862–

193. Marks. Mark of the Don Pottery after the firm became styled Samuel Barker & Son, c. 1841, less familiar than the demi-lion with a pennon; Belle Vue Pottery, Hull, 1825–41; phoenix mark of T. Forester & Sons, Longton, 1883–1959; impressed hand mark of Sir James Duke & Nephews, Burslem, 1859–63.

GRAINGER, *or* GRAINGER LEE & CO *See* Worcester entry, p. 331.

GREATBATCH William Greatbatch, Lane Delph. Modeller for Wedgwood, etc. and made transfer-printed earthenwares. About third quarter of 18th century.

GREEN *See* Sadler & Green, Liverpool, p. 296.

GRESLEY (*under church*) T. G. Green & Co., Church Gresley, Derbyshire. Stonewares, earthenwares. 1864– (Mark used from 1888).

G W T & S, *or* G W T S G. W. Turner & Sons, Tunstall. Earthenwares, 1873–95.

H, HF E. Hughes & Co., Fenton. Bone china. 1884–1953. (But H also used as a mark by one of the several Hackwood firms of the early and mid-19th century.)

H A & CO H. Adams & Co., Longton. Earthenware and bone china. 1870–85.

H A & CO H. Alcock & Co., Cobridge. Earthenware. 1860–1910.

H A & CO H. Aynsley & Co., Longton. Earthenware. 1869–

H & A   Hulse & Adderley, Longton. Earthenware, bone china. 1864–75.

H & B (*sometimes on pennon*) Harrop & Burgess, Hanley. Earthenware. 1895–1904.

H & B (*in garter*) Heath & Blackhurst, Burslem. Earthenware. 1859–80s.

194. Marks. TOP: three typical marks of Herculaneum Pottery, Liverpool, under successive owners, c. 1794–1841, earthenwares and bone china (the liver bird used alone by Case & Mort, *see* Fig. 192). BOTTOM: Green & Clay, Longton, c. 1886–91; Hicks & Meigh, c. 1805–22; (a royal arms mark with a more lively lion than similar marks by Hicks, Meigh & Johnson (1822–36) and other makers such as T. R. Boote in the 1840s when the Victorian coat-of-arms lacked the small central shield); crown mark of Hicks, Meigh & Johnson, 1822–36.

H & G (*sometimes with* LATE HARVEY) Holland & Green, Longton. Earthenware, granite ware, etc. 1853–82.

H & M   Hilditch & Martin, Lane End. Bone china. 1814–22.

H & S   Hilditch & Son (following above). Bone china and earthenware. 1822–30, when became Hilditch & Hopwood.

HARTLEY GREENS & CO *See* Leeds Pottery, p. 262.

H M J, *or* H M & J Hicks, Meigh & Johnson, Shelton. Ironstone china, earthenware, etc. 1822–35. (Successors to Hicks & Meigh, Fig. 194.)

H T (*monogram*) H. Tooth, manager of Linthorpe Pottery.

CHR DRESSER Freelance professional designer whose name appeared on some of Tooth's early Linthorpe pottery. Also on some of William Ault's Swadlincote pottery, 1892–6.

HYLTON POT WORKS Sunderland. Earthenwares. Under the Maling family, 1762–1815, and under John Phillips & Co. 1815–c. 1870.

I K Joseph Kishere, Mortlake, London. Salt glazed stoneware (*see* p. 260).

I R & CO, *or* J R & CO John Rose, Coalport. Mainly third quarter of 19th century (*see* p. 240 and Fig. 185).

INDIAN STONE CHINA Found on wares made at the Old Hall Works, Hanley, by Charles Meigh and successors (*see* p. 275 and Fig. 197).

I W & CO Isaac Wilson & Co., Middlesbrough, Yorks. Earthenware. 1852–1880s.

J & C W, J F & C W, *or* J F W Various members of the Wileman family, Foley China Works, Fenton. Bone china and earthenware. 1864–1925 (*see* Fig. 201).

J & M P B & CO J. & M. P. Bell., Glasgow. Earthenware, terracotta, parian, bone china, etc. 1840s–1920s. (*see* Fig. 190.)

J & R R John & Richard Riley, Burslem. Stone china, figures, earthenware (bone china from 1816). 1802–30.

J & W R, *or* J W R J. & W. Ridgway, Shelton. 1814–30, followed by W. Ridgway, 1830–55 (W R and W R & CO).

J B & S James Beech & Son, Longton. Bone china. 1860–1900.

195. Marks. TOP: Hollinshead & Griffiths, Burslem, 1890–1909; W. Hudson, Longton, c. 1890–1912; J. Maddock, Burslem, 1842–55. BOTTOM: Miles Mason, Lane Delph, c. 1800–16; early version of standard mark of G. M. & C. J. Mason, Lane Delph and successors, 1813–51, and used by G. L. Ashworth & Bros when they acquired the business, 1862, with Mason's name and later with their own; F. Grosvenor, Glasgow, 1868–1926.

J D & CO, *or* D   Dimmock & Co., Hanley. Good quality earthenware. 1830–1904.

J E & S (*sometimes with* D H)   James Edwards & Sons, Dale Hall, Burslem. Earthenware, ironstone china, white granite ware, etc. 1842–79.

J F W   *See* J & C W above.

J H   *See* James Hadley, Worcester, Fig. 189.

J H   Joseph Holdcroft, Longton. Earthenware, parian, etc. 1870–1939.

J M, *or* J M & S   John Meir (& Son), Tunstall. Bone china. c. 1810–1900.

J M & S   Job Meigh & Son, Old Hall Works, Hanley. Earthenware, caneware, red stoneware, etc. 1812–35.

J R   *See* I R p. 340.

J R, *or* J R & CO   John Ridgway (& Co.), Shelton. Earthenware, bone china. 1830–40, 1841–55.

J T (*sometimes monogram*), *or* J T & S   John Tams, Longton. General earthenware, lustre ware, etc. 1874–1903. Followed by J. Tams & Son.

J T H (*sometimes with anchor*)   J. T. Hudden, Longton. Printed earthenware, granite ware. 1859–84.

K & B   *See* Kerr & Binns, Worcester, p. 320 and Fig. 189.

K & CO (*sometimes 'late Mayers'*)   Keeling & Co., Burslem. Earthenware. 1886–1936.

K & W   Keeling & Walker, Longton. Gold and silver lustre, figures. 1850s.

LAKIN, LAKIN & POOLE, *or* L & P   *See* p. 260.

LEEDS POTTERY, *or* L P   *See* p. 262.

LOCKER & CO   *See* Derby, p. 250.

LONDON (*with anchor*), *or* M P CO (*with anchor*)   Middlesbrough Pottery Co., Yorks. Opaque china, lustre, printed earthenware, cream-coloured ware. 1831–44. Then Middlesbrough Earthenware Co., 1844–52 (*see* MEC, p. 344).

LOWESBY   Lowesby Pottery, Leicestershire. Terracotta. c. 1835–40.

M, MINTON, MINTONS, M & B, M & CO, M & H, *or* M H & CO   The Minton firm, Stoke, *see* p. 282 and Fig. 196.

M   John Maddock (& Sons), Burslem. Earthenware. 1842–55, 1855–   (*see* M & S below and Fig. 195).

M & C   Martin & Cope, Longton. Bone china, lustre. 1820s–30s.

M & E   Mayer & Elliott, Longport. Earthenware. c. 1860.

M & S   Maddock & Seddon, Burslem. Earthenwares. 1830s–42. (Followed by John Maddock).

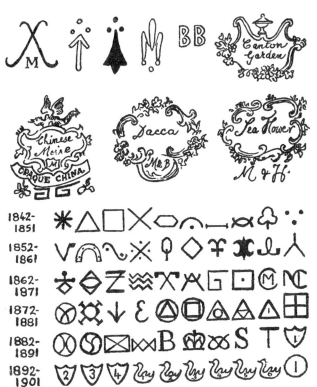

196. Marks. Minton marks (Thomas and his son Herbert), Stoke.
FIRST ROW: painted mark, c. 1800–15; three versions of the ermine
mark, incised or impressed, later 1840s, painted, 1850s onwards,
incised or impressed on some parian statuary; 'best body' mark on
mid-century earthenware; typical of many pattern title cartouches
on printed wares. SECOND ROW: printed ware pattern titles incorporating border initials: M, early 1820s–36; M & B (Minton &
Boyle), c. 1836–41; M & H (Minton & Hollins), c. 1845–68. LOWER
SIX ROWS: year symbols introduced in 1842, small impressed marks
that are easily overlooked.

343

M & S   Mayer & Sherratt, Longton. Earthenware. 20th century.

M & S   Charles Meigh & Son, Old Hall Works, Hanley. Bone china, earthenware, stone china, parian. 1851–61.

MASON'S   Mason & Co., Lane Delph. Ironstone china. Used by the Mason family, c. 1812–48, and by successors, F. Morley 1848–62 and G. L. Ashworth & Bros, 1862–   (*see* p. 273 and Fig. 195).

MAYER   *See* Fig. 202.

M E CO   Middlesbrough Earthenware Co., Yorks. Opaque china, lustre, earthenwares. 1844–52.

MORTLOCK   London china retailer. 1746–20th century (*see* p. 284).

N   *See* Derby, Fig. 188. *See also* New Hall, Fig. 187.

N C P CO   New Chelsea Porcelain Co., Longton. Porcelain reproductions. 20th century.

O H E C   Old Hall Earthenware Co., Hanley. Earthenwares. 1861–86 (*see* Fig. 197).

OLD HALL   Mark used by above and by its owners, the Meigh family, throughout practically the whole of the 19th century. (Job Meigh, Charles Meigh and the Old Hall Porcelain Works).

P   *See* Pinxton, Pennington, Fig. 187.

P & A, BRISTOL POTTERY, *or* P & CO   Marks of the Pountney firm, Temple Backs, Bristol. Earthenware. From about 1815 (*P & Co* from 1850).

P & B
P B & S   Powell & Bishop, and Powell, Bishop & Stonier, Hanley. Earthenwares, bone china, granite ware. 1865–78, 1878–91 when firm became Bishop & Stonier (*see* Fig. 191).

P B
 B   Price Bros, Burslem. Earthenware. 1897–1903.

P & U   Poole & Unwin, Longton. Figures, stonewares, earthenwares, gold and silver lustre, majolica. 1869–80.

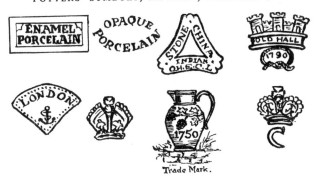

Trade Mark.

197. Marks. TOP: four marks of Job Meigh and successors—
Charles Meigh, etc.—Old Hall Pottery, Hanley, c. 1800–61, the
third and fourth subsequently used by the Old Hall Earthenware
Co., 1861–86, and the Old Hall Porcelain Works, 1886–1902, the
date 1790 being claimed at the date Job Meigh founded the pottery.
BOTTOM: two marks of the Middlesbro' Pottery, 1834–44, probably also used by the Middlesbrough Earthenware Co. and I.
Wilson & Co. at the same pottery to 1880s; 1880s mark of J.
Mortlock & Co., London, china and glass dealers who claimed
establishment in 1746; impressed mark of Neale & Co., Hanley,
1776–86 and their successors R. Wilson and D. Wilson, late 18th
century to c. 1820.

P B & CO   Pinder, Bourne & Co., Burslem. Bone china, red
      ware, Egyptian black. 1862–83.

P B & H   Pinder, Bourne & Hope. Predecessors to above.
      1850–62.

P & D   Poulson & Dale, Stoke. Bone china. 1816–20s.

PUBLISHED BY   followed by a firm's name and the date the
      design was first issued, not the date of the particular
      vessel bearing this mark. The intention was to copy-
      right the design under the Sculpture Copyright Act,
      1797, amended 1814. For example, W. Ridgway,

345

198. Marks. TOP: Pearson & Co., Chesterfield, founded 1808, mark used after 1875; impressed crown of T. Poole, Longton, 1880–1952; obscure monogram, early version, S. Radford, Fenton, 1880–1957. BOTTOM: two marks of W. Ratcliffe, Hanley, 1831–40; John Ridgway, Shelton, 1830–55, including the variable pattern title (other John Ridgway marks including the royal arms usually show the initials more clearly).

  Shelton and Hanley, often used this mark on relief-moulded jugs.

P S & W Poole, Stanway & Wood, Stoke. Parian, bone china, terracotta, stone china, caneware. 1873–90.

P W & CO Podmore, Walker & Co., Tunstall. Earthenware. 1834–55.

R *See* William Ratcliffe, Fig. 198.

R & L Robinson & Leadbeater, Stoke. Parian. 1865–1924.

RD., *or* RD. NO. *See* pp. 357, 358 and Fig. 192.

R H, *or* R H & S Ralph Hammersley (& Son), Burslem, Shelton and Tunstall. Earthenwares at Shelton. At Tunstall, earthenwares, Egyptian black, red ware, Rockingham-glazed ware. At Burslem, earthenware and stoneware jugs. 1860–1905.

199. Marks. Rockingham Pottery: typical griffin mark, this style dating 1830–42; embossed mark found on stoneware and some earthenware and china, the border composed of roses, thistles and shamrocks.

R S, R S & S, *or* R S & W   Ralph Stevenson (& Son), and Ralph Stevenson & Williams, Cobridge. Blue-printed earthenwares. c. 1810–35.

ROSE   *See* Coalport, p. 240.

ROYAL CHELSEA   *See* New Chelsea China Co. and New Chelsea Porcelain Co., Fig. 202.

R S R *(often in Staffordshire knot)*   Ridgway, Sparks & Ridgway, Hanley. Earthenware, stoneware, terracotta, jasper, all of fine quality. 1872–9.

S, *or* SO   *See* Caughley, p. 223 and Fig. 185.

S A & CO *(may be with beehive)*   Samuel Alcock & Co., Burslem. Fine earthenware, semi-porcelain, bone china, bisque figures, parian. c. 1830–59.

S & G   Shore & Goulding, Isleworth. Earthenware and slipware. 1760s–1830.

S & S   Daniel Sutherland & Sons, Longton. Majolica, parian and stone china. 1863–75. (Sutherland china mark, see below).

S & SONS, S B & CO   A. Scott & Co., and successors, South-wick Pottery, Sunderland. Earthenware. Throughout 19th century. A. Scott & Co., 1800–29; Scott & Sons, 1829–44; Scott Bros & Co., 1844–72; Scott & Son, 1872–96.

200. Marks. TOP: two marks of Ruskin Pottery, West Smethwick (W. Howson Taylor), 1898–1935; monogram of Louis Marc Solon, Minton decorator 1870–1904; Josiah Spode, 1770–1833, this mark c. 1800–24, but the name Spode in similar lettering was used later by successors W. T. Copeland. BOTTOM: impressed anchor attributed by Jewitt to Peter Stephan, Jackfield, first maker there of encaustic tiles, first half of 19th century; Andrew Stevenson, Cobridge, c. 1810–30; Felix Summerly's Art Manufactures, a raised mark found on some parian statuary, this example being taken from the John Bell figure of Dorothea made by Minton which bears additional marks showing the design's registration at the Patent Office in 1847, an incised Minton mark, a year symbol for 1853 and the number 189.

S H   *See* Derby, p. 250 and Fig. 188.

S H (*sometimes monogram*), *or* S H & S   Sampson Hancock (& Sons), Stoke. Earthenware. c. 1860–20th century.

SPODE   *See* p. 296 and Fig. 200.

S S   Sampson Smith, Longton. Earthenware figures, chimney ornaments, gold and silver lustre, etc. 1846– (Mark usually 20th century).

STAFFORDSHIRE (*under crown*)   Crown Staffordshire Porcelain Co. (*see* Fig. 192).

SUTHERLAND CHINA   W. Hudson, *see* Fig. 195.

SWANSEA   *See* p. 287 and Fig. 187.

T & B G, *or* T G   Thomas & Benjamin Godwin, Thomas Godwin, Burslem. Creamware and blue-glazed earthenware. 1809–34, and their descendants to c. 1860.

T & K (L *through the ampersand*)   Taylor & Kent, Longton. Bone china. 1867–

T & L   Tams & Lowe, Longton. Earthenware. 1865–74.

T & R B, *or* T B & S   Thomas & Richard Boote, Burslem. Parian, granite ware, earthenware. 1842–

T B   Thomas Baggeley, Lane Delph. Bone china. 1808–c. 1815.

T B   Thomas Bevington, Hanley. Bone china, parian, etc. 1877–92. Previously James & Thomas Bevington from 1865.

T B   Thomas Birks, Longton. Bone china, gold and silver lustre, earthenware. 1850–80.

T B & S, T G & F B, *or* BOOTH'S SILICON CHINA   Thomas Booth & Sons, Tunstall, 1872–76 and T. G. & F. Booth, 1884–90. Earthenwares. From 1891 including various 20th-century marks incorporating the name Silicon china.

T R & CO   Thomas Rathbone & Co., Portobello, Scotland. Earthenware. 1810–45.

T T H (*in Staffs knot*)   Thomas Twyford, Hanley. White granite and cane ware. 1860–98.

T T   Taylor, Tunnicliffe & Co., Hanley. Earthenware. 1868–75.

TURNERS   G. W. Turner & Sons, Tunstall. 1873–95.

TURNER   John Turner and his sons John and William, Longton. Creamwares, Wedgwood-type wares. c.1762–1806.

W   *See* Enoch Wood, Fig. 201. *See* Worcester, p. 315 and Fig. 189.

W A A   William Alsager Adderley, Longton. Bone china, earthenware. 1876–1905 (*see* Fig. 190).

Rᵈ Nº 88523

ROYAL STAFFORDSHIRE
POTTERY ENGLAND

201. Marks. TOP: Torquay Terra Cotta Co., impressed or printed, 1875–20th century; crowned w of Wardle & Co., Hanley, 1871–1910, used from c. 1890; crowned w of Wileman & Co., Foley Potteries, Fenton, 1864–1925, before ENGLAND was added 1891 (the registered number indicating a date in 1887). BOTTOM: misleading date under pattern title of A. J. Wilkinson, Ltd., Burslem, 1885–   , used late 19th century; impressed mark, Enoch Wood, used from c. 1784; another anchor, without initials, J. Woodward, Swadlincote, Derbyshire, 1859–88.

WALTON   *See* p. 308 and Fig. 176.

W & A   Wardle and Ash, Hanley. Parian, majolica, earthen-
W   ware. 1859–62. Wardle & Co., 1871–20th century
         (*see* Fig. 201).

W & B   Wood & Baggaley, Burslem. Earthenware. 1870–82.

W & B   Wood & Brownfield, Cobridge. 1838–50.

W & C   Wood and Caldwell, Burslem. Earthenware, cane-
         ware, Egyptian black. 1790–1818.

W & C (*monogram*)   Wileman & Co. (*see* Fig. 201).

W & C, *or* W C & C   Wood and Challinor, Wood, Challinor
         & Co., Tunstall. Earthenware. c. 1830–64.

350

202. Marks. Marks that may confuse the beginner. TOP: anchor mark of New Chelsea Porcelain Co., Longton, a 20th-century firm (for Chelsea porcelain marks *see* Fig. 186); 20th-century mark of F. Winkle & Co., Stoke, not associated with Thomas Whieldon; Wedgwood & Co., Tunstall, 1860– , sometimes attributed to Josiah Wedgwood & Sons Ltd. (Other confusing Wedgwood marks include some of '*J. Wedgwood*' and the *Wedgewood* marks of W. Smith & Co., Stockton on Tees from 1826.) CENTRE: typical marks of Meissen (Dresden) and Sèvres often incorporated into English marks; typical use of Dresden as a pattern name; T. Pcole, Longton, 1880–20th century. BOTTOM: confusing dates: Coalport, late 19th-century crown mark before addition of ENGLAND, the date referring to the earliest pottery site at Caughley; T. J. & J. Mayer, Dale Hall Pottery, Burslem, etc., 1843–55, a mark used with variations by their successors until 1888; early 20th-century mark of H. M. Williamson & Sons, Longton, 1870s–1941.

351

W & E C, *or* W E C (*sometimes with royal coat of arms*) W. & E. Corn, Burslem. Earthenware. 1864–91.

W & SONS (*monogram*) (*often with pattern name such as Sèvres*) H. M. Williamson & Sons, Longton. Bone china. 1880–20th century.

W B, *or* W B & S William Brownfield (& Son), Cobridge. Earthenware 1850–70; earthenware and bone china 1871–91 (*see* Fig. 192). Succeeded by Brownfield Guild Pottery Co. (B G P CO). 1891–1900.

WEDGWOOD *See* p. 311.

WEDGEWOOD *See* W S & Co below.

W H William Hudson, Longton. Bone china (*see* Fig. 195).

W H, *or* W H & S William Hackwood (& Son), Shelton. Earthenwares and figures, 1827–53.

W H G William Henry Goss, Stoke. Ivory porcelain, jewellery, armorial china. 1858–1944.

WILSON Robert Wilson, Hanley (formerly Neale & Wilson) and David Wilson. China. End of 18th century and to c. 1820 (*see* Fig. 197).

W N William Nutt, Lane End. Bone china. 1816–20s.
L E

W R *See* J W R above.

W S & CO (*sometimes with name* WEDGEWOOD) William Smith & Co., Stockton-on-Tees. Earthenware. 1826–50s (*see* Fig. 202).

W S & T R W. S. & T. Rathbone. Tunstall. Bone china. 1816–30s.

W W & CO Wiltshaw, Wood & Co., Burslem. White granite. 1869–20th century.

Y William Absolon, Yarmouth. Decorator. 1784–1815.

Z B Zachariah Boyle (& Son), Hanley and Stoke. Fine
Z B & S quality bone china and earthenware. 1823–8, 1828–50.

WOOD & SONS
ENGLAND

203. Marks that may confuse the beginner. Early 20th-century mark of Wiltshaw & Robinson, Stoke, from late 19th century; later 19th-century mark, but with flag dated 1746, of Mortlocks Ltd., china retailers 1746–1934; early 20th-century mark of Wood & Sons, Ltd., Burslem, founded 1865, with implications of the famous Ralph and Enoch Wood.

Worcester year marks. From 1867 these were printed under the trade mark. Note that letters F, J, O and Q were omitted.

LETTER	DATE	LETTER	DATE	LETTER	DATE
A	1867	K	1875	U	1883
B	1868	L	1876	V	1884
C	1869	M	1877	W	1885
D	1870	N	1878	X	1886
E	1871	P	1879	Y	1887
G	1872	R	1880	Z	1888
H	1873	S	1881	O	1889
I	1874	T	1882		

a in Old English script = 1890
No letter for 1891
In 1892 a dot was added above the R of Royal Worcester, 1893 two dots, 1894 three dots, and so on until by 1915 there were twenty-four dots.

Instead of a letter the last two figures of the date were sometimes used: e.g. 73 for 1873.

Wedgwood year letters. When a group of three impressed letters is found, the third letter indicates the year of manufacture. The letters of the alphabet from O to Z were used twice—from 1860 to 1871 and from 1886 to 1897. From 1872 to 1885 the letters used were from A to N. From 1898 to 1906 the letters were again the first part of the alphabet, A to I, but the mark also contained the word ENGLAND. From 1907 the first letter in the group was replaced by a figure 3.

LETTER	DATE	LETTER	DATE	LETTER	DATE
O	1860	E	1876	U	1892
P	1861	F	1877	V	1893
Q	1862	G	1878	W	1894
R	1863	H	1879	X	1895
S	1864	I	1880	Y	1896
T	1865	J	1881	Z	1897
U	1866	K	1882		
V	1867	L	1883	A	1898
W	1868	M	1884	B	1899
X	1869	N	1885	C	1900
Y	1870	O	1886	D	1901
Z	1871	P	1887	E	1902
		Q	1888	F	1903
A	1872	R	1889	G	1904
B	1873	S	1890	H	1905
C	1874	T	1891	I	1906
D	1875				

PART VIII

Registry of Designs and
Other Official Marks

Excise stamps. From 1824 every county and borough was required by law to verify the capacity of vessels in which liquor was sold by measure. Each article was tested brim-full and, if found accurate, was stamped with an excise mark composed of the royal crown, the monarch's cypher (G.R., W.R., or V.R.), a local badge or emblem, and letters or numerals indicating the year. From these the date of testing may sometimes be interpreted. Sometimes a plug of soft metal was rivetted into the base, side or handle of the vessel and upon this the excise officer struck his marks with a steel die. In 1877 excise stamps were standardised, to comprise of the royal crown, monarch's cypher, a number representing the county or borough testing office and a year numeral beneath.

In early days the potters embossed the denomination on an applied pad and the inspectors added their stamp. From late Victorian times it has been customary for the official stamp to include the denomination.

Registration marks and numbers. Diamond-shaped marks printed or impressed upon specimens of industrial art were used from 1842 to 1883 to show that the pattern or design had been registered at the Patent Office, thus securing three years of protection against industrial piracy. Rightly interpreted, the symbols contained in the diamond contribute interesting information regarding the piece. Reference to the accompanying key chart (Figs. 205 and 206) will reveal the exact date on which the design of any specimen so marked was

204. Excise marks. TOP LEFT: mocha pottery measure with imperial measure embossed in the earthenware; beside this are four typical underglaze symbols embossed by the potters in their measures, two without indicating the size. BELOW LEFT: two plainer marks embossed by the potters. CENTRE ROW: two typical symbols incorporated in the old verification marks—the shield of London and arrows of Sheffield—also a typical disc in soft metal such as was rivetted into the handle or base of a measure. BOTTOM: three typical marks post-dating the change of pattern in 1877, the number indicating the region such as 64 for Sunderland. These are sand blasted onto the vessels, some with the aid of stencils.

Registry of Designs

Index to the letters for each month & year from 1842 to 1867

1842	X	January	C
1843	H	February	G
1844	C	March	W
1845	A	April	H
1846	I	May	E
1847	F	June	M
1848	U	July	I
1849	S	August	R
1850	V	September	D
1851	P	October	B
1852	D	November	K
1853	Y	December	A
1854	J		
1855	E		
1856	L		
1857	K		
1858	B		
1859	M		
1860	Z		
1861	R		
1862	O		
1863	G		
1864	N		
1865	W		
1866	Q		
1867	T		

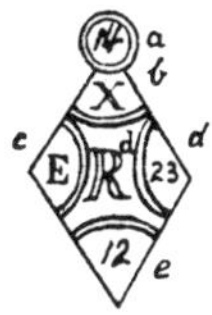

a - Class
b - Year
c - Month
d - Day
e - Bundle

For Sep 1857, 2ⁿ Letter R used from 1ˢᵗ to 19ᵗʰ Septr.

For Decʳ 1860 a very Letter K used

July 1ˢᵗ 1842

J Wong Registrar

205. Keys to the letters and figures found on diamond-shaped marks used for registering designs, 1842–67.

206. Keys to letters and figures, 1868–83.

registered at the Patent Office. If the potter's trade mark is not present it is possible to obtain full details from the Comptroller, Patent Office, Southampton Buildings, Chancery Lane,

London, W.C.2, for a small fee. Some of the early numbers are at the Public Record Office, Chancery Lane, London.

This method was abandoned from 1st January 1884 in favour of straightforward numbering. On that date the registered number 1 was entered and subsequent numbers appeared as follows:

January	1885	began with the entry of					Rd No. 19754
,,	1886	,,	,,	,,	,,	,,	Rd No. 40480
,,	1887	,,	,,	,,	,,	,,	Rd No. 64520
,,	1888	,,	,,	,,	,,	,,	Rd No. 90483
,,	1889	,,	,,	,,	,,	,,	Rd No. 116648
,,	1890	,,	,,	,,	,,	,,	Rd No. 141273
,,	1891	,,	,,	,,	,,	,,	Rd No. 163767
,,	1892	,,	,,	,,	,,	,,	Rd No. 185713
,,	1893	,,	,,	,,	,,	,,	Rd No. 205240
,,	1894	,,	,,	,,	,,	,,	Rd No. 224720
,,	1895	,,	,,	,,	,,	,,	Rd No. 246975
,,	1896	,,	,,	,,	,,	,,	Rd No. 268392
,,	1897	,,	,,	,,	,,	,,	Rd No. 291241
,,	1898	,,	,,	,,	,,	,,	Rd No. 311658
,,	1899	,,	,,	,,	,,	,,	Rd No. 331707
,,	1900	,,	,,	,,	,,	,,	Rd No. 351202

Index